ST. LUKE'S RECORDS

1829-early 1900's
Danville, Knox County, Ohio

Compiled by

Richard T. Koch

Phyllis I. Davidson

CLEARFIELD

Printed for
Clearfield Company, Inc. by
Genealogical Publishing Co., Inc.
Baltimore, Maryland
2001

International Standard Book Number: 0-8063-5108-X
Made in the United States of America

Table of Contents

PREFACE

St. Luke in Danville, Knox County, is considered to be the second oldest Catholic parish in Ohio, the first being St. Joseph of Somerset, Perry County. The founding members came shortly after Ohio became a state; and their children populated not only this region, but many also moved westward into Indiana, Illinois, and Iowa. Later their descendants could be found in communities throughout the United States. The compilers are numbered among their descendants, and thus this is the cause of our interest in these records.

Six years ago a unique opportunity arose when Father Homer Blubaugh, St. Paul Church, Westerville, Ohio, was allowed to make a photocopy of existing records with the blessing of Father F. Richard Snoke, pastor of St. Luke. Now Father "Blu" is an ardent genealogist and shared this information with three other genealogical enthusiasts, Phyllis Davidson, Westerville, Ohio; Jim Logsdon, Columbus, Ohio; and Richard Koch, Frostburg, Maryland. The compilers undertook the task of translating from the Latin, editing, and putting the material into a typescript document. Phyllis did the arduous task of proofing the draft copy against the original and an earlier translation by Rev. Carl Clagett and Martha Grassbaugh. Jim Logsdon, with his vast knowledge of Knox County residents, contributed in many ways. A copy of the typescript was supplied to St. Luke, along with the photocopy, now bound in a ledger that would allow copying of the handwritten records without damage to the fragile originals. Each of the four contibutors maintained a copy of the typescript.

Subsequently the compilers tackled the records of St. Ignatius of Mt. Savage, Maryland, and St. Mary of Cumberland, Maryland, the earliest Catholic churches in Allegany County. These two churches were, in effect, the home churches of the founders of St. Luke and as such included many of the same family names. Armed with more advanced software, we sought to have that data formally published. *Western Maryland Catholics 1819 - 1951* by Phyllis I. Davidson and Richard T. Koch was published by the Clearfield Company, Baltimore, Maryland in November, 1998. With that experience behind us, we were now ready to attempt publishing the St. Luke records.

ACKNOWLEDGMENTS

The compilers are very appreciative of the efforts of Father "Blu" (Rev. Homer Blubaugh), of Westerville, Ohio for copying the original records and his assistance in certain clerical Latin terminology. We are also greatful for the assistance of James M. Logsdon of Columbus, Ohio, in making corrections to the names and dates in the original rendition based upon his own genealogical efforts and knowledge of the Knox County families. We wish to publicly thank Father F. Richard Snoke, Pastor of Saint Luke Catholic Church, who gave permission to have formally published the sacramental records of this church.

ABBREVIATIONS

The abbreviations used are those familiar to genealogists, but bear listing:

abs	- absent	mo.	- months
abt.	- about	nee	- maiden name
aka	- also known as	prob.	- probable
b	- born	Sps:	- sponsor(s)
bapt.	- baptized	s/o	- son of
c	- circa	w/o	- wife of
?/o	- child of unknown sex	wid/o	- widow of
d	- died	wit.	- witnesses
da	- days	_____	- indistinguishable or
d/o	- daughter of		blank
FC	- First Communion	yr	- years
F-#	- Fragment number	name	- questionable rendition
	(loose pages in records)	<	- before
md	- married	>	- after

Variant surname spellings exist through the records, even within one entry. A listing of some more frequent variations is given in the following two pages.

PREFACE

Surname	Variants	Surname	Variants
Allerding	Allending	Dial	Doyle,
Armburst	Armbush		Dyle,
Bailes	Bales,		Dyil
	Bayles	Durbin	Derbin
Banbury	Banberry	Eckenrode	Akenroad,
Beam	Biem		Akinrode
Beckstel	Bechtel	Eifert	Ifert,
Bickel	Bickle		Iford
Blubaugh	Bluebaugh,	Engle	Ingle
	Bluebach	Ferenbaugh	Fenbach,
Boeshart	Boshard,		Firebaugh
	Boshart,	Fesler	Fassler,
	Popshot		Fessler
Bowman	Beauman	Fraiser	Frazer,
Boyle	Boile		Frazier
Breckler	Bregler	Guenther	Ginther,
Bricker	Brecker		Gunthie
Brosnaham	Brosenham,	Hammond	Hammon
	Brosenhard,	Harshberger	Harsperger
	Brosham	Headington	Heddington
Cocanover	Kukenaugh	Himes	Hymes
Colglesser	Calkglesser,	Hollet	Holler,
	Colclusser,		Haller
	Colehesser,	Homan	Homann
	Colgesser	Hosfeld	Hossephelt,
Colopy	Collopy		Hosephelt,
Connelly	Conley,		Hopsephett
	Conly,	Hosey	Hosea
	Connolly	Houck	Hawk,
Connor	Conner		Hock
Critchfield	Christfield	Kline	Cline,
Crownapple	Krownapple		Klein
	Kremimple	Kreakbaum	Crikbaum,
Crowner	Cronner		Krikbaum

Surname	Variants	Surname	Variants
Logsdon	Logston	Shafer	Shaffer
Logue	Log,	Shaub	Shaa,
	Loge		Schaub
Losh	Louche	Sheneberger	Schonenberger,
Lybarger	Lyberger		Schenebarger,
Magers	Majors		Shenebard
McGough	Mego	Shillinger	Steelinger,
McKinney	McKenny,		Stillinger,
	McKinny		Stoolmiller
McKenzie	McKinsie,	Shults	Shuls,
	McKinsey,		Shultz
	McKinzee	Smith	Smyth
Mumaw	Meumaugh,	Smithhisler	Smithhysler
	Moughmaw,	Stevens	Stephens
	Moomaw	Stoffer	Stofer
O'Hara	O'Heir	Swarts	Schwartz,
Payne	Pain,		Swartz
	Paine	Trullinger	Trollinger
Postlewait	Prestlerwaite,	Uhl	Ul
	Postelwait,	Waggoner	Wagoner,
	Posthelwait		Wagner
Quinn	Quin	Welker	Welcher
Reams	Riems	Whisler	Wisler

PREFACE

Within the text, where known, each entry includes the initials of that priest performing the specific rite. Below is a list of those priests names keyed to the initials used.

ADF - Anthony Dominic Fahy,
    O. P.
CDB - Charles Dominic Bowling,
    O. P.
DJO - Daniel Joseph O'Leary, O. P.
ESM - E. S. Murphy
FM - Francis Moitrier
HJB - Hugh J. McDevitt
JB - J. Brunemann, O. S. F.
JBD -John Baptist Vincent
    DeRaymaecker, O. P.

JBE - J. B. Eis
JBL - John Baptist Lamy
JBO - J. B. O' Connor
JFK - James F. Kramer
JGA - John Geo. Albert Alleman,
    O.P.

JHC - James Hyacinth Clarkson,
    O. P.
JJB - John Julius Brent
JSC - John Sylvester Collins
JVB - James Vincent Bullock, O. P.
JW - Joseph Wijsel
LM - Lawrence Muhane
MA - Michael Aherns
MM - Michael McAleer, O. P.
NDY - Nicholas Dominic Young,
    O. P.

PK - Phil Kummert
TJB - Thomas Joseph Boulger
TJO - Thomas J. O' Reilly
TM - Thomas Martin, O. P.
WC - W. Collins, O. P.
WM - William McDermott

INTRODUCTION

Ohio became the seventeenth state in 1803. In 1805 George Sapp and his wife Catherine (nee Arnold) left Allegany County, Maryland and came to Howard, Ohio. Three years later they settled in Knox County, Ohio, one mile from what became the town of Danville[1]. Other Catholic emigrants soon followed. In 1811 George Sapp's father, George Sapp Sr., died here leaving a will. Other settlers came, many from the Catholic congregations of Arnold's Settlement (Mt. Savage), Willstown, and Cumberland, Maryland, to start new farms in Knox County, near what became known as Sapp's Settlement. One might wonder why they would choose such hilly country for their farms, but it is strikingly similar to the areas of Allegany County and bordering Pennsylvania which they had left. The first Catholic missionary priest, Father Edward Fenwick, visited here in 1814, coming from Somerset County, Ohio. The first church was a log building, 20 ft by 30 ft, built on land donated by George and Catherine Sapp. This church was dedicated to St. Luke on 17 Oct 1824 by Rev. Nicholas Young[2]. The first surviving known baptismal register begins in August 1829. On 26 Mar 1831 the heads of families of St. Luke voluntarily agreed to build a new church, and this list is reproduced herein as the first entry.

The records included herein are basically baptisms initiating 29 Aug 1829, and in some cases identify the baptismal sponsors. Later records show birthdates. Existing marriage records (beyond those implied as parents of those being baptized) and witnesses to marriages are included if shown. Some deaths and burials were scattered throughout the records, with a separate listing beginning in 1876. These were collected together and are presented in one section. Where ages were given, one can identify some early members in these later years. Some lists of those children partaking of their first communion not only show the religious vigor of this church, but also give us the names and approximate ages (about 11 years) of these youth.

---

[1] Named for Daniel Sapp, one of four brothers who settled in this area.

[2] History principally from a small pamphlet: Grassbaugh, Martha "A Short History of St. Luke Church, Danville Ohio", May 1983.

ST. LUKE'S RECORDS

Inconsistency of record keeping is apparent throughout, but remembering the difficulty of living in those times, we wonder at the magnitude of the information contained therein. The rites were recorded in Latin. In some cases filium and filia identify the child as son or daughter respectively; however in many instances this would be abbreviated fil. and the sex of the child could not be ascertained, unless by the given name. Mariam or Elizabetha would be females Maria (aka Mary) and Elizabeth. Joannem could be John, James, Jane, Joan or Joanna. We tried to use clues where possible, i.e. if a sponsor had the same given name, and the sponsor's sex was known, we would assign the same sex to the child. Between spelling differences and sometimes illegible handwriting, it sometimes became a guess as to what the interpretation should be. We used an underlined if the name was in doubt. We have tried to use the most common form of both given and family names throughout, thus McKenzie is used for McKinsie, McKinzee, etc. This is to help in computer searches. Brackets [ ] are used for our insertions, while parentheses ( ) are those insertions in the handwritten records. The baptismal records are chronological, and we have repeated this order. In a few instants *italicized* birth dates were used in the baptizmal date column, if the latter was not given, to allow a chronological placement.

EARLY MEMBERSHIP

26 Mar 1831   Undersigned voluntarily agreed to build a new church
for the Catholic Congregation of Knox County on the
lot of ground where the old one now stands.

George Sapp	$10
Thomas J. Porter	10
Dan Durbin	10
Jonathan McKenzie	5
Elias Arnold	5
Aaron McKenzie	5
John Blubaugh	5
John Logue	5
Raphael Logue	5
Gabriel McKenzie	2.50
Jacob Blubaugh	5
George Payne	5
Nathan W. Magers	10
William N. Magers	10
Baptist Durbin	5
Benjamin Blubaugh	5
John Durbin Jr.	5
Daniel Logue	4
Simon H. Sapp	3
Jacob Collopy	5
Levi Sapp	5
John Carter	5
James McKenzie	5
William Starner	0.50
Martin Durbin	5
Jonathan A. Sapp	2
Benjamin Sapp	2.50
Richard Logue	5
John Logue of J.	10
Gabriel McKenzie Jr.	0
Aaron McKenzie	1
Revd. Mr. Bolin	~~10~~ 0
Isaac Dial	4
John Durbin	0
Samuel McKenzie	5
Caleb McKenzie	5
[total]	200.50

3

A List of Parish Members 19 May 1839

Jonathan McKenzie
Henry Akenroad [Eckenrode]
William Carter
Thomas Mego [McGough]
P. Mego [McGough]
James Mego [McGough]
David Akenroad [Eckenrode]
J. Logue
Ben Durbin
James White
George Durbin
Peter Hineman
James McKenzie
Raphael Payne
John Zumma Zimmerman
A. E. Quin [Queen ?]
Levi Sapp
Wm N Magers
Thomas J. Porter
____ Durbin
John Porter
Elijah Durbin
Jonathan S. Sapp
John Durbin
Martin Durbin
Nathan S. Magers
David Logsdon
Daniel Logue

John Logue
Moses McKenzie
Gabriel McKenzie
George Sapp Jr.
Hartley Sapp
Thos Whitt
Jacob Colopy
Aaron McKenzie
Thos Brosnathan
Baptist Durbin
Mary Draper
Wm Hinaman
Sam Durbin
Absolom Buckingham
Henry Morton
R. B. [Ralph Boyd] Payne
Jon Arnold
Senr. Ben Durbin
Sam of Ben Durbin
James Sapp Jr.
Gabriel McKenzie*
John Carter*
Elizabeth Blubaugh*
David Logsdon*
David Logsdon Jr.*
Elias Arnold

* Carried over on second sheet, some appear duplicated.

REGISTER OF BAPTISMS

29 Aug 1829	John McKenzie s/o John McKenzie & Margaret Logsdon alias McKenzie. Sps: Samuel McKenzie & Henrietta McKenzie -DJO [F-1a].
29 Aug 1829	Margaret White d/o Anthony White & Kesiah Wade. Sps: Caleb McKenzie & Margaret Magers -DJO [F-1a].
29 Aug 1829	Elizabeth [Logue] d/o John Logue & Elizabeth McKenzie alias Logue. Sps: John Durbin & Honora Logsdon -DJO [F-1a].
29 Aug 1829	Margaret Logue d/o Raphael Logue & Catherine McKenzie. Sps: John Durbin & Honora Logsdon -DJO [F-1a].
08 Nov 1829	Martha Magers d/o Peter Magers & Catherine Magers. Sps: Caleb McKenzie & Margaret Magers -DJO [F-1a].
08 Nov 1829	Benjamin Francis McKenzie s/o Gabriel McKenzie & Anna [Nancy] Logue. Sps: Moses McKenzie & Honora Logue -DJO [F-1a].
08 Nov 1829	(missing section) Elias Arnold ___eres Pain [Payne] alias [Arnold]. Sps: George Sapp & Mary Logsdon. [This must be William Arnold b 26 Feb 1828 s/o Elias Arnold & Rachel Payne] -DJO [F-1b].
08 Nov 1829	Sarah Dial d/o George Dial & Margaret Logue. Sps: Nathan Magers & Winifred Magers (nee Logsdon) -DJO [F-1b]
08 Nov 1829	Nathaniel [Nathan] Magers s/o____ [Nathan] Magers & Winifred Logsdon. Sps: _____ [William Magers & Margaret Sapp] -DJO [F-1a].
10 Nov 1829	Francis Ignatius Morton s/o David Morton & Bridget McArdle alias Mor[ton]. Sps: John Mo[rton &] Maria McArdle at Mt.Vernon -DJO [F-1c].
11 Nov 1829	___amttim [missing section] & Anne [missing section] DJO [F1-c]
15 Mar 1830	Sarah Jane Colopy d/o William Colopy & Maria Fitzpatrick alias Colopy. Sps: Sarah Colopy -DJO [F-1b].

16 Mar 1830	Luke Durbin s/o Martin Durbin & Sara Sapp alias Durbin. Sps: Basil Durbin & Joanna Durbin -DJO [F-1b].
17 Mar 1830	William McKenzie s/o Jonathan McKenzie & Sarah Mattingly alias McKenzie. Sps: Benjamin Durbin & () [Elizabeth Durbin] -DJO [F-1b].
17 Mar 1830	Martha Jane Sapp d/o Simon [Hartley] Sapp & Rachel Sapp. Sps: Jonathan Sapp & Maria Sapp -DJO [F-1c].
19 Mar 1830	Stephen Blubaugh s/o Jacob Blubaugh & Honora ~~Logsdon~~ [McKenzie] alias Blubaugh. Sps: Elizabeth Blubaugh & George Pain [Payne] -DJO [F-1c].
19 Mar 1830	Margaret [Dial] d/o Samuel Dial & Elizabeth Lawrence. Sps: William Carter & Sarah Logue -DJO [F-1c].
24 Mar 1830	Rosanne [Lybarger Walker] Durbin w/o Benjamin Durbin & d/o George Lybarger & _____; [Widow of Jesse Walker]. Sps: Catherine Sapp -DJO [F-1d].
24 Mar 1830	Edmund Walker s/o Jesse Walker & Rosanna Lybarger alias Walker. Sps: George Sapp & Catherine Sapp -DJO [F-1d]
24 Mar 1830	Samuel Walker s/o Jesse Walker & Rosanne Walker alias Lybarger. Sps: George Sapp & Catherine Sapp -DJO [F-1d].
27 Mar 1830	Anastasia Mary McKenzie d/o Samuel McKenzie & Henrietta McKenzie. Sps: Gabriel McKenzie & Anastasia McKenzie -DJO [F-1d].
28 Mar 1830	Sara Catharine Colopy d/o Jacob [Colopy] & Delila Sapp alias () [Colopy]. Sps: [Har]tly Sapp & Henrietta ____ [McKenzie] -DJO [F-1d]
20 May 1830	Joseph Trullinger s/o George Trullinger & Honora Durbin. Sps: Benjamin Durbin & Margaret Durbin. -DJO
20 May 1830	Elizabeth Logue d/o Richard Logue & Catherine Sapp. Sps: John Carter & Sarah Logue. -DJO
23 May 1830	Benjamin Durbin s/o Samuel Durbin & Helena [Hannah] McKenzie. Sps: Benjamin Durbin & Elizabeth Durbin. -DJO

6

BAPTISMS

04 Jan 1831	Simeon Sapp s/o Jonathan Sapp and Maria Durbin. Sps: Simeon Sapp & Rachel Sapp. -CDB
04 Jan 1831	Thomas Sapp s/o Samuel Sapp & Susanna [Magers] Sapp. Sps: Nathan Magers & Winifred Magers. -CDB
06 Jan 1831	Reason Welker d/o Solomon Welker & Elizabeth Welker. Sps: Daniel Durbin & Honora Dial. -CDB
06 Jan 1831	Jane Durbin b 14 Apr 1830 d/o Baptist Durbin & Catherine [King] Durbin. Sps: Abigail [Aparilla] Buckingham -CDB
06 Jan 1831	Eleanor Durbin d/o Daniel Durbin & Anna Hayden. Sps: Basil Durbin & Abigail [Aparilla] Buckingham -CDB
11 Mar 1831	Sarah Anna Hunt d/o Richard Hunt & Anna Colopy. Sps: Sara Colopy. -CDB
13 Mar 1831	Elizabeth Meumaugh [Mumaw] d/o Frederick Meaumaugh [Mumaw] & Honora [Logue] Meaumaugh. Sps: Moses McKenzie & Anna McKenzie -CDB
13 Mar 1831	Susanna McKenzie [daughter] & Hester McKenzie [mother]. Sps: Gabriel McKenzie & Susanna Sapp -CDB
13 Mar 1831	Catherine King d/o John King & Maria King. Sps: Margaret McKenzie -CDB
07 May 1831	Peter....[rest is blank].
08 May 1831	Eliza [Magers] d/o Peter Magers & Rachel Magers. Sps: Margaret McKenzie. -CDB
10 May 1831	Rachael Logue d/o Henry Logue & Maria Logue Sps: John Logue & Elizabeth Logue -CDB
11 May 1831	Mary Akens d/o James Adkins & Mary Adkins. Sps: Sarah McKenzie -CDB
11 May 1831	Lewis Durbin s/o Benjamin Durbin & Elizabeth [Reams] Durbin. Sps: Daniel Durbin and Anna Durbin -CDB
11 May 1831	Maria Durbin d/o Lawrence Durbin & Honora Durbin. Sps: Cath. Sapp -CDB
12 May 1831	Martin Ward s/o Stephen Ward & Sarah [McGough] Ward. Sps: Daniel Durbin & Elphina Durbin -CDB

7

10 Jul 1831	Emily Coleman d/o Jacob Coleman & Barbara Coleman. Sps: Simon Sapp & Elizabeth McDermott -CDB
10 Jul 1831	Margaret Logue d/o Richard Logue & Catherine [Sapp] Logue. Sps: Samuel McKenzie & Henrietta McKenzie -CDB
11 Jul 1831	Benjamin Dial s/o Jesse & Maria Dial. Sps: Benjamin & Elizabeth Durbin -CDB
11 Jul 1831	Joseph Bowser s/o John & Elizabeth [Ewing] Bowser. Sps: Nathan & Winifred Magers -CDB
11 Jul 1831	Lucinda Sapp d/o Levi Sapp & Maria [Colopy] Sapp. Sps: George & Catherine Sapp -CDB
11 Jul 1831	Winifred Magers d/o William [R.] Magers & Margaret [Sapp] Magers. Sps: George & Catherine Sapp -CDB
11 Sep 1831	Daniel Phillips s/o Bertie & Honora Phillips. Sps: Daniel Durbin & Anna Durbin -CDB
11 Sep 1831	John Dial s/o Samuel Dial & Elizabeth [Lawrence] Dial. Sps: Gabriel McKenzie & Anna McKenzie -CDB
06 Jan 1832	Francis Blubaugh s/o Jacob [Blubaugh] & ~~Onora~~ Honora [McKenzie] Blubaugh. Sps: Elias Arnold -CDB
06 Jan 1832	William ~~Loge~~ [Logue] s/o John & Elizabeth [McKenzie] ~~Loge~~ [Logue]. Sps: Caleb & Margaret McKenzie -CDB
06 Jan 1832	Elizabeth Metcalf d/o Thomas & Anna Metcalf. Sps: Absolem Buckingham & Anna Durbin -CDB
11 Mar 1832	Elias [Arnold] s/o John & Christina [Sapp] Arnold. Sps: Winnie Magers -CDB
11 Mar 1832	Maria [Durbin] d/o Joseph & Elizabeth [Lybarger] Durbin. Sps: Benjamin & Rosanna Durbin -CDB
11 Mar 1832	John [Magers] s/o Nathaniel & Winifred Magers. Sps: Caleb & Margaret McKenzie -CDB
11 Mar 1832	Sara [Kreakbaum] d/o Conrad & Priscilla [Blair]Kreakbaum. Sps: Daniel Loge [Logue] & Elizabeth Magers -CDB
11 Mar 1832	Elias Stoffer s/o John & Harriet [Durbin] Stoffer. Sps: Samuel & Helen Durbin -CDB

8

BAPTISMS

11 Mar 1832	Honora [McKenzie] d/o Jonathan & Sara McKenzie. Sps: Daniel & Henrietta McKenzie -CDB
11 Mar 1832	Baptist [Durbin] s/o John [Jr.] & Maria [Winebrenner] Durbin. Sps: Baptist & Catherine Durbin -CDB
13 Mar 1832	Maria Abigail Miller d/o Jacob & Anna Miller. Sps: Thomas & Maria [Mary] Porter -CDB
10 May 1832	Catherine Sapp d/o Jonathan & Maria [Durbin] Sapp. Sps: Benjamin & Rosanna Durbin -CDB
12 May 1832	Siril [Cyril McKenzie] s/o Ignatius & Elizabeth [Magers] McKenzie. Sps: Caleb & Margaret McKenzie -CDB
__ May 1832	George Edward Colopy s/o Jacob & Delila Colopy. Sps: Moses McKenzie & Elizabeth Blubaugh -CDB
14 May 1832	Anna ~~Loge~~ [Logue] d/o Raphael & Catherine ~~Loge~~ Logue. Sps: Thomas White & Lydia Porter -CDB
20 May 1832	Margaret Shafer d/o Peter & Anna [Nancy White] Shafer. Sps: Winifred White -CDB
20 May 1832	Francis M. Durbin s/o Martin & Sarah [Sapp] Durbin. Sps: Moses & Hester McKenzie -CDB
12 Aug 1832	John [Miller] s/o Frederick Miller & Rachel Daniels. Sps: Thomas White & Elizabeth Blubaugh -DJO
12 Aug 1832	Sarah Margaret Dial d/o William Dial & Rebecca Arnold. Sps: Nathan Majors [Magers] and Winifred Majors [Magers] -DJO
12 Aug 1832	William (Henry) Porter s/o John Porter & Lenora Albright. Sps: John Durbin & Maria Porter -DJO
14 Aug 1832	William Porter [Carter] s/o John Carter & Sarah Logue. Sps: William Carter & Eliza Blubaugh -DJO
15 Aug 1832	Robert Jacob Sapp s/o Samuel Sapp & Susanna Majors [Magers]. Sps: Caleb McKenzie & Margaret McKenzie -DJO
15 Aug 1832	Catherine Durbin d/o Benjamin Durbin & Rosanna Lybarger. Sps: Nathan Majors [Magers] and Winifred Majors [Magers] -DJO

9

15 Aug 1832	Maria Emily Ward d/o Stephen Ward & Sara McGough. Sps: Patrick McGough & Helen McGough -DJO
15 Aug 1832	Catherine Bowser (born in 1810). Sps: none given -DJO
17 Aug 1832	Joseph Hyacinthas McKenzie s/o Samuel McKenzie & Henrietta McKenzie. Sps: George Sapp & Catherine Sapp -DJO
10 Mar 1833	Susanna McKenzie d/o Aaron McKenzie & Maria Logue. Sps: Daniel Durbin & Anna Durbin -JVB
10 Mar 1833	Richard F. Magers s/o William Magers & Drusy [Drusilla] Sapp. Sps: Conrad Kreakbaum & Priscilla Kreakbaum -JVB
10 Mar 1833	Nathan McKenzie s/o Gabriel McKenzie & Nancy Logue. Sps: Aaron McKenzie & Mary McKenzie -JVB
10 Mar 1833	Daniel Mumaw s/o Frederick Mumaw & Honora Logue. Sps: William Carter & Rachel Logue -JBD
10 Mar 1833	Sylvester McKenzie s/o Moses McKenzie & Hester Sapp. Sps: Benjamin Blubaugh & Elizabeth Blubaugh—JBD
11 Mar 1833	James [Sapp] s/o Simon [Hartley] Sapp & Rachel Sapp. Sps: Jacob Sapp & Anna Sapp -JBD
11 Mar 1833	Sara Helen [McKenzie] d/o Caleb McKenzie & Margaret Magers. Sps: Sam Durbin & Helen Durbin -JBD
11 Mar 1833	Sarah McKenzie b 11 Aug 1832, d/o Maria Dial McKenzie, w/o Nathaniel McKenzie. [Sarah born after Nathaniel's death.] Sps: Sam Durbin & Helen Durbin - JBD.
11 Mar 1833	James Dial s/o George Dial [Jr.] & Margaret [Logue]. Sps: Eleanor Hartley -JVB
12 Apr 1833	Absalom Durbin s/o Bazil Durbin & Aparilla Buckingham. Sps: Daniel Durbin and Anna Durbin-JVB
15 May 1833	Hilary Blubaugh s/o John Blubaugh & Elizabeth Sapp. Sps: George Sapp & Anna Sapp -JVB

BAPTISMS

16 May 1833	Parmelia Anna Durbin d/o Joseph Durbin & Elizabeth Durbin nee Lybarger. Sps: John Durbin & Maria Durbin -JVB
16 May 1833	John Henry Porter s/o David Porter & Lydia Sapp. Sps: William Carter & Anna Sapp -JVB
16 May 1833	Delila Helen Durbin d/o Samuel Durbin & Helena McKenzie. Sps: Samuel McKenzie & Anna Dial -TM
11 Aug 1833	Sarah Anna [Logue] d/o Richard Logue & Catherine Sapp. Sps: Nathan Major (Magers) & Winifred Logsdon -TM
11 Aug 1833	Charles Bowling [Buckingham] s/o Absalom Buckingham & Anna [Nancy] Murphy. Sps: Basil Durbin & Aparilla Buckingham -TM
11 Aug 1833	Matilda Ann Bowser d/o John Bowser & Eliza Ewing. Sps: Jacob Walsh & Elizabeth McGaw [McGough] -TM
11 Aug 1833	Winifred [Porter] d/o John Porter & Rachel Arnold. Sps: Stephen Blubaugh & Susanna Sapp -TM
11 Aug 1833	Julia Anna [Arnold] d/o John Arnold & Christina Sapp. Sps: William Carter & Rachel Logue -TM
12 Aug 1833	Leo Sapp s/o Levi Sapp & Maria Colopy. Sps: Nathan Magers & Winifred Logsdon -TM
12 Aug 1833	Matilda [Welker] d/o Solomon Welker & Elizabeth Richardson. Sps: Daniel Durbin & Hanna Dial -TM
12 Aug 1833	Patience [Blubaugh] d/o Stephen Blubaugh & Honora Logsdon. Sps: Thomas Porter & Maria Parker -TM
12 Aug 1833	Benjamin Sapp s/o Frederick Sapp [Jr.] & Mary Parker.
02 Sep 1833	Emily [Durbin] d/o Benjamin Durbin & Eliz. Reams. Sps: Henry & Hanna [Honora] Durbin -TM
04 Sep 1833	Elizabeth [McGough] d/o Henry McGough & Margaret Arnold. Sps: Dan Logue & Liddie [Lydia] Porter -TM
09 Feb 1834	William Kreakbaum s/o Conrad & Priscilla [Blair] Kreakbaum. Sps: Benjamin Durbin & Rosann Durbin -NDY

11

09 Feb 1834	Eleanor Miller d/o Jacob & Honora Miller. Sps: George Sapp -NDY
10 Feb 1834	Solomon Durbin s/o Martin Durbin & Sarah Durbin [nee Sapp]. Sps: Stephen Blubaugh & Elizabeth Blubaugh -NDY
11 Feb 1834	[Irene] Eleanor Rolman d/o Ichabod Rolman & Barbara _____ . Sps: Daniel Durbin & Anna McDermott -NDY
12 Feb 1834	Susanna Elizabeth Sapp d/o Jonathan & Maria [Durbin] Sapp. Sps: Levi Sapp & Priscilla Kreakbaum -NDY
24 Mar 1834	In Utica, Ohio Henry William Glassberger s/o Thomas Glassberger & Catherine Mitchell. Sps: Walter Mitchell & Maria <u>Deciver</u> -DJO
28 Mar 1834	John Trullinger s/o George Trullinger & Honora Durbin. Sps: Benjamin & Rosanna Durbin -DJO
29 Mar 1834	Sylvestor Stoffer s/o John Stoffer & Harriet Durbin. Sps: Daniel & Elizabeth Durbin -DJO
29 Mar 1834	Matilda Anna Dial d/o Isaac Dial & Anna [Nancy] Durbin. Sps: Daniel & Elizabeth Durbin -DJO
29 Mar 1834	Raphael Carter s/o John Carter & Sarah [Logue] Carter. Sps: Daniel & Elizabeth Durbin -DJO
01 Feb 1835	Thomas [Shafer] s/o Peter Shafer & Anna [Nancy] White. Sps: Benjamin & Elizabeth Blubaugh -WC
05 Apr 1835	Benjamin [Bowser] s/o Michael Bowser & Catherine Bowser nee Wilson. Sps: John McDermott & Elizabeth McDermott.-WC
05 Jul 1835	Maria [Hunt] d/o Richard Hunt & Nancy Hunt at Mt.Vernon. Sps: Tim & Sara Colopy -ADF
05 Jul 1835	Catherine [Magers] d/o William & Margaret Majors [Magers]. Sps: Alexander and Ann O'Brien -ADF
05 Jul 1835	William [Durbin] s/o Elijah and Margaret [Logsdon] Durbin. Sps: Stephen & Honor Blubaugh -ADF
05 Jul 1835	Elizabeth [Porter] d/o David & Liddy [Lydia] Porter. Sps: Stephen & Honor Blubaugh -ADF

05 Jul 1835	Edward [Blubaugh] s/o Benjamin & Elizabeth [Durbin] Blubaugh. Sps: Martin & Sara Durbin -ADF
05 Jul 1835	Henry [Durbin] s/o Bazil & Aparilla [Buckingham] Durbin. Sps: Benjamin & Betsy Derbin [Durbin] -ADF
05 Jul 1835	Maria [McGough] d/o Patrick & Ellen [Durbin] McKeogh [McGough]. Sps: Benjamin & Elizabeth Blubaugh -ADF
05 Jul 1835	Ann Mariah [Smith] d/o Isaac & Maria Smith Sps: John Derbin [Durbin] & Honor Hettinger -ADF
06 Jul 1835	Mary Ann [Sapp] d/o Simon Hartley and Rachel Sap [Sapp]. Sps: George & Anna Sap [Sapp] -ADF
06 Jul 1835	Rachel [Blubaugh] d/o Jacob & Honor [Logsdon] Blubaugh. Sps: Stephen & Honor Blubaugh -ADF
06 Jul 1835	Sera [Sara McGough] d/o Henry & Margaret [Arnold] McGough. Sps: Patrick McGough and Becky Dial -ADF
06 Jul 1835	Isaac [Dial] s/o George & Margaret [Logue] Dial. Sps: George Pain [Payne] & Sara Carter -ADF
04 Oct 1835	Caleb [McKenzie] s/o Samuel and Henrietta McKenzie. Sps: Jacob & Margaret McKenzie -ADF
04 Oct 1835	Maria [Porter] d/o John & Rachel [Arnold] Porter. Sps: Benjamin & Elizabeth Blubaugh -ADF
04 Oct 1835	John [Irvin] s/o Joseph & Sara Irvin. Sps: Ambrose Hayden & Honor Blubaugh -ADF
04 Oct 1835	Sara [Arnold] d/o John & Christina [Sapp] Arnold. Sps. Nathan Magers & Rachel Pain [Payne] -ADF
04 Oct 1835	Mary [Magers] d/o William & Drusilla Majors [Magers]. Sps: John & Maria Durbin -ADF
04 Oct 1835	Timothy [Sapp] s/o Levi & Maria [Colopy] Sap [Sapp]. Sps: Jacob & Delila Colopy -ADF
04 Oct 1835	Joseph [Colopy] s/o Jacob & Delila Colopy. Sps: Levi Sap [Sapp] & Maria Sapp -ADF
04 Oct 1835	William [Magers] s/o Nathan & Winifred Majors [Magers]. Sps: Benjamin & Rosanna Derbin [Durbin] -ADF

04 Oct 1835	Sylvester [Waggoner] s/o Henry & Hanna Waggoner. Sps: Daniel & Honor Derbin [Durbin] -ADF
05 Oct 1835	Henry [Stoffer] s/o John & Hariett [Durbin] Stofer [Stoffer]. Sps: Dan Durbin & Hanna Dial -ADF
05 Oct 1835	Louisa [Logue] d/o Richard & Catherine Louge [Logue]. Sps: Aaron & Polly McKenzie -ADF
10 Jan 1836	Margarite [Durbin] d/o Elias & Maria [Gorsage] Durbin. Sps: John Durbin and Anna Durbin nee Hayden -JGA
10 Jan 1836	Martha Eleanor [Blubaugh] d/o John Blubaugh & Elizabeth Bluebaugh nee Sapp. Sps George Sapp & Martha Sapp -JGA
26 Mar 1836	John [Durbin] s/o Henry Durbin & Nancy Durbin nee Stoffer. Sps: Peter Kreakbaum & Flora Durbin -JGA
26 Mar 1836	Jacob [Durbin] s/o Benjamin Durbin & Elizabeth Durbin nee Riems [Reams]. Sps: Samuel Durbin & Helena Durbin -JGA
28 Mar 1836	Caroline Elizabeth [Durbin] d/o Martin Durbin & Sarah Durbin nee Sapp. Sps: John Durbin & Anna Durbin nee Hayden -JGA
28 Mar 1836	Henrietta Eleanor [Kreakbaum] d/o Conrad Kreakbaum & Priscilla Kreakbaum nee Blair. Sps: Catherine Sapp nee Arnold -JGA
30 Mar 1836	William Francis [Sapp] s/o Jonathan Sapp & Maria Sapp nee Durbin. Sps: Anna Sapp -JGA
03 Apr 1836	Dan Basil [Durbin] s/o Basil Durbin & Maria Durbin nee Rowland. Sps: Dan Durbin & Catharine Margaret Durbin -JGA
03 Apr 1836	John Baptist [McKenzie] b 8 Mar [1836] s/o Aaron McKenzie & Maria McKenzie nee Logue. Sps: Jacob McKenzie & Maria McKenzie -JGA
04 Apr 1836	Richard [Carter] s/o John Carter & Sara Carter nee Logue. Sps: William Carter & Rachel Log [Logue] -JGA
10 Jun 1836	Anna Elizabeth [Hardt] d/o Ephraim Hardt & Eliza Hardt nee Gordan. Sps: Edward Gallagher & Maria Gordan -JGA

BAPTISMS

12 Jun 1836	Maria Magdalena [Beam] d/o Jacob Beam & Maria Beam nee Krough. Sps: Jacob Holler & Magdalena Holler nee Linebert -JGA
12 Jun 1836	Catherine Margaret [Bowser] d/o John Bauser [Bowser] & Elizabeth Bauser nee Ewing. Sps: David Logsdon & Sara McKenzie -JGA
12 Jun 1836	Thomas Major [McCarthy] s/o Henry McCarthy & Martha McCarthy nee Curry. Sps: Jonathan McKenzie & Sarah McKenzie -JGA
13 Jun 1836	Phillip [Dial] s/o William Dial & Rebecca Dial nee Arnold. Sps: Jacob Logue & Rachel Payne -JGA
14 Jun 1836	Benjamin [Zimmerman] s/o Frederick Zimmerman [Jr.] & Sarah Zimmerman nee Colopy. Sps: Timothy Colopy & Sarah Colopy at Mt.Vernon -JGA
09 Aug 1836	Martha Joanna [Jane] [Trullinger] d/o George Trullinger & Honora Trullinger nee Durbin. Sps: Levi Sapp & Maria Sapp -JGA
10 Aug 1836	Theresa Honora [Durbin] d/o John Baptist Durbin & Catherine Durbin nee King. Sps: John Durbin & Theresa Durbin -JGA
11 Aug 1836	Michael [McNamara] s/o William McNamara & Bridget McNamara nee McNamara [?] Sps: Elijah Durbin & Catherine McNamara -JGA
12 Aug 1836	Maria [Durbin] b 1834 d/o John Baptist Durbin & Catherine Durbin nee King. Sps: Moses McKenzie & Martha Sapp -JGA
14 Aug 1836	James [Daniels] s/o David Daniels & Rebecca Daniels nee McKenzie. Sps: Jacob McKenzie & Maria McKenzie -JGA
14 Aug 1836	Solomon James [Shafer] s/o Peter Shafer & Maria [Nancy] Shafer nee White. Sps: Benjamin Blubaugh & Eliza ____ -JGA
14 Aug 1836	Benjamin [Sapp] s/o Samuel Sapp & Susanna Sapp nee Magers. Sps: William Magers & Margaret Sapp -JGA

15

14 Aug 1836	Lydia [Magers] d/o William Majors [Magers] & Margaret Magers nee Sapp. Sps: Samuel Durbin & Helen Durbin -JGA
14 Aug 1836	George [Dial] s/o Isaac Dial & Nancy Dial nee Durbin. Sps: Samuel Durbin & Margaret Magers -JGA
14 Aug 1836	Raphael Howard [Loney] s/o Wallas Loney & Sara Loney nee Howard. Sps: Raphael Logsdon & Agnes Durbin -JGA
14 Aug 1836	Joseph Anthony [Ferenbaugh] s/o Fidelis Ferenbaugh & Eliza Ferenbaugh nee Draper. Sps: Raphael Payne & Mary Durbin -JGA
15 Aug 1836	Sara Margaret [Buckingham] d/o Absalom Buckingham & Nancy [Murphy] Buckingham. Sps: David Morton & ____ _____ -JGA
15 Aug 1836	John Baptist [Uhm] s/o Michael Ul [Uhm] & Catherine Ul [Uhm] nee Weyerback. Sps: John Hunt & Magdalena _____.-JGA
15 Aug 1836	Phillip [Smithhisler] s/o Philip Smithhisler & Maria Smithhisler nee Uhm. Sps: John Hartman & Maria Hartman nee Grace -JGA
15 Aug 1836	Anna Penelope [Pratt] d/o Henry Pratt & Penelope Buckingham. Sps: Daniel Durbin & Rachel Sapp -JGA
15 Aug 1836	Eliza [Jane Bricker] d/o Lewis [Christopher] Bricker & wife Anna [Nancy]. Sps: Bazil Durbin & Aparilla Durbin -JGA
26 Oct 1836	Rachel [Durbin] d/o Joseph Derbin [Durbin] & Elizabeth Lybarger. Sps: Benjamin Durbin and wife Rosanna [Lybarger] Durbin -TM
18 Jan 1837	Rebecca Maria [McKenzie] d/o Moses McKenzie & Hester McKenzie nee Sapp. Sps: Daniel Logue & Honora Logue -JGA
18 Jan 1837	Lewis [McKenzie] s/o Gabriel McKenzie & Anna [Nancy] McKenzie nee Logue. Sps: Moses McKenzie & Esther McKenzie -JGA

16

BAPTISMS

18 Jan 1837	Joseph [White] s/o Joseph White & Susanna Sapp. Sps: Daniel Logue & Anna Blubaugh -JGA
18 Jan 1837	Rachel Margaret [McGough] d/o Henry McGough & Margaret [Arnold] McGough. Sps: Benjamin Blubaugh & Eliza Blubaugh -JGA
10 Mar 1837	Noe Sylvester [Boyle] s/o Daniel Boyle & Anna Boyle nee Edgington. Sps: David Boyle -JGA
10 Mar 1837	Maria [Boyle] d/o Daniel Boyle & Anna Boyle nee Edgington. Sps: Jacob Boyle -JGA
16 Mar 1837	Joseph [Logue] s/o Richard Logue & Catherine Logue nee Sapp. Sps: Stephen Blubaugh & Honora [Logsdon] Blubaugh -JGA
16 Mar 1837	John Valentine [Porter] s/o John Porter & Rachel Porter nee Arnold. Sps: Nathan Majors [Magers] & Winifred [Logsdon] Majors [Magers] -JGA
16 Mar 1837	Phillip [Dial] s/o George Dial and Margaret Dial nee Logue. Sps: George Sapp & Maria McKenzie -JGA
17 Mar 1837	John Baptist [Spiker] s/o Jacob Spiker & Eva Spiker nee Winebrenner. Sps: John Baptist Durbin & Catherine Durbin nee King -JGA
20 Mar 1837	John Baptist [McKenzie] s/o Nathan McKenzie & Eliza McKenzie nee Magers. Sps: John Durbin & Anna Sapp -JGA
07 Jun 1837	Sarah Margaret Bricker b 7 Jun 1837 d/o Christopher Bricker & Nancy [Buckingham]. Sps: Absalom Buckingham & wife [F-4] -JGA
30 Jul 1837	Sara Agnes [Durbin] d/o Bazil Durbin & Aparilla Durbin nee Buckingham. Sps: John Durbin & Sara Buckingham -JGA
30 Jul 1837	Rebecca [McKenzie] d/o James McKenzie & E.[Elsie] McKenzie nee Arnold. Sps: Thomas Porter & Maria Porter -JGA
30 Jul 1837	Maria Catherine [Durbin] d/o John Durbin & Maria Durbin nee Winebrenner. Sps: Nathan Magers & Winifred Magers -JGA

17

18 Aug 1837	George [Logsdon] s/o David Logstone [Logsdon] and Rebecca nee Uhl. Sps: Nathan Magers & Winifred [Logsdon] Magers -JHC
22 Aug 1837	Nancy Jane [Porter] d/o David Porter & Lydia Sapp. Sps: Martha Sapp -JHC
23 Aug 1837	Edward Landon [Welker] s/o Solomon Welker & Elizabeth Richardson. Sps Martin & Anna Sapp -JHC
23 Aug 1837	Edmund Virtue Brent -JHC
21 Nov 1837	George Durbin b 21 Nov 1837 s/o Elijah Durbin & Margaret [Logsdon]. Sps: Ben Durbin & wife. [F-4] -JHC
14 Jan 1838	John Arnold s/o John Arnold & Christina Sapp. Sps: Simeon Sapp & Sara Durbin -MM
15 Jan 1838	Martha Frances Eckenrode d/o Henry Eckenrode & Maria Case. Sps: Bazil H. Durbin & Aparilla Durbin -MM
15 Jan 1838	George Trullinger s/o George Trullinger & Honora Durbin. Sps: John Durbin & Maria Durbin -MM
15 Jan 1838	Solomon Sapp s/o Levi Sapp & Maria Colopy. Sps: E. V. Brent & M. [Mary Ann] Sapp -MM
06 Jan 1838	John Magers s/o William Magers & Margaret Sapp. Sps: Nathan Magers & Winifred Magers -MM
>24 Feb 1838	Esther Jane Buckingham b 24 Feb 1838 d/o Absalom Buckingham & Nancy [Murphy]. Sps: Levi Sapp & Mrs. Pratt. [F-4] -MM
>02 Mar 1838	Delila Sapp b 2 Mar 1838 d/o [Simon] Hartley Sapp & Rachel [Sapp]. Sps Delila Colopy & Jacob Colopy [F-4] -MM
>13 Mar 1838	Joseph Valentine Shafer b 13 Mar 1838 s/o Peter Shafer & Nancy [White]. Sps: Elijah Durbin & wife Margaret. [F-4] -MM
20 May 1838	Emma Brent b 21 Jun 1815 d/o Samuel Brent & Anna Virtue. -MM
20 May 1838	William Jacob Bailes b 3 Nov 1837 s/o John Bailes & Allison Hopkins. Sps: Elijah Durbin & Mrs. Trullinger -MM

11 Aug 1838	Charles [Logsdon] s/o David Logsdon & Rebecca Logsdon aka Uhl. Sps: David Logsdon & Honora Durbin [F-9] -MM
11 Aug 1838	Henry Purcell [Pratt] s/o Henry Pratt & Penelope Pratt nee Buckingham. Sps: Dan Durbin & Sara Buckingham [F-9] -MM
04 Sep 1838	Elizabeth Ann Pyatt Logsdon b 1 Feb 1838 d/o John Logsdon & Elizabeth Hardy. Sps: Nathan W. Magers & wife. [F-5] -MM
04 Sep 1838	George [Jerome] Logsdon b 26 Jul 1838 [?] s/o John Logsdon & Elizabeth Hardy. Sps: Benjamin Blubaugh. [F-5] -MM

- The following are apparent baptisms written on a sheet identified as fragment number 3, [F-3], which also contained the list of members dated   19-20 MAY 1839. [see page 4]   The actual baptismal dates are unknown, but occurred on-or after- the birthdates, or before the next entry of 28 Jul 1839. The names of the officiating priest or priests are unknown.

1819	Catherine Devise w/o Joseph [John] Jones b 1819. [F-3] Elizabeth Jones d/o Joseph Jones & Catherine Devise.Sps: Mary Shults. [F-3]
>06 Oct 1836	Mary Shults b 6 Oct 1836 d/o Jacob Shults & Mary Breckler. Sps: Francis Breckler & Marianna his mother. [F-3]
>19 Mar 1837	Mary Jane Swarts b 19 Mar 1837 d/o Jacob Swarts & Margaret Breckler. Sps: Francis Breckler. [F-3]
>07 Dec 1837	Rebecca Durbin b 7 Dec 1837 d/o Elias Durbin & Mary Gorsage. Sps: Benjamin Durbin & wife. [F-3]
>13 Jun 1838	Richard Dial b 13 Jun 1838 s/o William Dial & Rebecca Arnold. Sps: Samuel McKenzie & wife. [F-3]

>*11 Aug 1838*   Sarah Catherine McGough b 11 Aug 1838 d/o Thomas McGough & Drusilla Losh. Sps: Rev. M. McAleer & Mrs. Trullinger. [F-3]

>*26 Aug 1838*   Henry Sapp b 26 Aug 1838 s/o Samuel Sapp & Susanna Magers. Sps: Thomas White & wife. [F-3]

>*07 Sep 1838*   Keziah Lorena White b 7 Sep 1838 d/o Anthony White & Keziah Wade. Sps: George Sapp Sr. & Mrs. Mary Draper. [F-3]

>*08 Sep 1838*   Dennis Durbin b 8 Sep 1838 s/o Joseph Durbin & Elizabeth Lybarger. Sps: Benjamin Durbin & wife. [F-3]

>*22 Sep 1838*   Catherine Margaret McKenzie b 22 Sep 1838 d/o Gabriel McKenzie & Ann Logue. Sps: Benjamin Blubaugh & Honora Blubaugh. [F-3]

>*20 Oct 1838*   John Peter Magers b 20 Oct 1838 s/o William Magers & Drusilla Sapp. Sps: Wm Magers & Catherine Durbin. [F-3]

>*01 Jan 1839*   Levi Francis Colopy b 1 Jan 1839 s/o Jacob Colopy & Delila Sapp. Sps: Jonathan Sapp & wife Mary. [F-3]

>*11 Jan 1839*   Catherine Isabel Payne b 11 Jan 1839 d/o Raphael Payne & Winifred Porter. Sps: Mr. Andreas Quin & wife. [F-3]

>*11 Jan 1839*   Bazil Durbin b 11 Jan 1839 s/o Samuel W. Durbin & Anna Blubaugh. Sps: Stephen Blubaugh & Winifred Blubaugh. [F-3]

>*27 Jan 1839*   Elias Porter b 27 Jan 1839 s/o John Porter & Rachel Arnold. Sps: Benjamin Durbin & wife. [F-3]

>*31 Jan 1839*   Peter McKenzie b 31 Jan 1839 s/o Ignatius McKenzie & Eliza McKenzie. Sps: Elizabeth Durbin & Stephen Elias McKenzie. [F-3]

>*10 Feb 1839*   Stephen Jerome Blubaugh b 10 Feb 1839 s/o Stephen Blubaugh & Honora his wife. Sps: Benjamin Blubaugh & wife. [F-3]

>*11 Apr 1839*   Mary Matilda Arnold b 11 Apr 1839 d/o John Arnold & Christina Sapp. Sps: William Carter & Rebecca Dial [F-3]

BAPTISMS

20 May 1839	Drusilla Losh b 27 Oct 1815 w/o Thomas McGough. Druscilla & Thomas were remarried by church this day. [F-3] -JGA
28 Jul 1839	Benjamin [Swarts] s/o Jacob Schwarz & Margaret Swarts nee Breckler. Sps: Benjamin Blubaugh & Esther McKenzie. [F-3] -JGA
28 Jul 1839	Raphael Hilary [McKenzie] s/o Moses McKenzie & Esther McKenzie nee Logue [Sapp]. Sps: Jacob Sapp & Mary Blubaugh. [F-3] -JGA
28 Jul 1839	Sara [McGough] d/o Patrick McGough & Ellen [Helen Durbin] McGough. Sps: Dan Durbin & Winifred Blubaugh. [F-3] -JGA
11 Aug 1839	Theodore [Allerding] b 27 Jan 1838 s/o Michael & Elizabeth [Anthony] Allerding Sps: Theodore Smithhisler & Mary Allerding -JGA
11 Aug 1839	Mary [Stoffer] b 1 Oct 1827 d/o John Stoffer & Harriet Stoffer nee Durbin Sps: Samuel Durbin & Helen Durbin [F-9] -JGA.
>18 Sep 1839	Elizabeth Durbin b 18 Sep 1839 d/o Henry Durbin & Nancy Stoffer Sps: Elias Durbin & Christina Arnold. [F-3]
17 Oct 1839	David Alfred Mitten s/o Lewis & Amelia Magers. Sps: Timothy Colopy & Barbara Helen Brophy -JBL
23 Oct 1839	Anna Durbin d/o Martin & Sara [Sapp] Durbin. Sps: Jonathan Sapp & Anna Sapp -JBL
>30 Oct 1839	Henry Alexander Blubaugh b 30 Oct 1839 [?] s/o Benjamin Blubaugh & Elizabeth Durbin Sps: Stephen Durbin & wife. [F-3]
1 Nov 1839	Jonathan David [McKenzie] s/o James McKenzie & Elsie [Ellen] Arnold. Sps: Jacob Ploubac & Rebecca Ploubac -JBL [See marriage 11 May 1833]
13 Nov 1839	Rufus Rowley. Sps: J. Lamy -JBL
14 Nov 1839	Martin Limert s/o Henry Limert & Bridget Work Sps: J. Lamy -JBL

21

17 Nov 1839	Elizabeth Losh d/o Joseph A. [Losh] & [Frances] Anna Balsher. -JBL
17 Nov 1839	Catherine Eifert d/o Michael Eifert & Elizabeth Brell. -JBL
17 Nov 1839	Henry Shaub s/o Adam [Shaub] & Martha Hunt. -JBL
17 Nov 1839	Margaret Helen [Jumbard] d/o George & Regina Jumbard. -JBL
17 Nov 1839	John Beam s/o Jacob Beam & Maria Kroughler -JBL
17 Nov 1839	Jacob Beam s/o Jacob & Maria Kroughler -JBL
07 Dec 1839	Maria [Zimmerman] s/o Frederick [Zimmerman Jr.] & Sara Colopy. Sps: Levi Sapp & Maria Colopy -JBL
07 Dec 1839	Matilda Hunt d/o Richard Hunt & Nancy Colopy. Sps: Levi Sapp & Maria Colopy -JBL
07 Dec 1839	William Hunt s/o Richard Hunt & Nancy Colopy. Sps: Levi Sapp & Anna Sapp -JBL
08 Dec 1839	John Willenpuc s/o John Willenpuc & Helen Koor. Sps: Edward Hook & Maria Fretke -JBL
25 Dec 1839	Samuel Brent s/o Edward [Brent] & Rebecca Magers. Sps: Samuel Sapp & Anne Brent -JBL
26 Dec 1839	Raphael Logue b 26 Dec 1839 [?] s/o John Logue & Elizabeth McKenzie. Sps: Benjamin Blubaugh & wife. [F-3] -JBL
06 Jan 1840	Caroline Postlewait b 6 May [1839] d/o Joseph [Postlewait] and Margaret Glesson. Sps: M. Morton & Mrs. Colopy -JBL
06 Jan 1840	Debora Postlewait b 4 May [1839] d/o Joseph Postlewait Sps: M. Morton & Mrs. Colopy -JBL
12 Feb 1840	Edward Brent b 2 Nov [1839] s/o Edmund Brent & Fanny [Frances Isabella] Sapp. Sps: George Sapp & Martha Sapp -JBL
18 Feb 1840	Sarah Catherine [Durbin] d/o Baptist [Durbin] & Catherine King. Sps: Absalom Buckingham & Maria Murphy -JBL

22

BAPTISMS

23 Feb 1840	Frances _____ d/o _____ McCarren & _____ Sps: ___ Morton & wife -JBL
29 Mar 1840	Mary Frances Critchfield d/o Hiram [Critchfield] & Harriet Porter. Sps: Nathan Magers & wife -JBL
29 Mar 1840	Jane Critchfield d/o Jesse [Critchfield] & Maria Horton. Sps: George Sapp & Honoura Trullinger -JBL
18 Apr 1840	Francis Brent (Adult) s/o Samuel Brent & Anna Virtue. Sps: Levi Sapp & Anna Brent -JBL
18 Apr 1840	Maria Brent (Adult). -JBL
19 Apr 1840	Elizabeth Magers d/o William Magers & Margaret Sapp. Sps: Simon H. Sapp & Maria McKenzie -JBL
19 Apr 1840	Mary Isabella Davidson d/o George [Davidson] & Rachel Payne. Sps: Raphael Payne & wife -JBL
19 Apr 1840	Richard Durbin d/o Samuel [Durbin] & Helen McKenzie. Sps: Benjamin Durbin & _____ -JBL
19 Apr 1840	Joseph Dial s/o Isaac [Dial & Nancy Durbin]. Sps: Elias Durbin -JBL
20 Apr 1840	Christina Gardner d/o Anthony [Gardner] & Barbara Lazarus. Sps: Stephen Blubaugh & wife -JBL
21 Apr 1840	Magdalena Earnst d/o Jacob [Earnst] & Eva Rich. Sps: Adam Schaub & Magdalena Schaub -JBL
21 Apr 1840	Mary Fesler d/o Joseph & Salome [Stark] Fesler. Sps: Laurence Fesler & Mary Baumy -JBL
21 Apr 1840	Sophia Eifert d/o Michael & Maria Eifert. Sps: Joseph Losh & Ferdinand Losh -JBL.
21 Apr 1840	Maria Bersang d/o Joseph & Anna Bersang Sps: Ignatius Shenenberger & Mary Baer -JBL
21 Apr 1840	Joseph Bersang s/o Michael [Bersang] & ~~Regina~~ ~~Sheneberger~~. Sps: Michael Schonenberger & Regina Schonenberger -JBL
21 Apr 1840	_____ Tramerle s/o Adam & Anna Tramerle. Sps: Paul Pullin & Agatha Reschner -JBL
16 May 1840	_____ Durbin ?/o Benjamin & Susan Durbin [F-7] -JBL

24 May 1840	Henry Eckenrode s/o Henry [Eckenrode] & [Mary Case]. Sps: Nathan Magers & wife [F-7] -JBL
28 May 1840	Frances Welker d/o Solomon [Welker] & Elizabeth Richardson. Sps: Benjamin Durbin & wife [F-7] -JBL
31 May 1840	Pauline Leoto d/o John Baptist [Leoto] & Josephine Inslow. Sps: Michael Uhl & Colettina Leota. [F-7] -JBL
31 May 1840	Margaret Joanna McGlaune d/o Jacob McGlaune & Fabi Warby. Sps: David Rowley & Nancy Agent [F-7] -JBL
07 Jun 1840	_____ Buckingham ?/o Absalom [Buckingham] and one of his sister. Sps: Ben Durbin & wife Rosanne Lybarger [F-7] -JBL.
08 Jun 1840	Michael Trullinger s/o George [Trullinger] & Honora Durbin. Sps: Ben Durbin & wife [F-7]. -JBL
11 Jun 1840	_____ Dial [See below]. Sps: Ben Durbin & wife.
11 Jun 1840	Rebecca Bricker d/o Christopher [Bricker] & Anna Buckingham. Sps: Ben Durbin & wife -JBL
11 Jun 1840	Rebecca Rachel Dial d/o William Dial & Rebecca Arnold. Sps: Ben Durbin & wife -JBL
17 Jun 1840	Nancy Jane Buckingham d/o Daniel [Buchingham] & Rebecca Bricker. Sps: Basil Durbin & wife Rosanne Buckingham -JBL
04 Jul 1840	Jacob Earnest b in May s/o Jacob Earnest & Eve Rich. Sps: Joseph Earnest & Christina Moser -JBL
12 Jul 1840	John Carter b 12 Jun [1840] s/o John [Carter] & Sarah Logue. Sps: John Logue & Rachel Logue -JBL
12 Jul 1840	Emilia Kreakbaum b 26 May 1838 d/o Conrad Kreakbaum & Priscilla Blair. Sps: Ben Durbin & _____ Krigbaum -JBL
12 Jul 1840	Priscilla Kreakbaum b 7 Feb 1820 w/o Conrad Kreakbaum. -JBL
23 Jul 1840	Benjamin Jones s/o John Jones & Catherine Devise. Sps: George Sapp & Maria Beachy -JBL
23 Jul 1840	Joseph Jones, brother preceeding. -JBL

BAPTISMS

23 Jul 1840	Jacob Jones s/o Michael Jones & Elizabeth Gaye. Sps: Christopher Beachy & wife Mary -JBL
23 Jul 1840	Mary Anna Jones. -JBL
23 Jul 1840	Nancy Jones, sister of preceeding. -JBL
07 Aug 1840	Anna White d/o ____ White. -JBL
15 Aug 1840	Paul Smith b 13 Jun 1840 s/o Isaac [Smith] & Mary Kreakbaum. Sps: Eve Brosnaham & Honora Trullinger -JBL
16 Aug 1840	Maria Frances Waggoner b 28 Apr 1840 d/o Henry [Waggoner] & Hanna Durbin. Sps: Ben Durbin & wife -JBL
22 Aug 1840	John Haas b 22 Apr 1838 s/o Francis Haas & Julia Cooper. Sps: Daniel Boyle & wife -JBL
22 Aug 1840	Elizabeth Haas b 10 Mar 1840. -JBL
22 Aug 1840	Martin Homan b 4 Aug 1840 s/o Paul [Homan] & Elizabeth Smith. Sps: Martin Sheneberger & Margarey Emerick -JBL
22 Aug 1840	Gaspar Bolger s/o David [Bolger] & Mariann Cammen. Sps: Gasper Keller & Susanna Cammon -JBL
25 Aug 1840	Anna Caroline Shults b 7 Feb 1840 d/o Jacob Shults & Mary Breckler. Sps: Christopher Breckler & Margaret Breckler -JBL
25 Aug 1840	Anthony Allerding b 21 Jul 1840 s/o Michael Allerding & Hyacinth Anthony. Sps: Anthony Whisler & Barbara Fairasen -JBL
25 Aug 1840	Catherine Whisler b 17 Jul 1840 d/o Anthony [Whisler] & Maria Fit[zpatrick] Sps: Michael Allerding & Catherine Allerding -JBL
25 Aug 1840	Anthony Whisler s/o Theodore [Whisler] & Barbara Fairasen. Sps: Anthony Whisler & Theodora Anthony -JBL
30 Aug 1840	Thomas Henry McMullen b 20 Aug 1840 s/o Thomas [McMullen] and Margaret Fitzpatrick. Sps: Henry Linhart & Bergetta Boret -JBL

20 Sep 1840	Honora Mumaw b 16 May 1840 d/o Frederick [Mumaw] & Honora Log[ue]. Sps: John Log[ue] & Rachel Log[ue] -JBL
20 Sep 1840	Emila Baugher b 24 May 1838 d/o Michael Baugher & Catherine Wilson. Sps: George Sapp & Catherine Arnold -JBL
17 Oct 1840	Leander Durbin b 5 Sep 1840 s/o Samuel W. Durbin & Anna Blubaugh. Sps Ben Blubaugh & Rosa Durbin -JBL
31 Oct 1840	Elizabeth Boeshart b 20 Aug 1840 d/o Joseph Boeshart & Barbara Morgan. Sps: Peter Kiner & Rachel Sheneberger -JBL
31 Oct 1840	Joseph Gillane b 25 oct 1840 s/o Paul Gillane & Rachel Huotts. Sps: Joseph Paulson & Susanna Caumer -JBL
01 Nov 1840	Catherine Durbin b 17 Sep 1840 d/o Bazil [Durbin] & Margaret [Aparilla] Buckingham. Sps: Nathan Magers & wife -JBL
01 Jan 1841	Catherine Sapp b 1 Oct 1840 d/o Simon Hartley [Sapp] & Lady [Rachel] Sapp. Sps: Benjamin Draper & Anna Sapp -JBL
01 Jan 1841	Sarah Elizabeth Porter b 18 Nov 1840 d/o John [Porter] & [Rachel] Arnold. Sps: George Trullinger & Honora Durbin -JBL
06 Jan 1841	Magdalena Homan b 16 Dec 1840 d/o Michael & Elizabeth [Neuth] [Homan] Sps: Adam Shaub & Magdalena Shaub -JBL
05 Jan 1841	Martha Frances Porter b 15 Oct 1840 d/o David [Porter] & Lady [Lydia] Sapp. Sps: Levi Sapp & Martha Sapp -JBL
17 Jan 1841	John [Boyle] b 7 Oct 1840 s/o Michael & Margaret Boyle. Sps: David Martin & wife Bridget -JBL
21 Jan 1841	Samuel White s/o [David White] & Rebecca Magers. Sps: Benjamin Durbin & Catherine Arnold -JBL
27 Jan 1841	Benjamin Blubaugh [Jr.] b 6 Jan 1841 s/o Benjamin [Blubaugh] & Elizabeth Durbin. Sps: Jacob Blubaugh and wife -JBL

BAPTISMS

06 Feb 1841   Joseph Fesler [Jr.]b 17 Nov 1840 s/o Joseph [Fesler] & Salome Stark. Sps: Laurence Fesler & Margaret Shenebarger -JBL

06 Feb 1841   Joseph ~~Crops~~ [Shaup] b 3 Jan 1841 s/o Joseph [Shaup] & Elizabeth Medrick. Sps: Joseph Boeshart & Barbara Morgan -JBL

07 Feb 1841   ~~Joanna Fisdora Christfield~~ [Phedora Jane Critchfield] b 5 Dec 1840 d/o Hiram Critchfield & Harriet Porter. Sps: George Sapp & Catherine Arnold -JBL

09 Mar 1841   Catherine Logsdon b 29 Oct 1840 d/o Daniel & Catherine Logsdon. Sps: Elias Arnold [Jr.] & wife [A. Lovina Logsdon] -JBL

25 Mar 1841   Jane [Eliza Jane] Davidson b 7 Oct 1840 d/o George [Davidson] & Rachel Payne. Sps: Levi Sapp & wife Mary Colopy -JBL

25 Mar 1841   George Payne's dau [Possibly Susanna Payne d/o George Payne & Anna Croy; 1850 census shows Susanna age 9 (b 1841)] -JBL

01 Apr 1841   Abalona Buck b 27 Apr 1840 d/o Eberhart Buck & Adaline Draper. Sps: _____ Breckler & _____ -JBL

11 Apr 1841   Jacob Shults. Sps: Levi Sapp & Anna Brent -JBL

11 Apr 1841   John Julius Brent. Sps: Levi Sapp & Anna Brent -JBL

11 Apr 1841   Julius Johns b 20 ___ 1840 s/o Gabriel [Johns] & Catherine Huits. Sps: Jacob Holler & Catherine Trobley. -JBL

11 Apr 1841   Mary Miller b 27 Jan 1841 d/o Martin & Margaret Miller. Sps: Jacob Swarts & Maria Hess -JBL

12 Apr 1841   Magdalena Losh b 9 Oct 1840 d/o Joseph [A. Losh] & Frances Balsher. Sps: Henry Nosfeld & Magdalena Nosfeld -JBL

12 Apr 1841   Margaret Sheneberger b 9 Mar 1841 d/o Michael [Sheneberger] & Margaret Richard. Sps: Michael Sheneberger & Margaret Sheneberger -JBL

21 Apr 1841	Anna Maria Croy w/o George Payne. Sps: Jacob Blubaugh & Maria Blubaugh -JBL
25 Apr 1841	____ Rowley s/o Rufus [Rowley] ____ Welch. Sps: Michael Boyle & wife Margaret -JBL
06 May 1841	Maria Logsdon b 1 Oct 1840 d/o John Logsdon & Elizabeth Hardy. Sps: Nathan Magers & Maria Durbin w/o Samuel -JBL
23 May 1841	Mary Eifert b 28 Mar 1841 d/o Michael [Eifert] & Elizabeth Brell. Sps: Henry Nosfeld & Margaret Nosfeld -JBL
30 May 1841	Celeste Brosnaham b 24 Jan 1841 d/o Thomas [Brosnaham] & Anna [McNamee]. Sps: Nathan Magers & Margaret Smith -JBL
30 May 1841	Francis Logsdon b 23 Apr 1841 s/o David [Logsdon] & Rebecca Houls [Uhl]. Sps: David Durbin & Rosa Durbin -JBL
30 May 1841	Stephen McKenzie b 6 Apr 1841 s/o Nathan McKenzie & Eliza Magers. Sps: Jacob Sapp & Maria Blubaugh -JBL
31 May 1841	Catherine Douche b 7 Feb 1835 d/o Joseph [Douche] & Catherine Holler. Sps: Christopher Breckler & Maria Hess -JBL
31 May 1841	Elisabeth b 29 Mar 1841 Douche b 7 Feb 1835 d/o Joseph [Douche] & Catherine Holler. -JBL
31 May 1841	~~Elizabeth~~ [Catherine Douche] Joseph's wife.
10 Jun 1841	Anna Stoffer b 15 Aug 1840 d/o John [Stoffer] & Anna [Harriet] Durbin. Sps: Benjamin Durbin & wife _____ -JBL
10 Jun 1841	Jacob Shults b 7 May 1841 s/o Jacob [Shults] & Catherine Breckler. Sps: Jacob Swarts & ____ Gardner -JBL
03 Jul 1841	Christopher Eifert s/o Michael [Eifert] & Elizabeth Brell. Sps: Gaspard Sheneberger & Rachel Sheneberger -JBL
03 Jul 1841	Amy Sarah Hosfeld b 01 Jun 1840 d/o Henry [Hosfeld] & Mary Veronica Bichof. Sps: Joseph Losh & Anna Fritz -JBL

BAPTISMS

12 Jul 1841   Maria Keiler [Keller] d/o Michael ~~Keiler~~ [Keller] & Maria Morning. Sps: Jacob Wollensneider & wife -JBL

18 Jul 1841   Winifred White d/o Lewis White & [Rebecca Welchammer]. Sps: George Trullinger & wife Honora Durbin -JBL

18 Jul 1841   Joan Frances Brent b 3 Jun 1841 d/o Edmund [Brent] & Rebecca Magers. Sps: Gabriel Magers & Frances Brent -JBL

18 Jul 1841   Anna Arnold b 27 May 1841 d/o John [Arnold] & Christina Sapp. Sps: William Magers & Sarah Ann Durbin -JBL

18 Jul 1841   Edward Payne b 15 Jun 1841 s/o Raphael [Payne] & Winifred Porter. Sps: Elias Arnold & wife -JBL

01 Aug 1841   Simon Blubaugh b 8 Mar 1841 s/o Stephen [Blubaugh] & Honora Logsdon. Sps: Anthony Gardner & wife Maria Barbara -JBL

15 Aug 1841   Norman McGough b 6 Jul 1841 s/o Patrick McGough & Helen Durbin. Sps: Benjamin Blubaugh & wife Elizabeth Durbin -JBL

22 Aug 1841   Barbara Sheneberger b 7 Jul 1834 d/o Martin Sheneberger & Margaret Emerick. Sps: Jacob Earnest & Barbara Morgan -JBL

27 Aug 1841   Rebecca Jane Bricker b 17 Sep 1831 d/o George Bricker & Catherine Buckingham Sps: Absolam Buckingham & Honora Trullinger [F-8] -JBL

27 Aug 1841   Mary [Aparilla] Bricker b 18 Feb 1835 d/o George Bricker & Catherine Buckingham Sps: Basil Durbin & Maria Buckingham [F-8] -JBL

02 Sep 1841   George Thomas Christian b 24 Nov 1840 s/o Thomas Christian & Susanna Shink. Sps: Peter Morton & Brigett Morton -JBL

05 Sep 1841   Anna Fesler b 16 Feb 1841 d/o Joseph Fesler & Phoebe Ann Priess. Sps: William Miller & Catherine McFarland -JBL

05 Sep 1841   Elizabeth O'Hara d/o Thomas & Anna O'Hara.
               Sps: John Wallensneider & Brigett O'Henry -JBL

05 Sep 1841   Marianna Etrick b 19 Aug 1841 d/o Joseph Etrick &
               Marianna Letsler. Sps: Demetrius Thomas & Catherine
               Emberish -JBL

11 Sep 1841   Anna Connely b 14 Aug 1841 d/o Patrick Connely &
               Margaret Eagan. Sps: Michael McFarland & Maria
               McFarland -JBL

11 Sep 1841   Adam Sapp b 11 Sep 1811 s/o Frederick Sapp [Jr.] &
               Mary Parker. Sps: John Lamy & Elizabeth McKenzie
               -JBL

13 Sep 1841   John Absolam Pratt b 6 Jun 1841 s/o Henry [Pratt] &
               Penelope Buckingham. Sps: David Morton & Brigett
               Morton -JBL

03 Oct 1841   Peter McCarren b 21 Sep 1841 s/o Jacob McCarren &
               Susanna Nerret. Sps: David Nerret & Matilda Colopy
               -JBL

31 Oct 1841   Adam Kinter b 30 Sep 1841 s/o Peter Kinter & Delila
               Morgan. Sps: Philip Morgan & Margaret Sheneburger
               -JBL

01 Sep 1841   Delila Ann Colopy b 7 Jun [1841] d/o Jacob Colopy &
               Delila Sapp. Sps: Levi Sapp & Maria Colopy -JBL

08 Oct 1841   Joseph Close b 17 Jul 1836 s/o Jacob Close & Mary
               Arnold. Sps: George Sapp & [wife] Catherine Arnold
               -JBL

08 Oct 1841   Marianne Close b 24 Jan 1837 d/o Jacob Close & Mary
               Arnold. -JBL

08 Oct 1841   Catherine Elizabeth Close b 29 Jun 1840 s/o Jacob Close
               & Mary Arnold -JBL

15 Oct 1841   Elizabeth Hardy w/o John Logdon
               Sps: Paul Blubaugh -JBL

01 Jan 1842   Silvern Sapp b 21 Oct 1841 s/o Jacob [Sapp] & Winifred
               Blubaugh. Sps: Simon Sapp & Maria Blubaugh -JBL

BAPTISMS

02 Jan 1842	Mariann Starner d/o Silvern [Starner] & Theresa Chinie [Chaney]. Sps: Joseph Chinie [Chaney] & Mariann Chiney [Chaney]. GERMAN CONGREGRATION.
02 Feb 1842	Marianna Starner d/o Sid [Starner] & Theresa Chaney. Sps: Joseph Chaney & Mariann Chaney -JBL
10 Jan 1842	Isaac Johns b 3 Nov 1841 s/o Benjamin [Johns] & Elizabeth Richards. Sps: Christopher Breckler & Margaret Allending -JBL
10 Jan 1842	Caroline Beam b 23 Oct 1841 d/o Jacob [Beam] & Maria Kroughler. Sps: Henry Shenebarger & Margaret Kroughler -JBL
11 Jan 1842	Elias Shannon b 23 Feb 1841 s/o _____ [Shannon] & Elizabeth Sapp. Sps: Elias Arnold [Jr.] & Rachel Porter -JBL
13 Jan 1842	Thomas Bourner b 11 Jun 1841 s/o John [Bourner] & Anna Carr. Sps: William Milley & Elizabeth Wollensneider -JBL
13 Jan 1842	John Helm b 2 Jan 1842 s/o Lawrence [Helm] & Theresa Ascot. Sps: Martin Ferry & Maria Offmyer -JBL
24 Jan 1842	Alexander Queen b 12 Apr 1826 s/o Jacob [Queen] & Mariann Butler. Sps: Joseph Henry & Sarah Walker -JBL
24 Jan 1842	Elizabeth Queen b 12 May 1829 d/o Jacob [Queen] & Mariann Butler. Sps: Joseph Henry & Sarah Walker -JBL
30 Jan 1842	John Wilton Bowser b 28 Aug 1841 s/o Michael [Bowser] & Catherine Wilton. Sps: Ben Durbin & Rosa Durbin -JBL
13 Feb 1842	Benjamin Horn b 13 Jan 1842 s/o Daniel [Horn] & Joanna Durbin. Sps: Ben Durbin & Rosa Durbin -JBL
17 Feb 1842	Herman White b 1 Jan 1842 s/o Joseph [White] & [Hannah DeWitt]. Sps: Thomas Garety & Elizabeth Garety -JBL
11 Mar 1842	Priscilla Kreakbaum b 18 Jan 1842 d/o Conrad [Kreakbaum] & Priscilla Blair. Sps: Stephen Blubaugh & Honora Trullinger -JBL

20 Mar 1842	Normanda Sapp b 1842 d/o Levi [Sapp] & Maria Colopy. Sps: Jacob Colopy -JBL
20 Mar 1842	_____ Buckingham b 1842 ?/0 Daniel [Buckingham] & [Rebecca] Bricker. Sps: Ben Durbin & Rosa Durbin -JBL
20 Mar 1842	_____ White b 1835 d/o Lewis [White] & Rebecca Welshammer. Sps: David Durbin & Anna Sapp -JBL
26 Mar 1842	Peter Shafer b 12 Jul 1801. Sps: George Sapp & Catherine Arnold [F-2] -JBL
26 Mar 1842	George Albert Draper b 6 Feb 1842 s/o Benjamin [Draper] & Martha Sapp. Sps: Edmund Brent & Frances Brent [F-2] -JBL
27 Mar 1842	George Oliver Lepley b 2 Feb 1840 s/o Francis [Lepley] & Jane Arnold. Sps: David Logsdon & Rebecca Dial [F-2] -JBL
27 Mar 1842	Eliza Lepley b 20 Feb 1840 s/o Francis [Lepley] & Joanna Arnold. Sps: David Logsdon & Rebecca Dial -JBL
27 Mar 1842	Eliza Dial b 18 Jan 1842 d/o William & Rebecca [Arnold] Dial. Sps: Elias Arnold & wife [F-2] -JBL
27 Mar 1842	Lucinda McCarthy b 26 Jul 1841 d/o Henry [McCarthy] & Martha Curry. Sps: George Trullinger & Honora Trullinger [F-2] -JBL
27 Mar 1842	Christopher Swarts b 28 Oct 1841 s/o Jacob [Swarts] & Margaret Breckler. Sps: Christopher & Margaret Sheneberger [F-2] -JBL.
27 Mar 1842	Rachel Susanna McKenzie b 1 Jan 1842 d/o James [McKenzie] & Elsie [Ellen] Arnold. Sps: Jacob McKenzie & Maria McKenzie -JBL
28 Mar 1842	Margaret Ernest b 7 Jan 1842 d/o Jacob Ernest & wife Eva Rich. Sps: Martin Sheneberger & Margaret Emerick [F-2] -JBL
28 Mar 1842	Elizabeth Homan b Mar 1842 d/o Michael [Homan] & Elizabeth *Neuth.* Sps Paul Homan & Elizabeth Homan [F-2] -JBL

BAPTISMS

28 Mar 1842	John Andrew Gramore b 6 Sep 1841 s/o William Gramore & M. Draper. Sps: Andrew Gramore & Athifer Kemble -JBL
28 Mar 1842	Phillip Boeshart b 1 Mar 1842 s/o Joseph [Boeshart] & Barbara Morgan. Sps: Philip Morgan & Margaret Sheneberger [F-2] -JBL
28 Mar 1842	Felicia Payson b 6 Jan 1842 s/o Joseph [Payson] & Anne Speiker. Sps: ____ Shenberger & Margaret Garner [F-2] -JBL
03 Apr 1842	Elizabeth Goring b 20 Mar 1842 d/o John [Goring] & Barbara Weaver. Sps: John Weaver & Elizabeth Weaver [F-6] -JBL
03 Apr 1842	Julianna R. Lafferty b 18 Mar 1842 d/o Roddy Lafferty & Rosanna Paton. Sps: Thomas Lafferty & Marianne Brown [F-6] -JBL
07 Apr 1842	James Martin s/o John [Martin] & Bridget McFarland. Sps: [illegible] [F-6] -JBL
10 Apr 1842	William Henry McGough b 7 Feb 1842 s/o Henry [McGough] & Margaret Arnold. Sps: ____ Boyle & Margaret Boyle [F-6] -JBL

No records found between 10 Apr 1842 and 11 Feb 1844.

Start book 2

11 Feb 1844	Christopher Bricker b 1810. -JBL
19 Apr 1844	Elizabeth Magers w/o David White. -JBL
30 Apr 1844	Marie Hess w/o Francis Hess. -JBL
17 Mar 1844	William McGraw b 24 Feb 1844 s/o Patrick [McGraw] & Catherine Johnson. Sps: Catherine McGraw—JBL
21 Apr 1844	Marie Isabelle Draper b 18 Mar 1844 d/o Benjamin [Draper] & Martha Sapp. Sps: Simon H. Sapp & Isabella Brent -JBL

21 Apr 1844	Thomas Payne b 12 Mar 1844 s/o George Payne [& Anna Croy]. Sps: Benjamin Blubaugh & Rachel Logue -JBL
06 Jun 1844	Jacob Carter b 17 Nov 1843 s/o John [Carter] & Sarah Logue. Sps: John Logue & Anna Logue -JBL
09 Jun 1844	Levi Francis Swarts b 12 May 1844 s/o Jacob [Swarts] & Margaret Breckler. Sps: Anthony Gardner & Maria Gardner -JBL
09 Jun 1844	David Blubaugh b 9 Mar 1844 s/o Benjamin [Blubaugh] & Charlotte Heckler. Sps: Francis Breckler & Rachel Blubaugh -JBL
09 Jun 1844	Maria Penelope Pratt b 17 Nov 1843 d/o Henry [Pratt] & Penelope Buckingham. Sps: William Magers & Jane Buckingham -JBL
24 Jul 1844	Catherine Breckler b 29 Feb 1815.
24 Jul 1844	Martha Durbin b 9 Jun 1844 d/o [John] Baptist [Durbin] & Catherine King. Sps: Benedict Magers & Rebecca Durbin -JBL
24 Jul 1844	Maria Catherine Durbin b 17 Jun 1844 d/o Samuel [Durbin] & Anna Blubaugh. Sps: John Durbin & Margaret Durbin -JBL
02 Aug 1844	Joseph Miller b 27 Jul 1842 s/o Vincent [Miller] & Margaret Stillinger. Sps: Henry Hosfeld & Veronica Hosfeld -JBL
02 Aug 1844	Christina [Miller] b 8 Apr 1844 d/o Vincent Miller [& Margaret Stillinger]. Sps: Joseph Miller -JBL
04 Aug 1844	James Leo [Ferenbaugh] b 20 Aug 1843 s/o Fidele Ferenbaugh & Eliza Draper. Sps: Benjamin Draper & Martha Draper -JBL
11 Aug 1844	John Davidson b 18 Apr 1842 s/o George [Davidson] & Rachel Payne. Sps: Richard Arnold & Jane Payne -JBL
11 Aug 1844	Elias Davidson b 17 Jan 1844 s/o George Davidson & Rachel Payne. Sps: Benedict Magers & Joanna Smith -JBL
11 Aug 1844	Matilda Dial b 3 May 1844 d/o William [Dial] & Rebecca Arnold. Sps: Lewis Sapp & Sarah Sapp -JBL

11 Aug 1844	Thomas McKenzie b 5 Jul 1844 s/o Jacob [McKenzie] & ~~Louisa~~ Ellen Arnold. Sps: Lawrence Sprague [?] & Matilda Arnold -JBL
01 Sep 1844	Joseph Buckingham b 1780, sub-conditional, by Bishop of Cincinnati.
01 Sep 1844	Frederick Zimmerman b 1816, sub-conditional, by Bishop of Cincinnati.
01 Sep 1844	Isaac Dial, sub-conditional, by Bishop of Cincinnati.
13 Oct 1844	Catherine Gardner b 22 Aug [1844] d/o Anthony [Gardner] & Barbara Lazarus. Sps: Joseph King & Catherine Gardner -JBL
20 Oct 1844	Sarah Anna Sapp b 30 Aug 1844 d/o Jonathan [Sapp] & Maria Durbin. Sps: George Sapp & Sara Ann Sapp -JBL
10 Nov 1844	Frances Ann Porter b 27 Sep 1843/4 d/o John Porter & Rachel Arnold. Sps: Benedict Magers & Maria Blubaugh -JBL
31 Nov 1844	Joseph Sapp s/o Robert [Sapp] & Rosanna Lore. Sps: Henry Porter & Lucinda Porter -JBL
25 Dec 1844	Emeline Augusta [Payne] b 13 Oct 1844 d/o John Payne & Joan Rundle. Sps: John Durbin & Rachel Davidson -JBL
29 Dec 1844	John Baptist Bricker b 26 Oct 1844 s/o Christopher [Bricker] & Anna [Nancy] Buckingham. Sps Dan Buckingham & Rebecca Buckingham -JBL
01 Jan 1845	Elizabeth Warden Sps: Benjamin Durbin & Rosa Durbin -JBL
02 Jan 1845	Anna Kreakbaum b 25 Jul 1844 d/o Conrad [Kreakbaum] & Priscilla Blair. Sps: Ben Durbin & Rachel Durbin -JBL
06 Jan 1845	John Haverick b 15 Oct 1844 s/o Joseph Haverick & Elizabeth Dixon. Sps: Ulysses Haverick & Mariann Haverick -JBL
20 Jan 1845	Sara Helen Beachy b 18 Jul 1844 d/o Jonathan Beachy & Sarah Draper. Sps: Frederick Zimmerman & Maria Parr -JBL

13 Mar 1845	Isaac Dial b 30 Oct 1845 s/o Lewis [Dial] & Rachel Reems. Sps: Samuel Durbin & Miranda Dial -JBL
14 Mar 1845	Maria Matilda Colopy b 29 Jul 1844 d/o Jacob Colopy & Delila Sapp. Sps: Leo Sapp & Ann Sapp -JBL
23 Mar 1845	Martha Ogg b 23 Dec 1844 d/o James J. Ogg & Julia [Ann] Logsdon. Sps: Absalom Buckingham & Maria Sapp -JBL
30 Mar 1845	Joseph Smith b 24 Jan 1845 s/o Isaac Smith & Maria Kreakbaum. Sps: Jonathan Sapp & Harriet Critchfield -JBL
30 Mar 1845	Margaret Sapp b 7 Feb 1845 d/o James Sapp & Winnie Blubaugh. Sps: Jacob McKenzie & Esther McKenzie -JBL
31 Mar 1845	Maria Starner b 25 Jan 1845 d/o Lewis [Starner] & Carol Myers. Sps: Adam Shaub & Maria Shaub -JBL
31 Mar 1845	Eva Catherine Homan b 6 Jan 1845 d/o Michael Homan & Elizabeth Neuth. Sps: Jacob Wiley & Catharine Moser -JBL
20 Apr 1845	Lucinda Logsdon b 15 Feb 1845 d/o David [Logsdon] & Rebecca [Uhl]. Sps: John Blubaugh & Maria Blubaugh -JBL
11 May 1845	Francis Xavier McKenzie b 30 Mar 1845 s/o Elias Stephen [McKenzie] & Maria Blubaugh. Sps: Henry & Rebecca Blubaugh -JBL
11 May 1845	Honora Frances Hess b 11 Apr 1845 d/o Samuel [Hess] & Sara Anna Eckenrode. Sps: Benedict Magers & Henrietta Eckenrode -JBL
18 May 1845	Absolam Sapp b 14 Dec 1827 s/o Adam Sapp & Mary Magdalena Lybarger. -JBL
18 May 1845	Benjamin Flatz b 9 Apr 1845 s/o Joseph [Flatz] & Eva Eckenrode. Sps: Daniel Buckingham & Ann Bricker -JBL
21 May 1845	Druscilla McGough b 16 Nov 1844 d/o Patrick [McGough] & Helen Durbin. Sps: James Sapp & Winifred Sapp -JBL

25 May 1845	William Francis McKenzie b 3 Dec 1844 s/o Samuel & Henrietta McKenzie. Sps: John Logue & Maria Dial -JBL
25 May 1845	Ambrose Logue b 17 Apr 1845 s/o Francis [Logue] & Honora Dial. Sps: Samuel McKenzie & Paula McKenzie -JBL
26 May 1845	Apolonia Whisler b 22 Apr 1845 d/o Anthony [Whisler] & Margaret Sheneberger. Sps: Theodore Whisler & Apollonia Sheneberger -JBL
26 May 1845	Anna Myers b 10 Jul 1844 d/o Peter [Myers] & Maria Anna Keller. Sps: Christopher Breckler & Maria Anna Krough -JBL
01 Jun 1845	John Ryan [Jr.] b 17 Jan 1845 s/o John [Ryan] & Maria Payne. Sps: George Payne & Rachel Davidson -JBL
08 Jun 1845	John Logsdon b 31 Jan 1845 s/o William Logsdon & Elizabeth Magers. Sps: John Magers & Lydia Porter -JBL
22 Jun 1845	Maurice Welsh b 16 Jun 1845 s/o Maurice Welsh & Julia Duboy. Sps: William Magers & Margaret Magers -JBL
02 Jul 1845	Barbara McNamara b 22 May 1845 d/o Francis [McNamara] & Christine Weber. Sps: William Cummins & Margaret McNamara -JBL
17 Jul 1845	William Farell b ___ 1845 s/o Henry [Farell]. -JBL
20 Jul 1845	Angeline Shults b 9 Apr 1845 d/o Jacob Shults & Maria Breckler. Sps: Benjamin & Naomi Hessler -JBL
20 Jul 1845	Jacob Smith b 14 Jul 1845 s/o Aloysius [Smith] & Catherine Harlett. Sps: Jacob Shults & Maria Breckler -JBL.
02 Aug 1845	Maria McNamara b 9 Apr 1845 d/o William McNamara & Anna Brigett Donnell. Sps: John Welsh & Catherine Welsh -JBL
03 Aug 1845	Helen Brosnaham b 23 Jan 1845 d/o Thomas [Brosnaham] & Anna McNamara. Sps: Maurice Welsh & Rachel Arnold -JBL
11 Aug 1845	Peter Carr b 15 Jun 1845 s/o Francis [Carr] & Catherine Cassellton. Sps: Michael Hughes & Sarah Hughes -JBL

21 Aug 1845	Anna Levina White b 9 Apr 1844 d/o Joseph [White] & Joanne DeWitt Sps: George Sapp & Catherine Sapp.
25 Aug 1845	Philip Shaub b 7 Jul 1845 s/o Adam [Shaub] & Magdalena Smithhisler. Sps: Phillip Smithhisler & Mary Ann Ulm -JBL
25 Aug 1845	Peter Sheneberger b 17 Jun 1845 s/o Martin [Sheneberger] & Margaret Emerick. Sps: Peter Rinter & Violet his wife -JBL
07 Sep 1845	Druscilla [Sapp] b 19 Jan 1840 d/o Robert Sapp & Rose Anna Lore. Sps: William Magers & Harriet Critchfield -JBL
07 Sep 1845	Maria Elizabeth Sapp b 2 Mar 1845 d/o Robert Sapp & Rose Anna Lore. Sps: Raphael Payne & Lydia Porter -JBL
11 Sep 1845	Sara Maria Chapin b 1827 d/o Audy [Chapin] & Annie Durn. -JBL
11 Sep 1845	Jacob Welsh b 7 Sep 1825. -JBL
14 Sep 1845	Margaret Elizabeth Buckingham b 11 Aug 1845 d/o Daniel [Buckingham] & Rebecca Bricker. Sps: Lawrence Magers & Joan Buckingham -JBL
19 Oct 1845	Moses McKenzie b 26 Aug 1845 s/o Jacob [McKenzie] & Effie [Esther] Sapp. Sps: Maria Durbin & Sarah Durbin -JBL
19 Oct 1845	George [Washington] Sapp b 18 Aug 1845 s/o Simon [Hartley] Sapp & Rachel Sapp. Sps: Edgar Brent & Martha Draper -JBL
19 Oct 1845	George Solomon Arnold b Sep 1845 s/o John Arnold & Christina Sapp. Sps: Jacob McKenzie & Esther McKenzie -JBL
16 Nov 1845	Sarah Margaret Logsdon b 27 Oct 1845 d/o Zachary [Logsdon] & Sarah Buckingham. Sps: Dan Buckingham & Rebecca Buckingham. -JBL
__ Dec 1845	_____ Engle -JBL
15 Dec 1845	_____ Brophy s/o William [Brophy] -JBL

BAPTISMS

25 Dec 1845	Maria Welsh b 27 Jul 1845 d/o Peter [Welsh] & Barbara Sergent. Sps: William Walker & Anna Walker -JBL
04 Jan 1846	Alice Brent b 8 Sep 1845 d/o Edmund [Brent] & ~~Anna~~ [Frances] Sapp. Sps: Edgar Brent & Emma Brent -JBL
06 Jan 1846	Charles Henry Warden b 17 May 1843 s/o Henry Warden & Elizabeth Burr. Sps: Edmund Brent & Emma Brent -JBL
18 Jan 1846	John Lyman Durbin b 13 Oct [1845] s/o Samuel [Durbin] & Anne Blubaugh. Sps: Martin Durbin & Maria Blubaugh -JBL
25 Jan 1846	Margaret Sapp d/o Robert [Sapp] & [Rosanne] Lore Sps: Jacob Swarts & Margaret Swarts.
25 Jan 1846	Helen White b 22 Jul 1843 d/o Lewis White & Rebecca Welchhammer Sps: George Trullinger & Honora his wife.
27 Jan 1846	Apollonia Sheneberger b Jan [1846] d/o Gaspar [Sheneberger] & Apollonia Fritz his wife. Sps: Martin Sheneberger & Maria Fritz -JBL
27 Jan 1846	Joseph Losh s/o Joseph [Losh] & Frances Balzer. Sps: Joseph [Henry] Hosfeld & Veronica his wife -JBL
02 Feb 1846	_____ Croy -JBL
13 Feb 1846	Benjamin Magers -JBL
22 Feb 1846	William Allen White b 22 Jul 1845 s/o Anthony [White] & Keziah Wade. Sps: Laurence Magers & Elizabeth Dial -JBL
02 Mar 1846	Maria Shaub b 18 Aug 1839 d/o John [Shaub] & Maria Cocanower. Sps: Theodore Whisler & Helen Yunker -JBL
25 Mar 1846	Francis Blubaugh b 10 Dec 1845 s/o Benjamin [Blubaugh] & Charlotte Heckler. Sps: George Sapp & Anna Sapp -JBL
31 Mar 1846	Emily Elmore b 18 Jun 1845 d/o Jacob [Elmore] & Eliza King. Sps: John Farrell & wife Laura -JBL

39

03 Apr 1846	Helen McGough b 17 Nov 1845 d/o Patrick [McGough] & Helena Durbin. Sps: Jacob Blubaugh & wife Honora -JBL
05 Apr 1846	Margaret Hollet b 14 Dec 1845 d/o Nicholas [Hollet] & Ursula Kleiman. Sps: Alvin Smidt & Rachel Colglesser -JBL
19 Apr 1846	Francis Shults b 26 Mar 1838 s/o Jacob [Shults] & Maria Breckler. Sps: Francis Breckler & Charlotte Blubaugh -JBL
20 Apr 1846	John Kilkenny [Jr.] b 1 Apr 1846 s/o John Kilkenny & Maria Donahue. Sps: Michael Boyle & Brigett Johnson -JBL
03 May 1846	Maria Breckler b 3 Mar 1846 d/o Francis [Breckler] & Catherine Heckler. Sps: Jacob Shults & wife -JBL
03 May 1846	John Waggoner b 20 Feb 1846 s/o Henry Waggoner & Hannah Durbin. Sps: Martin Durbin & wife -JBL
03 May 1846	Mary Angela Horn b 21 Mar 1846 d/o Daniel Horn & Jane Durbin. Sps: Raphael Magers & Elizabeth Logsdon -JBL
30 May 1846	William Thomas Critchfield b 20 Apr 1846 s/o Hiram [Critchfield] & Harriet Porter. Sps: Robert Sapp & Lucinda Magers -JBL
31 May 1846	Lydia Colglesser d/o John [Colglesser] & Elizabeth Blubaugh. Sps: George Sapp & Anna Sapp; [Lydia married Zachary Blubaugh] -JBL
06 Jun 1846	Joseph Kinny b __ Jan 1846. -JBL
14 Jun 1846	Benedict Perfectus Durbin b 18 Apr 1846 s/o John [Durbin] & Margaret Logsdon. Sps: Benedict Magers & wife -JBL
21 Jun 1846	Thomas Porter b 19 May 1846 s/o David [Porter] & Lydia Sapp. Sps: Simon H. Sapp & Elizabeth Colopy -JBL
30 Jun 1846	Augustine Gallagher b 2 Jul 1845 s/o Edward [Gallagher] & Lucinda _____ [illegible] -JBL
05 Jul 1846	Maria Welsh b 8 May 1846 d/o John [Welsh] and Catherine McNamara. Sps: Jacob Welsh & Jane Payne -JBL

40

BAPTISMS

05 Jul 1846	John Baptist Durbin b 4 Mar 1846 s/o Baptist [Durbin] & Catherine King. Sps: Samuel Walker & Marianna Durbin -JBL
19 Jul 1846	Charles Robert Bradfield b 31 May 1846 s/o James W [Bradfield] & Sara Ann Sapp. Sps: Levi Sapp & Lucinda Sapp -JBL
19 Jul 1846	Eliza Porter b 6 May 1846 d/o John [Porter] & Rachel Arnold. Sps: Leo Logsdon & Matilda Arnold -JBL
19 Jul 1846	Margaret McKenzie b 29 May 1846 d/o James McKenzie & Elsa Ellen Anna Arnold. Sps: John Porter & Margaret Magers -JBL
26 Jul 1846	Melissa Anna Durbin b 4 Jun 1841 d/o Bazil [Durbin] & Maria Aparilla Buckingham. Sps: Dan Buckingham & Joanna Buckingham -JBL
23 Aug 1846	Julian Sapp b 25 Jun 1846 s/o Levi [Sapp] & Maria Colopy. Sps: Edmund Brent & Emma Brent -JBL
23 Aug 1846	Anna Brent b 24 Jul 1846 d/o Edgar [Brent] & Rebecca Magers. Sps: Julius Brent & Anna Brent -JBL
23 Aug 1846	Samuel Warden b 3 Jul 1846 s/o Henry Warden & Elizabeth Burr. Sps: Edgar Brent & Isabella Brent -JBL
15 Sep 1846	Anna Louise Elmore b 4 Jan 1842 d/o Jacob Elmore & Elise King. Sps: John Farrell & Emily King -JBL
15 Sep 1846	Sara Catherine Elmore b 1844 d/o Jacob Elmore & Elise King. -JBL
15 Sep 1846	Maria Hatfield d/o Sara Hatfield. Sps: John Farrell & Sara Evans -JBL
28 Sep 1846	Mary Jane Sherry b 20 Sep 1845 d/o John [Sherry] & Lucinda Harder. Sps: Henry Best & Elizabeth Eberling -JBL
30 Sep 1846	Julianna Sheehy b 25 Sep 1844 d/o Edward Sheehy & Marianna Stout. Sps: Michael Hogan & Helen Hogan -JBL
04 Oct 1846	Elizabeth Stoffer b 14 Sep 1845 d/o John [Stoffer] & Henrietta Durbin. Sps: Samuel Durbin & Elizabeth Dial -JBL

ST. LUKE'S RECORDS

04 Oct 1846   Martha Ashburn b 24 Aug 1846 d/o Ellis [Ashburn] & Rebecca Durbin. Sps: John Durbin & Elizabeth Durbin -JBL

11 Oct 1846   Charles Metzger b 13 Sep 1846 s/o Joseph [Metzger] & Marianna Bechtel. Sps: Charles Bechtel & Catherine King -JBL

11 Oct 1846   Maria Buckingham b 6 Aug 1846 d/o Absalom Buckingham & Nancy Murphy. Sps: John Morton & wife Catherine -JBL

25 Oct 1846   Martin Sheneberger b 15 Sep 1846 s/o Henry [Sheneberger] & Susanna Camel. Sps: Martin Sheneberger & wife Margaret -JBL

25 Oct 1846   Laurence King b 15 Sep 1846 s/o Anthony King & CatherineKeefer. Sps: Laurence King & wife Catharine Lore -JBL

25 Oct 1846   Angelina Boeshart b 1 Sep 1846 d/o Joseph [Boeshart] & Barbara Morgan Sps: Phillip Morgan & Maria Starner.

01 Nov 1846   Henry Sapp b 5 Jul 1846 s/o Adam [Sapp] & Maria Roush [Lybarger ?] Sps: Thomas Porter & wife _____.-JBL

03 Nov 1846   Susanna Bailes b 1 Sep 1846 d/o Joseph [Bailes] and Anna Spechler. Sps: Ferdinand Fritz & Susanna Fritzmeyer -JBL

08 Nov 1846   Lucinda Carter b 23 Sep 1846 d/o William [Carter] & Rachel Logue. Sps: Henry Blubaugh & Sally Blubaugh -JBL

20 Nov 1846   Susanna Sapp b 6 Aug 1846 d/o Jonathan [Sapp] & Maria Durbin. Sps: John Durbin & Margaret Durbin -JBL

06 Dec 1846   Charles Emmanuel Sapp b 2 Aug 1846 s/o Lewis [Sapp] & Sara Arnold. Sps: Leo Logsdon & Mathilda Arnold -JBL

15 Dec 1846   Peter Sholl b 26 Nov 1846 s/o Jacob [Sholl] & Elizabeth Kerol. Sps: Francis Buckhart & Maria Sholl -JBL

15 Dec 1846   Henry Crabaugh b 13 Dec 1846 s/o William [Crabaugh] & Barbara Yunkawig. Sps: Francis Buckhart -JBL

BAPTISMS

15 Dec 1846	John Henry Shoemaker b 13 Nov 1846 s/o John [Shoemaker] & Magdalena Eberling. Sps Joseph Eberling & Catherine Eberling -JBL
03 Jan 1847	Isaac Engle b 9 May 1835 s/o Elias Engle & Carol Hull. Sps: Ben Durbin & wife Rosa Anna -JBL
03 Jan 1847	Clarence Warden b 1 Mar 1838 s/o John Warden & Delila Engle. Sps: Ben Durbin & wife Rosa Anna -JBL
15 Jan 1847	Theresa Caroline Chey b 23 Dec 1846 d/o Anthony Chey & Theresa Yunker. Sps: John Popiker & wife Catarina -JBL
17 Jan 1847	Rachel Anna Payne b 17 Nov 1846 d/o Raphael [Boyd] Payne & Maria Parr Sps: Frederick Zimmerman & Maria [Payne] Ryan -JBL
27 Jan 1847	Christina Fesler b 30 Nov 1846 d/o Joseph [Fesler] & Saloma Stark. Sps: _____ Earnest & wife -JBL
27 Jan 1847	Caroline Keller b 18 Dec 1846 d/o John [Keller] & Catharine Kerich. Sps: Martin Weber & wife -JBL
07 Feb 1847	Elizabeth Lawler b 3 Feb 1847 d/o Thomas [Lawler] & Mariann Evysnoly. Sps: Peter Welsh & wife -JBL
25 Feb 1847	Jeremiah Edmund Kerrity b 15 Feb 1847 s/o Ivan [Kerrity] & Honor McCarthy. Sps: Edmund Shelby & Margaret Hogan -JBL
25 Feb 1847	Jacob Valentine Kerrity [twin] brother of Edmund [s/o Ivan [Kerrity] & Honor McCarthy]. Sps: Michael Crown & Anna Hogan -JBL
25 Feb 1847	William Dial [Jr.] b 25 Apr 1846 s/o William [Dial] & Rebecca Arnold. Sps: Levi Sapp & wife -JBL
25 Mar 1847	Samuel Draper b 17 Sep 1846 s/o Benjamin [Draper] & Martha Sapp. Sps: Timothy Colopy & Emma Sapp -JBL
02 Apr 1847	Ambrose Porter b 26 Jan 1847 s/o Francis [Porter] & Maria Parker. Sps: Robert Sapp & Levina Logsdon -JBL
03 Apr 1847	Henry Milton Magers b 19 Nov 1846 s/o Benjamin [Magers] & Lucinda Porter. Sps: William Ridgely Porter & Jane Magers -JBL

04 Apr 1847	Barbara Frances Bricker b 3 Nov 1846 d/o George [Bricker] & Catherine Buckingham. Sps: Dan Buckingham & Maria Penelope Pratt -JBL
05 Apr 1847	Anthony Bernard Starner b 10 Dec 1846 s/o Silvern [Starner] & Theresa King [Chaney?] Sps: Bernard Phillips & Rosanna King -JBL
07 Apr 1847	George Crowner b 6 Dec 1846 s/o Michael Crowner & Phebe Wizernandt. Sps: William Crownapple [Krownapple] & wife Maria -JBL
07 Apr 1847	Joan Elsie Stark b 26 Aug 1844 d/o Cyrus [Stark] & Maria Crown. Sps: Jacob Hopkins & wife Maria -JBL
08 Apr 1847	[Styles] Matthew Stevens b 20 Feb 1847 s/o Cyrus [Stevens] & Mary Jane Smith. Sps: Elias Arnold & Anna [Nancy] Joan Hopwood -JBL
11 Apr 1847	Elias Engle -JBL
11 Apr 1847	Joseph Florin McNamara s/o _____ McNamara & ____ Alvin. Sps: Ben Durbin Sr. & N. Durbin w/o Samuel Durbin -JBL
25 Apr 1847	Margaret Shults b 11 Mar 1847 d/o Jacob [Shults] & Maria Breckler. Sps: Jacob Swarts & wife Margaret -JBL
26 Apr 1847	Elizabeth Allerding b 23 Mar 1847 d/o Lewis [Allerding] & Catherine Lewis. Sps: John Vogler & Elizabeth Allerding -JBL
16 May 1847	Mary Jane Hosey b 29 Dec 1837 d/o William Hosey & Martha Spartfield. Sps: Frederick Zimmerman & Matilda Colopy -JBL
22 May 1847	Maria [Parker] Porter b 25 Mar 1825 [w/o Francis D. Porter] d/o Robert Parker & Margaret Miller. Sps: Thomas White & Susanna Magers -JBL
23 May 1847	George Leander [Payne] b 9 Apr 1847 s/o George Payne & Anna Croy. Sps: Raphael Payne & Honora Blubaugh -JBL
23 May 1847	Rachel Louise [Payne] d/o John Payne & Jane Rambo -JBL

44

BAPTISMS

23 May 1847	William Louis [Logsdon] s/o David Logsdon & Rebecca ~~Hull~~ [Uhl]. -JBL
26 May 1847	Jacob Kelley b 15 Mar 1847 s/o William Kelley & Eliza Welker. Sps: Felix Kelley & wife -JBL
27 May 1847	John Kelley b 13 Feb 1847 s/o Patrick Kelley & Sara McHurd. Sps: William Kelley & Sara Kelley -JBL
06 Jun 1847	Catherine Isabelle Arnold b 6 Apr 1847 d/o Richard Arnold & Eliza Hardin. Sps: Elias Arnold & wife Lovina -JBL
20 Jun 1847	Mary Magdalena Gardner d/o Anthony Gardner & Barbara Lazarus. Sps: Francis Gardner & Maria Anna Gardner -JBL
21 Jun 1847	Catherine McMullen b 31 Mar 1847 d/o Thomas McMullen & Margaret Fritzpatrick. Sps: Michael McMullen & Matilda Colopy -JBL
05 Jul 1847	Anthony Fisher b 8 Jun 1847 s/o Martin Fisher & Mary Ann King. Sps: Laurence King & Gertrude Keefer -JBL
25 Jul 1847	Maria Elizabeth Sapp b 20 May 1847 d/o James [Sapp] & Winifred Blubaugh. Sps: George Blubaugh & wife Nora -JBL
08 Aug 1847	Elizabeth Hosfeld b 01 Jan 1839 d/o Henry C. [Hosfeld] & Maria Veronica Bishoff. Sps: Michael Keefer & wife Elizabeth -JBL
15 Aug 1847	Peter Miller b 9 Jul 1847 s/o Vincent [Miller] & Margaret Shillinger. Sps: Peter Ferenbaugh & wife Josephine -JBL
15 Aug 1847	Simon Miller b 26 Nov 1845 s/o Vincent [Miller] & Margaret Shillinger. Sps: Francis Breckler & wife Catherine -JBL
15 Aug 1847	Barbara Buck b 26 Dec 1847 d/o Eberhart Buck & Adeline [Draper] Buck. Sps: Peter Ferenbaugh & wife Josephine -JBL
15 Aug 1847	Maria Buck b 24 Mar 1844 d/o Eberhart Buck & Adeline [Draper] Buck. Sps: Martin Fisher Jr. & wife _____. -JBL

15 Aug 1847	Joseph Buck b 21 Aug 1846 s/o Eberhart Buck & Adeline [Draper] Buck. Sps: Joseph Riberg & Maria Fisher -JBL
21 Aug 1847	Jeremiah Smith b 22 Aug 1845 s/o Ivan Henry [Smith] & Rebecca Draper. Sps: George Sapp & Anna Sapp -JBL
27 Aug 1847	Elizabeth Helen Logsdon b 7 Jan 1847 d/o William Logsdon & Elizabeth Magers. Sps: James White & Catherine Logsdon -JBL
31 Aug 1847	Maria Delila Engle b 13 Dec 1815 d/o Eli [Engle] & Charity Hull. Sps: Isaac Dial & Rosa Durbin -JBL
01 Sep 1847	Lydia Huck [Houck?] (adult) -JBL
12 Sep 1847	Margaret Anna Crowner b 3 Sep 1825 d/o Michael Crowner & Anna Nisbit. Sps: Benedict Magers & Maria Eckenrode -JBL
12 Sep 1847	Charles Sapp b 16 Dec 1826 s/o Adam [Sapp] & Mary Lybarger. Sps: Edmund Brent & Else McKenzie -JBL
12 Sep 1847	John Stoffer [Jr.] b 16 Jun 1847 s/o John [Stoffer] & Harriet Durbin. Sps: Benjamin Durbin & wife Elizabeth -JBL
14 Sep 1847	Mary McNamara b 13 Jul 1841 d/o Francis McNamara & Christine Weber. Sps: Ivan Welsh & Margaret McNamara -JBL
14 Sep 1847	Francis K. McNamara b 6 Apr 1843 s/o Francis McNamara & Christine Weber . -JBL
14 Sep 1847	Bridget McNamara b 26 Jun 1847 d/o Francis McNamara & Christine Weber. -JBL
26 Sep 1847	John Thomas Parker s/o George B. Parker & Henrietta Magers. Sps: William Magers & Honora Durbin -JBL
17 Oct 1847	John Frederick [Zimmerman] s/o Frederick Zimmerman & Sarah Colopy. -TJB
17 Oct 1847	Lucinda [Logsdon] d/o William Zachary Logsdon & Sarah Buckingham. Sps: ____ & Lucinda White -TJB
27 Oct 1847	Anna [Horn] d/o Daniel Horn & Jane Durbin. Sps: George Durbin & Lucy Mattingly -TJB

BAPTISMS

31 Oct 1847	John Baptist (new conversion) s/o [blank]. Sps: Laurence Magers -TJB
31 Oct 1847	Mary Helen [McKenzie] d/o Jacob McKenzie & Esther Sapp. Sps: Jacob Blubaugh & Honora Blubaugh -TJB
04 Nov 1847	_____ d/o John Welch & Catherine McNamara -TJB
07 Nov 1847	Anna [Bradfield] d/o James W. Bradfield (non cath) & Sarah Ann Sapp. Sps: Benjamin Draper & wife Martha Sapp -TJB
14 Nov 1847	Anna Margaret [Gray] b this year, d/o John Gray & [Susan] Green (non cath). Sps: William Walker & wife Anna Durbin -TJB
15 Nov 1847	Jacob (Monroe). Sps: Frederick Zimmerman & Rachel Blubaugh -TJB
15 Nov 1847	Charles [Bechtel] s/o Joseph Bechtel & Maria Brophy. Sps: Michael Boyle & _____ -TJB
21 Nov 1847	Emma Jane [Headington] d/o Laban Headington (non cath] & _____. Sps: John Frederick Zimmerman & Sarah Colopy -TJB
28 Nov 1847	Anna Magers d/o Ambrose Magers & [Susanna O'Brien]. Sps: Benedict Magers & Maria Trullinger -TJB
28 Nov 1847	_____ d/o John Welch & Catherine McNamara. Sps: Thomas Joseph Bougler & _____ -TJB
28 Nov 1847	Louisa Jane Durbin d/o Samuel Durbin & Anna Blubaugh. -TJB
28 Nov 1847	Maria Anna [Walsh] d/o Michael Walsh & wife Elizabeth Crawford. Sps: Jacob White & Maria Blubaugh -TJB
26 Dec 1847	Andrew [Welker] s/o Elet [William Elliott] Welker (non cath) & wife Rachel Durbin. Sps: Laurence Magers & Maria Durbin -TJB
08 Jan 1848	Michael [Boyle] s/o Michael Boyle & wife Margaret. Sps: T. J. Boulger & Eliza Boyle -TJB
12 Jan 1848	Charles White s/o Lewis White & Rebecca Welchhammer. Sps: Jacob White & Lydia White -TJB

16 Jan 1848	Edward Kilkenny s/o John Kilkenny & Marie Donahue. Sps: Bernard O'Connor & Brigett <u>Hunt</u> -TJB
25 Jan 1848	Joseph Yeager s/o Bernard Yeager & Catherine Fisher. Sps: Laurence King & Marianna King -TJB
25 Jan 1848	Sarah Catherine [Buckingham] d/o Daniel Buckingham & Rebecca Bricker. Sps: Baptist Durbin & Catherine King -TJB
25 Jan 1848	Catherine [Mitchell] d/o Michael Mitchell & Maria ____. Sps: Michael McMullen & Margaret McMullen, at Fredericktown, Ohio -TJB
15 Feb 1848	Jacob Laurence [Haverick] s/o Vincent Haverick & Hester Ann Magers. Sps: Laurence Magers & Jane Buckingham -TJB
20 Feb 1848	____ [Gray] d/o John Gray & Susan Green (non cath) Sps: William Walker & wife Anna Durbin.
26 Feb 1848	____ [McKenzie] s/o Elias McKenzie & Maria Blubaugh. -TJB
27 Feb 1848	Maria Elizabeth [Sapp] d/o Levi Sapp & Matilda Arnold. Sps: Elias Arnold & wife Levina Logsdon -TJB
31 Mar 1848	Sarah Frances Hopwood d/o Samuel Hopwood & ~~Anna Joanna~~ [Nancy Jane] Payne. Sps: Francis Payne & Lucinda Sapp -TJB
31 Mar 1848	Maria Bricker d/o Christopher Bricker & wife Nancy Buckingham. Sps: George Trullinger & wife Honora Durbin -TJB
16 Apr 1848	John Peter [Breckler] s/o Francis Breckler & wife Catherine Heckler. Sps: John Breckler & Eliza Allerding -TJB
17 Apr 1848	Maria [Metzger] d/o Joseph Metzger & Marianna Bechtel. Sps: ____ Bechtel & Maria Brophy -TJB
23 Apr 1848	Thomas Bishop by conversion. -TJB
23 Apr 1848	Maria [Bishop] w/o Thomas Bishop. -TJB
23 Apr 1848	Elizabeth Bishop d/o Thomas & Maria Bishop. -TJB

BAPTISMS

27 Apr 1848	Andrew Alexander [Durbin] s/o Baptist Durbin & wife Catherine King. Sps: Benjamin Durbin & wife Rosanna.
07 May 1848	Pius Gregory Durbin s/o John Durbin & wife [Margaret] Logsdon Sps: William Walker & Joan Durbin -TJB
13 May 1848	_____ Fleming (non cath). -TJB
15 May 1848	Edward [Lawler] s/o Thomas Lawler & wife Maria Anna Cassidy. Sps: Michael Boyle & wife Margaret Boyle -TJB
21 May 1848	Martha [Critchfield] d/o Hiram Critchfield & Harriett Porter. Sps: George Trullinger & wife Honora -TJB
04 Jun 1848	John [Fisher] s/o Martin Fisher & wife [Mary Ann King]. -TJB
04 Jun 1848	Sarah Winifred [Davidson] d/o George Payne [Davidson] & Rachel [Payne]. Sps: [not listed] -TJB
04 Jun 1848	Sarah Catherine [Arnold] d/o Elias Arnold & Lovina Logsdon. Sps: John Durbin & Catherine Logsdon -TJB
04 Jun 1848	Isabella [McKenzie] d/o Gabriel McKenzie & wife Anna Logue. Sps: Raphael Logue & wife Catherine McKenzie -TJB
04 Jun 1848	Charles [Blair] s/o Ivan Blair (non cath) and wife Anna Cecila Hanlon. Sps: Joseph Bechtel & Bridgett Morton -TJB
15 Jun 1848	Thomas [Baker] s/o Nicholas Baker & Catherine Mansfield. Sps: John Graham & Catherine Sullivan -TJB
25 Jun 1848	John Henry [Sherry] s/o John Sherry & Lucinda Harding. Sps: Edward Cramer & Helena McCarthy. [written 25 Jul] -TJB
02 Jul 1848	Anna Elizabeth [Ogg] d/o James J. Ogg & wife Julia Anna Logsdon. Sps: David Logsdon & wife [Nancy Mattingly] -TJB
02 Jul 1848	Sarah Anna [Rafferty] d/o Jacob Rafferty & Hannah Cole. Sps: Edward McCormick & Catherine Montgomery -TJB
09 Jul 1848	Levi [Ashburn] s/o Ellis Ashburn (non cath) & Rebecca Durbin. Sps: Benjamin Durbin & wife Rosa -TJB

09 Jul 1848   John Thomas [Walsh] s/o Jacob Walsh & Briget Walsh.
Sps: Thomas J. Boulger & Bridgett Hunt -TJB

15 Jul 1848   Elizabeth Anna _____ conversion
Sps: Joanna Buckingham -TJB

23 Jul 1848   James H. Waggoner b 1 Jun 1848 s/o Henry Waggoner &
Hannah [Durbin]. Sps: James White & wife Anna Sapp.
[Child's name in different handwriting.] -TJB

23 Jul 1848   Thomas Francis [Blubaugh] b 18 Apr [1848] s/o Stephen
Blubaugh & Honora Logsdon, [wife's name in different
handwriting.] Sps: Francis Gardner & M. Anna Gardner
-TJB

15 Aug 1848   Hiram Ignatius [Rowley] s/o [Olney] Perry Rowley & wife
Maria Elizabeth McKenzie. Sps: Ignatius McKenzie &
wife Eliza -TJB

27 Aug 1848   John (Nelson) Sapp by conversion. Sps: John Porter &
wife Rachel -TJB

03 Sep 1848   Michael [Smith] s/o Aloysius Smith & Catherine Harlett.
Sps: Nicholas Harlett & Ursala _____ -TJB

03 Sep 1848   Emila [Emma Sapp] b 4 Mar 1843 d/o Robert Sapp &
[Rosanna Lore] (non cath). -TJB

03 Sep 1848   Harriet Ellen [Sapp] b 30 Oct 1846 d/o Robert Sapp &
[Rosanna Lore] (non cath). -TJB

03 Sep 1848   Henry Thomas [Sapp] b 3 Mar 1848 s/o Robert Sapp &
[Rosanna Lore] (non cath). -TJB

01 Oct 1848   Elias William [Ogg] s/o John Thomas Ogg & Susanna
Myers. Sps: Bazil Durbin & Jane Buckingham -TJB

06 Oct 1848   Catherine Isabella [McGough] d/o Patrick ~~McGow~~
[McGough] & ~~Helen~~ [Ellen] Durbin. Sps: Miranda
Durbin -TJB

09 Oct 1848   Timothy [Warden] s/o Henry Warden (non cath) &
Elizabeth Burr. Sps: Bridgett Morton -TJB

22 Oct 1848   Ambrose [Welker] s/o John B. (Jackson) Welker & Sarah
Miranda Dial. Sps: Bazil Durbin & Maria Dial -TJB

BAPTISMS

19 Nov 1848	Honora Eleanor [Blubaugh] d/o Benjamin Blubaugh & Elizabeth Durbin. Sps: John Porter & wife Rachel -TJB
17 Dec 1848	George W. [Porter] s/o David Porter & Lydia Sapp Sps: George Sapp & wife Lucinda -TJB
17 Dec 1848	Frances Isabella [Stevens] d/o Cyrus Stevens (non cath) & wife Mary Jane Smith. Sps: William Walker & wife Anna Margaret -TJB
11 Feb 1849	Henry Hiram [White] s/o James White & Anna Sapp. Sps: Daniel Buckingham & wife Jane -TJB
11 Feb 1849	John Thomas [Durbin] s/o Basil Durbin & Maria Buckingham. Sps: Richard Arnold & Joanna Buckingham -TJB
11 Feb 1849	Sarah Margaret [McKenzie] d/o Elias McKenzie & Maria Blubaugh. Sps: Jacob Blubaugh & wife Honora -TJB
01 Apr 1849	Margaret Frances [Welch] d/o John Welch & Catherine McNamara. Sps: Samuel Walker & Maria Teresa Bougler -TJB
08 Apr 1849	Clement [Draper] s/o Benjamin Draper & Martha Sapp. Sps: William Walker & wife Anna Durbin -TJB
23 May 1849	Maria Elizabeth [Breckler] d/o John Breckler & Elizabeth Allerding. Sps: Michael Allerding & Marianna Hess -TJB
23 May 1849	Theodore [Allerding] s/o Aloysius Allerding & Catherine La Croix. Sps: Theodore Whisler & Nichol Milly -TJB
23 May 1849	John [Blubaugh] s/o Zachary Blubaugh & Lydia Ann Colglesser. Sps: Benjamin Draper & wife Martha [Sapp] -TJB
23 May 1849	Alice Helen [Porter] d/o Henry T. Porter & Eliza Headington. -TJB
07 Jun 1849	Vincent Haverick & Hester Ann Magers, (adults)
07 Jun 1849	Israel _____. Sps: David Logsdon & [Nancy Ann Mattingly. Some Logsdon researcher have Israel as a s/o David & Nancy.] -TJB
07 Jun 1849	_____ Ferenbaugh & _____. -TJB

51

07 Jun 1849	Adam [Sapp] s/o Lewis Sapp & wife Sara Arnold. Sps: Elias Arnold & wife Rachel [Payne] -TJB
10 Jun 1849	Maria Elizabeth [King] d/o Lawrence King & Hannah Draper. Sps: Benjamin Draper & wife Martha [Sapp] -TJB
10 Jun 1849	Sarah Catherine [Colopy] d/o Jacob Colopy & Delila Sapp. Sps: Hilary Blubaugh & Maria Bougler -TJB
24 Jun 1849	Bernard [Fisher] b 8 May 1849 s/o Martin Fisher & Maria King. Sps: Laurence King & Catherine Keefer -TJB
24 Jun 1849	Andrew [King] s/o Anthony King & Catherine Keefer. Sps: Vincent Miller & Maria Fisher -TJB
01 Jul 1849	Maria Isabella [Magers] d/o Ambrose Magers & Susanna O'Brien. Sps: Nathan Magers & Lydia White -TJB
06 Jul 1849	Rebecca Joanna [Packsin] d/o Benjamin Packsin (non cath) & Maria Elizabeth Mckenzie. Sps: Elias Dial & Anna McKenzie aka Durbin -TJB
06 Jul 1849	Elias [Payne] s/o John Payne & Joanna Reynolds. Sps: John Porter & Winifred Payne -TJB
06 Jul 1849	Maria Isabella [Hess] b 1847 d/o Samuel Hess (non cath) & Sarah Eckenrode. Sps: Daniel Buckingham & wife Joanna -TJB
06 Jul 1849	Elizabeth [Hess] d/o Samuel Hess (non cath) & wife Sarah Eckenrode. Sps: Maria Eckenrode -TJB
06 Jul 1849	Emily Jane [Sapp] d/o Levi Sapp & Matilda Arnold. Sps: Nathan Magers & Winifred Porter -TJB
15 Jul 1849	Levi Thomas [Logsdon] s/o David Logsdon & Rebecca Uhl. Sps: Martin Durbin & wife Sarah -TJB
02 Aug 1849	Demetrius [Shafer] s/o George Shafer (non cath) & Rachel McKenzie. Sps: Elias McKenzie -TJB
05 Aug 1849	Lucy Emila [Magers] d/o Laurence Magers & Susanna McKenzie. Sps: Martin Durbin & wife Sarah -TJB
29 Aug 1849	Laurence Joseph [Miller] s/o Vincent Miller & Margaret Shillinger. Sps: Eberhart Buck & Margaret Shillinger -JB

BAPTISMS

29 Aug 1849	Thomas Jerome [White] s/o Joseph White & Hanna DeWit. Sps: George Trullinger & wife Honora Durbin -JB
01 Sep 1849	Rosanne [Logsdon] d/o [William] Zachary Logsdon & Sarah Buckingham. Sps: Daniel Buckingham & Rosella Kelly -TJB
20 Sep 1849	Celestine Edward [Mattingly] s/o Nathan Mattingly & Maria Durbin. Sps: Benjamin Draper & wife Martha [Sapp] -TJB
21 Sep 1849	John Albert [Arnold] s/o Jonathan Arnold & Maria Blubaugh. Sps: Jonathan Dial & wife Martha Frances Sapp -TJB
28 Sep 1849	_____ [Durbin] s/o Samuel Durbin & Anna Blubaugh. Sps: John Porter & wife Rachel Arnold -TJB
28 Sep 1849	Emily [Ann Jacobs] Blubaugh w/o William Blubaugh. -TJB
28 Dec 1849	John Fritz s/o Ferdinand Fritz & Thecle Grim. Sps: John Fritz & wife Maria Hosfeld -TJB
28 Dec 1849	_____ [Bradfield] ?/o James W. Bradfield & Sara Anna Sapp. Sps: Levi Sapp & wife Maria -TJB
09 Feb 1850	Eliza [Harden] Arnold w/o Richard Arnold. Sps: Levina [Logsdon] Arnold -TJB
18 Feb 1850	Sarah F. [White] d/o James White & Anna Sapp. Sps: Jacob Sapp & _____ Durbin -TJB
19 Feb 1850	George [Rowley] s/o [Olney] Perry Rowley & Mary Elizabeth McKenzie. Sps: Cyril McKenzie & wife Elizabeth -TJB
27 Feb 1850	Jacob [Walsh] s/o Jacob Walsh & Bridget Walsh. Sps: Peter Walsh & Helen Boulger -TJB
27 Apr 1850	James Henry [Critchfield] b 26 Jan 1850 s/o Hiram Critchfield & Harriet Porter. Sps: Levi & Hanna Sapp -JFK
27 Apr 1850	Sara Elizabeth [Sapp] b 16 Mar 1850 d/o Charles Sapp & Winifred Porter. Sps: Levi Sapp & Diana Dial -JFK

53

27 Apr 1850   Elizabeth [Durbin] b 2 Feb 1850 d/o Baptist Durbin & Catherine King. Sps: Gabriel Walker & Susanna Durbin -JFK

28 Apr 1850   Isaac [Arnold] s/o Richard Arnold & Elizabeth Hardin. Sps: George Trullinger & Honora Durbin -TJB

12 May 1850   Edward [Davidson] s/o George H. Davidson (non cath) & Rachel Payne. Sps: Ambrose Magers & Mary Ryan [Payne] -TJB

07 Jun 1850   Stephen [O'Neil] s/o Patrick O'Neil & Brigett McNamara (in Delaware County). Sps: Thomas O'Neil & wife Catherine Barry -TJB

16 Jun 1850   Matthew [McNamara] s/o Francis McNamara & Christine Weber. Sps: Patrick Kennedy & Bridget Walsh [widow] -TJB

16 Jun 1850   Henrietta [Packsin] d/o Benjamin Packsin (non cath) & wife Eliza McKenzie. Sps: Ignatius McKenzie & wife -TJB

20 Jun 1850   _____ [Stevens] ?/o Cyrus Stevens (non cath) & Mary Jane Smith. Sps: Stephen Blubaugh & Maria Smith -TJB

30 Jun 1850   Peter [Fischer] s/o Martin Fischer & Maria King (Koenig). Sps: Eberhart Buck & Ursula Harlett -TJB

10 Aug 1850   Jacob [Ignatius McKenzie] s/o Elias McKenzie & Maria Blubaugh. Sps: Honora Blubaugh -TJB

11 Aug 1850   Maria [White] d/o Anthony White & Keziah Wade. Sps: Lucinda White -TJB

12 Aug 1850   Hanna Philomena [Tucker] d/o John Tucker & Helena Beam. (at St. Michael) Sps: Jacob Holler & Catherine Allerding -TJB

12 Aug 1850   Henry _____ s/o Jacob _____ & Maria _____. Sps: Enoch Sheneberger -TJB

15 Aug 1850   Catherine [Buck] d/o Eberhart Buck & Adeline [Draper] Sps: Anthony King & Catherine Keefer (at St Michael) -TJB

BAPTISMS

15 Aug 1850	Julianna [King] d/o Anthony King & Catherine Keefer. Sps: Eberhart Buck & wife Adeline [Draper].
15 Aug 1850	Maria Elizabeth [Ashburn] d/o Ellis Ashburn & Rebecca Durbin. Sps: Benjamin Durbin & wife Rosanna -TJB
15 Aug 1850	William [Arnold] s/o Elias Arnold & Lovina Logsdon. Sps: Benedict Magers & wife Maria -TJB
18 Aug 1850	Thomas [Brosenham Jr.] s/o Thomas Brosenham & Anna McNamara. Sps: William Magers & Elizabeth Welker -TJB
18 Aug 1850	Maria Elizabeth [Kelly] d/o William Kelly & Eliza Welker. Sps: William N. Magers & Elizabeth Welker -TJB
15 Sep 1850	Rosanna [Walker] d/o Samuel Walker & Margaret Kelly. Sps: Edwin Walker & Rosanna Durbin -TJB
15 Sep 1850	Amanda Helen [Blubaugh] d/o Rachel Blubaugh. Sps: Jacob Colopy & Rachel Davidson -TJB
01 Dec 1850	Maria Frances [Dial] d/o Jonathan Dial & Martha J. Sapp. Sps: John B. Welker & Rachel Sapp -TJB
15 Dec 1850	_____ [Magers] ?/o Ambrose Magers & Susanna O'Brien. Sps: Laurence Magers & mother Winifred [Magers] -TJB
15 Dec 1850	John (Milton) [Steel] s/o _____ Steel & _____ (non cath). Sps: Francis Magers -TJB
01 Jan 1851	Lewis [Carter] s/o Sarah Carter. Sps: Maurice Walsh -TJB
11 Jan 1851	William Joseph [Welch] s/o James Welch & Catherine McNamara. Sps: Ambrose Magers & Jane Buckingham -TJB
14 Jan 1851	Catherine Melissa [Blubaugh] d/o Benjamin Blubaugh & Eliza Durbin. Sps: John Blubaugh & wife Maria Dial -TJB
28 Jan 1851	Edward [Smart] s/o Edward Smart & Elizabeth (non cath). Sps: William Walker & wife Anna -TJB
08 Feb 1851	Margaret Helen Headington by conversion. -TJB

55

09 Feb 1851	Jane [Waggoner] d/o Henry Waggoner & Hannah ~~Dial~~ [Durbin]. Sps: Bazil Durbin & Mary Sapp -TJB
09 Feb 1851	Jerome [Blubaugh] s/o Zachary Blubaugh & Lydia Colglesser. Sps: Benjamin Blubaugh & wife Charlotte -TJB
23 Feb 1851	Martha Jane [Blubaugh] d/o Benjamin Blubaugh & Charlotte Heckler. Sps: Nicholas Hollet & wife Ursula -TJB
12 Mar 1851	John Adam [Sapp] s/o Levi Sapp & Matilda Arnold. Sps: Jonathan Dial & wife Margaret -TJB
21 Mar 1851	William [Brent] s/o Edmund Brent & [Frances] Fanny Sapp. Sps: Leo & Lucinda Sapp -TJB
22 Mar 1851	George [Marshall] s/o John Marshall & Louisa Trullinger. Sps: Honora Trullinger -TJB
27 Apr 1851	Casper [Miller] s/o Vincent Miller & Margaret Shillinger. Sps: Anthony King & Rosella Harlett -TJB
29 Jun 1851	Eugene & Lucinda [Bresnahan] children of Thomas Bresnahan & Anna McNamara. Sps: Henry Eckenrode & wife -TJB
19 Jul 1851	Christina [Arnold] d/o John Alton Arnold & Christina Sapp. Sps: Sarah Anna Thompson -TJB
20 Jul 1851	John Martin [Smith] s/o Aloysius Smith & Catherine Harlett. Sps: Martin Fisher & wife Mary -TJB
26 Jul 1851	Miriam L. [Hopkins] d/o William Hopkins & wife ~~Maria~~ [Rachel Payne] (non cath). Sps: Jacob Colopy & wife Mary -TJB
02 Aug 1851	_____ [McGough] d/o Patrick McGough & Helen Durbin. Sps: Rosanna Durbin -TJB
03 Aug 1851	Charles [Durbin] s/o Samuel Durbin & Anna Blubaugh. Sps: Benedict Magers & wife Maria -TJB
03 Aug 1851	George G. [McNamara] s/o Francis McNamara & Christina Weber. Sps: Jacob Ritchman & Catherine Walsh -TJB

03 Aug 1851   Marianna [Haverick] d/o Vincent Haverick & Hester Ann
Magers. Sps: Henry Rodock & wife Mary Anna -TJB
Emeline [Haverick]
Harriet Helen [Haverick]
Benjamin Thomas [Haverick]
Phedora [Haverick]
[These are probably other children of Vincent & Hester.]

21 Sep 1851   Francis Anthony [Gardner] s/o Francis Gardner &
Catherine Stuhlmiller Sps: Anthony & Maria Gardner.

End Book 2

26 Oct 1851   Matthew King b 28 Jul [1851] s/o Anthony King &
Gertrude Keefer. Sps: Eberhart Buck & Adaline Buck
-JJB

26 Oct 1851   Peter King b 1 Oct [1851] d/o Anthony King & Catherine
Keefer. Sps: Eberhart Buck & Adaline Buck -JJB

26 Oct 1851   John Dorrer b 10 Oct [1851] s/o Fidel Dorrer & Adaline
Glazer. Sps: Eberhart Buck & Adaline Buck -JJB

26 Oct 1851   Sarah Waddle b 11 Oct 1848 adopted d/o George Payne.
Sps: Ben Durbin & Anna Payne -JJB

26 Oct 1851   Anna Maria Payne b 20 Sep [1851] d/o George Payne &
Anna Croy. Sps: Ben Durbin & Maria Thompson -JJB

01 Nov 1851   Mary Moxley b 20 Oct 1847 adopted d/o Elias Arnold.
Sps: John Porter & Maria Porter -JJB

01 Nov 1851   Mariah Blubaugh b 20 Sep [1851] d/o John [J.] Blubaugh
& Mary Dial. Sps: Jonathan Dial & Rebecca Dial -JJB

15 Nov 1851   George Jerome [McKenzie] s/o Elias Stephen McKenzie.
& Maria Blubaugh. Sps: Benedict Magers & Maria Elias
Magers -JJB

07 Dec 1851   Elizabeth Ellen Payne b 11 Dec 1850 d/o John Payne &
Jane Randell. Sps: Henry Porter & Eliza Ann Porter -JJB

07 Dec 1851   [Hulda] Anna Davidson b 30 Oct [1851] d/o George H.
Davidson & Rachel Payne. Sps: Aloysius Smith & Nancy
Jane Hopwood -JJB

07 Dec 1851	Thomas Hopwood b 19 Nov [1851] s/o Samuel Hopwood & Nancy Jane Hopwood. Sps: Ambrose Magers & Rachel Davidson -JJB
25 Dec 1851	Elizabeth [Fisher] b 15 Nov 1851 d/o Martin Fisher & Mary King. Sps: Aloysius Smith & Willomena Smith -JJB
05 Jan 1852	Martin [King] b 11 Nov [1851] s/o John King & Catherine Harden. Sps: Martin Fisher & Maria Shults -JJB
07 Jan 1852	Harriet Helen [Bradfield] b 25 Nov [1852] d/o James W. Bradfield & Sarah Ann Sapp. Sps: Edmund Brent & Martha Sapp -JJB
28 Jan 1852	Isaac [Stephens] b 24 Nov 1851 s/o Cyrus Stephens & Mary Jane Smith. Sps: Anna Maria Smith & Nelson Sapp -JJB
01 Feb 1852	William [White] b 23 Jan [1852] s/o James White & Anna Sapp. Sps: Nathan Mattingly & wife -JJB
17 Feb 1852	Jacob Austin [Arnold] b 4 Nov [1851] s/o Richard Arnold & Elizabeth Harden. Sps: John Blubaugh & wife -JJB
11 Mar 1852	Jeremiah Joseph Durbin b 2 Feb [1852] s/o Ben Durbin & Honora Blubaugh. Sps: Samuel Blubaugh & Maria McKenzie -JJB
25 Mar 1852	Mary Ellen [Sapp] d/o Charles Sapp & Winifred Porter. Sps: John Porter & wife -JJB
04 May 1852	Mary [Parr] Payne by conversion [w/o Raphael Boyd Payne]. -JJB
06 May 1852	John [Porter] b 24 Mar [1852] s/o David Porter & Lydia Sapp. Sps: Leo Sapp & Lucinda Sapp -JJB
16 May 1852	George [Ashburn] b 22 Feb [1852] s/o Ellis Ashburn & Rebecca Durbin Sps: Maria Anna Durbin & Joh. John Durbin -JJB
16 May 1852	Joseph [Blubaugh] b 22 Sep 1851 s/o Benjamin Blubaugh & Charlotte Heckler. Sps: Aloysius Smith & _____ -JJB
30 May 1852	Anthony White b 3 Jan [1852] s/o James White & Alice Smith. Sps: William Walker & wife -JJB

BAPTISMS

30 May 1852	Albina Helen Schaffer b 28 Feb [1852] d/o ~~John~~ George Schaffer & Rachel McKenzie. Sps: Jean Nicholas Allerding & Jean Allerding -JJB
10 Jun 1852	Rachel Normanda [Sapp] b 20 Feb [1852] d/o Levi Sapp & Matilda Arnold. Sps: John Porter & wife -JJB
16 Jun 1852	Julius and Julia Josephine Bricker b 8 Oct 1851 twins of George Bricker & C. Buckingham. Sps: N. Mattingly, Bazil Durbin, Jane Buckingham, & Penelope Bricker -JJB
20 Jun 1852	William Miller b 8 Apr [1852] s/o Vincent Miller & Margaret Stillinger. Sps: Anthony King & wife -JJB
20 Jun 1852	Nathan Benedict [McKenzie] b 1 May [1852] s/o Laurence & Susanna McKenzie. Sps: Benedict Magers & wife -JJB
04 Jul 1852	Joanna [Smith] b 4 Mar 1849 d/o John H. [Henry] Smith & Rebecca Draper. Sps: Mrs. Welker & David Logsdon -JJB
04 Jul 1852	Thomas [Logsdon] b 15 May [1852] s/o Francis Logsdon & Susanna Headington. Sps: Susanna Durbin & W. Magers -JJB
04 Jul 1852	James Rigly [Ridgely] Sapp b 19 May [1852] s/o Nelson Sapp & Elizabeth Porter. Sps: Nathan Mattingly & wife -JBO
04 Jul 1852	Norman [Welker] b 13 Aug 1851 s/o [John B.] Jackson Welker & Miranda Dial. Sps: William Walker & wife -JBO
18 Jul 1852	John Joseph [Losh] b 21 Jun [1852] s/o Joseph Losh & Frances Balzer. Sps: Victor & Catherine Eifert -JBO
18 Jul 1852	Leo [Arnold] b 25 May [1852] s/o Elias Arnold & Lovina Logsdon . Sps: Benjamin Durbin & Susanna Durbin -JBO
22 Aug 1852	Daniel Absalom [Bricker] b 14 Jul [1852] s/o Christopher Bricker & Anna Buckingham. Sps: Daniel Buckingham & wife -JJB
22 Aug 1852	Eliza Ellen [Bricker] b 14 Jul [1852] d/o Christopher Bricker & Anna Buckingham. Sps: Basil Durbin & Jane Buckingham -JJB

05 Sep 1852	Catherine [McGue] b __ Jun 1847 d/o James McGue & Eliza Losh. Sps: Martha McGue & Jacob Colopy -JJB
05 Sep 1852	Martha [McGue] b 7 Aug 1844 d/o James McGue & Eliza Losh. Sps: George Payne & wife [Anna Croy] -JJB
19 Sep 1852	Sarah Elizabeth [Sapp] b 1 Jul [1852] d/o Lewis Sapp & Sarah Arnold. Sps: Richard Arnold & Maria Porter -JJB
03 Oct 1852	Timothy [Sapp] b 25 Aug [1852] s/o Jonathan Sapp & Maria Durbin. Sps: Jacob Colopy & wife -JJB
03 Oct 1852	John Julian [Sapp] b 10 Aug [1852] s/o Jacob Sapp & Winifred Blubaugh. Sps: Benedict Magers & wife -JJB
04 Oct 1852	Caroline [McGough] b 22 Aug [1852] d/o Patrick McGough & Ellen Durbin. Sps: Maria McGough -JJB
01 Nov 1852	Emma Cecila [Durbin] b25 Sep [1852] d/o Baptist Durbin & Catherine King. Sps: George Sapp & Emma Brent -JJB
01 Nov 1852	Ellen Rebecca [Magers] b 12 Jul [1852] d/o Ambrose Magers & Susanna O'Brien. Sps: Benedict Magers & wife -JJB
12 Dec 1852	Michael [Fisher] b 15 Nov [1852] s/o Martin Fisher & Maria King. Sps: Maria Gardner & Enos King -JJB
29 Dec 1852	Joanna [or John] Bolan b 1 Dec 1834 by conversion ?/o Ferdinand Bolan & Harriet Bradfield. Sps: Emma Brent -JJB
10 Jan 1853	John [Arnold] b 20 Sep [1852] s/o Jonathan Arnold & Maria Sarah Blubaugh. Sps: Maria Dial & Elias Arnold Jr. -JJB
06 Feb 1853	Joseph Reuben Cook by conversion [husband of Sarah Arnold]. Sps: John Arnold & Susanna Brent -JJB
20 Mar 1853	John [Payne] b 11 Sep [1852] s/o John Payne & Joanna Reynolds. Sps: Elias Arnold Jr. & Eliza Anna Porter -JJB
20 Mar 1853	Eugene [Porter] b 8 Feb [1853] s/o Henry Porter & Eliza Ann Headington. Sps: George Trullinger & wife -JJB

60

21 Apr 1853	Stephen Aloysius [McKenzie] b 21 Feb [1853] s/o Elias McKenzie & Maria Blubaugh. Sps: Stephen Blubaugh & Emma Brent -JJB
01 May 1853	Theodore Francis [____] b 23 May 1852 adopted s/o William Walker & wife. Sps: Jonathan Sapp & wife -JJB
01 May 1853	Catherine Winkle b 6 Nov 1852 d/o Thomas Winkle & Catherine Robinson. Sps: Robert & Ann Richmond -JJB
13 May 1853	Rachel Loretta [Durbin] b 12 Apr [1853] d/o Benjamin Durbin & Honora Blubaugh. Sps: John & Emma Brent -JJB
15 May 1853	Isaac [Welker] b 31 Mar [1853] s/o [John B.] Jackson Welker & [Sarah] Miranda Dial. Sps: Benedict Magers & wife -JJB
15 May 1853	Maria Agnes [Blubaugh] b 27 Mar [1853] d/o Henry Blubaugh & Hannah Arnold (Gilbert). Sps: George Blubaugh & Maria McGough -JJB
02 Jun 1853	Catherine Apolonia [Boeshart] b 18 Mar [1853] d/o Joseph Boeshart & Barbara Homan. Sps: George Henley & Apolina Fritz -JJB
02 Jun 1853	Francis [Steel] b 16 Apr [1853] s/o Francis Steel & Susanna Beam. Sps: John & Maria Beam -JJB
19 Jun 1853	Raymond [Brent] b 24 May [1853] s/o Edmund Brent & Frances Sapp. Sps: Jacob Colopy & wife -JJB
03 Jul 1853	Francis Xavier [Magers] b 27 May [1853] s/o John Magers & Christina Ruhl. Sps: John Durbin & Winifred Magers -JJB
15 Aug 1853	Phedora Jane [Blubaugh] b 12 Jun d/o John J. Blubaugh & Maria Dial. Sps: John Porter & wife -JJB
15 Aug 1853	Isabella [Kelly] b 7 Jul [1853] d/o William Kelly & Elizabeth Welker. Sps: William Walker & Anna Maria Smith -JJB
18 Aug 1853	Rosella [McGue] b 11 Jan 1850 d/o James McGue & Elizabeth Losh. Sps: Thomas White & Martha McGue -JJB

18 Aug 1853	Elizabeth [McGue] b 25 Jun 1852 d/o James McGue & Elizabeth Losh. Sps: Thomas White & Margaret Durbin -JJB
28 Aug 1853	John Julius [Blubaugh] b 12 Jun [1853] s/o William Blubaugh & Emily Anna Jacobs. Sps: John & Rachel Blubaugh -JJB
28 Aug 1853	Maria Elizabeth [Gardner] b 12 Jul [1853] d/o Francis Gardner & Catherine Stuhlmiller. Sps: Peter Marshall & wife -JJB
25 Sep 1853	Rosanna [Walker] b 23 Aug [1853] d/o Edmund Walker & Rebecca Engle. Sps: Ben Durbin & wife -JJB
09 Oct 1853	George Henry [Haverick] b 28 Aug [1853] s/o Vincent Haverick & Hester Ann Magers. Sps: Jonathan Dial & wife -JJB
09 Oct 1853	Lillian Frances [King] b 3 Mar [1853] d/o Laurence King & Hanna Draper. Sps: Dol Richmond & wife -JJB
11 Oct 1853	Gregory Henry [Paul] b 9 Aug [1853] s/o Michael Paul & Mary Henley. Sps: Jos Boeshart & Jennifer Henley -JJB
11 Oct 1853	Elizabeth Isabella [Morgan] b 5 Oct [1853] d/o Philip Morgan & Rosanna Clark. Sps: Adam Stephens & wife -JJB
23 Oct 1853	Clara [Sapp] b 15 Aug [1853] d/o Simon [Hartley] Sapp & Rachel Sapp. Sps: Jonathan Dial & wife -JJB
10 Nov 1853	Cecilia [Stevens] b 7 Sep [1853] d/o Cyrus Stevens & Mary Jane Smith. Sps: Ambrose Magers & D. Smith -JJB
11 Nov 1853	Benjamin Jerome [Marshall] b 11 Oct [1853] s/o John Marshall & Louise Trullinger. Sps: Benedict Magers & wife -JJB
13 Nov 1853	John Hiram [Porter] b 9 Nov 1852] s/o Thomas Porter & Phoebe Anna Stull. Sps: George Trullinger & wife -JJB
13 Nov 1853	Florence [Blubaugh] b 4 Aug [1853] d/o Benjamin Blubaugh & Charlotte Heckler. Sps: Andrew Gimble & wife -JJB
27 Nov 1853	William [Weaver] b 20 Oct [1853] s/o Adam Weaver & Maria Ernest. Sps: William Walker & Maria Fisher -JJB

BAPTISMS

13 Dec 1853	Jacob [Griffith] b 6 Nov [1853] s/o William Griffith & Ellen O'Hearn. Sps: Timothy Holligan & Catherine Leary -JJB
13 Dec 1853	John Clement [Breckler] b 18 Jun [1853] s/o Christopher Breckler & Magdalena Hosfeld. Sps: Clemens Hosfeld & Wife -JJB
08 Jan 1854	Sarah Frances [Bradfield] b 9 Oct [1853] d/o James W. Bradfield & Sara Anna Sapp. Sps: George Sapp & wife -JJB
09 Mar 1854	Ellen Anna [McGue] w/o James McGue. Sps: Levi Sapp & Winifred Magers -JJB
02 Apr 1854	Mary Catherine [Durbin] b 19 Mar 1854 d/o John Durbin & Lucinda Sapp. Sps: John Mattingly & wife-JJB
10 May 1854	Ignatius Jefferies age 25 ? by conversion. -JJB
16 May 1854	Jonathan [Arnold] b 11 Oct 1853 s/o John Arnold & Christina Sapp. Sps: John Whitman & Eliz. Marshall -JJB
27 May 1854	Elizabeth Jane [Dial] b 21 Nov 1853 d/o William Dial & Rebecca Arnold. Sps: Jacob Blubaugh & Honora Trullinger -JJB
29 May 1854	Catherine [Sapp] b 9 Feb [1854] d/o Charles Sapp & Winifred Porter. Sps: John Porter & wife -JJB
29 May 1854	Henry Basil [McKenzie] b 15 Apr [1854] s/o Elias McKenzie & Maria Blubaugh. Sps: Jacob Blubaugh & wife -JJB
29 May 1854	George Swingle & children: John, Christian, Jacob, George Martin by conversion. -JJB
11 Jun 1854	Mary Elizabeth [Blubaugh] b 4 Sep 1853 d/o Zachary Blubaugh & Lydia Colglesser. Sps: Jonathan Colopy & Martha Blubaugh -JJB
11 Jun 1854	William [Sapp] b 14 Dec 1853 s/o Lewis Sapp & Sarah Arnold. Sps: John Porter & Matilda Arnold -JJB
11 Jun 1854	Lewis [Sapp] b 11 Nov 1853 s/o Levi Sapp Jr. & Matilda Arnold. Sps: Nathan Magers & Rebecca McKenzie -JJB

11 Jun 1854   Maria [King] b 1 May [1854] d/o Anthony King & Gertrude Keefer. Sps: Aloysius Smith & Maria Fisher -JJB

11 Jun 1854   William [Walker] b 31 Mar [1854] s/o Samuel Walker & Margaret Kelly. Sps: William Walker & Rosa Durbin -JJB

16 Jun 1854   Aloysius [Mattingly] b 12 Jun [1854] s/o Nathan Mattingly & Maria Durbin. Sps: John & Emma Brent -JJB

12 Jul 1854   Flora Anna [Sapp] b 20 Jun [1854] d/o George Sapp & Delia A. White Sps: Levi Sapp & Normanda Sapp.

23 Jul 1854   [Althea Louise] Genevieve [Davidson] b 10 Dec 1853 d/o George H. Davidson & Rachel Payne. Sps: Nancy Jane Hopwood & Francis McNamara -JJB

23 Jul 1854   Benjamin [Arnold] b 17 May [1854] s/o Jonathan Arnold & Maria Blubaugh. Sps: John & Elizabeth Blubaugh -JJB

23 Jul 1854   Thomas [Robinson] b 19 May [1854] s/o Madison Robinson & ~~Hester~~ Esther Jane White. Sps: W. Walker & Rachel Davidson -JJB

15 Aug 1854   John Absalom [Buckingham] b 6 Jul [1854] s/o Daniel Buckingham & Rebecca Bricker. Sps: Absalom & Joanna Buckingham -JJB

27 Aug 1854   Edward Fenwick [Payne] b 4 Jul [1854] s/o John Payne & Joanna Reynolds. Sps: William Walker & Anna Joanna Hopwood -JJB

27 Aug 1854   Emma Florence [Blubaugh] b 13 Dec 1853 d/o Joseph Blubaugh & Maria Anna Linebaugh. Sps: Jonathan Colopy & Martha Blubaugh -JJB

10 Sep 1854   Winifred [Magers] b 25 Jun [1854] d/o Ambrose Magers & Susanna O'Brien. Sps: John & Winifred Magers -JJB

22 Sep 1854   John Francis Durbin b 28 Aug [1854] s/o Ben Durbin & Honora Blubaugh. Sps: Basil Durbin & Sarah Blubaugh -JJB

24 Sep 1854	Maria Elizabeth [Magers] b 6 Aug [1854] d/o John Magers & Christina Ruhl. Sps: Francis & Winifred Magers -JJB
28 Sep 1854	Maria Elizabeth [Losh] b 17 Aug [1854] leg. d/o Elizabeth Losh. Sps: Thomas White & Margaret Durbin -JJB
08 Oct 1854	Theresa [Dorrer] b 15 May 1853 d/o Fidelis Dorrer & Adeline Glazer. Sps: Martin Fisher & wife -JJB
08 Oct 1854	Susanna [Porter] b 21 Sep [1854] d/o John Porter & Rachel Arnold. Sps: Winifred Magers & Nathan Mattingly -JJB
09 Oct 1854	Cecila [Magers] b 23 Aug [1854] d/o Laurence Magers & Susanna McKenzie. Sps: Basil & Margaret Durbin -JJB
12 Nov 1854	John [Engle] b 15 Oct [1854] s/o Joseph Engle & Susanna Durbin. Sps: Raphael & Maria Anna Durbin -JJB
12 Nov 1854	Martha Jane [Logsdon] b 28 Sep [1854] d/o David Logsdon & Rebecca Uhl. Sps: Laurence Magers & wife -JJB
12 Nov 1854	Michael Jefferies by conversion. -JJB
28 Nov 1854	Roman [Arnold] b 17 Sep [1854] s/o Elias Arnold & Levina Logsdon. Sps: Elias Arnold Sr. & wife -JJB
30 Dec 1854	Mary Ellen [Henley] b 17 Dec [1854] d/o George Henley & Barbara Boeshart. Sps: Jos Boeshart & wife -JJB
02 Jan 1855	Ischyrion [Mattingly] b 22 Dec [1854] s/o John Mattingly & Jane Durbin. Sps: Peter & Maria Durbin -JJB
06 Jan 1855	Martha Florence [Parker] b 5 Sep 1854 d/o Philip Parker & Maria Elizabeth Torman. Sps: Levi Sapp & wife -JJB
08 Apr 1855	Celestius Peter [Fisher] b 26 Jan [1855] s/o Martin Fisher & Mary Ann King. Sps: Alexander Starner & Gertrude King -JJB
08 Apr 1855	John [Homan] b 27 Feb [1855] s/o Paul Homan & Elizabeth Smith. Sps: Michael Millis & wife -JJB

09 Apr 1855	Sarah Anna [Headington] b 10 Feb 1836 d/o Leban Headington & Sarah Williams. Sps: J. Brent & David Logsdon -JJB
22 Apr 1855	Prudence [Payne] b 6 Feb 1855 d/o George Payne & Anna Croy. Sps: Jacob Colopy & wife -JJB
25 Apr 1855	James Augustine [Blubaugh] b 24 Mar [1855] s/o John [J.] Blubaugh & Mary P. Dial. Sps: Jacob & Sarah Blubaugh -JJB
06 May 1855	Margaret Alexis [Ella Porter] b 5 Feb [1855] d/o Henry T. Porter & Elizabeth Headington. Sps: Levi Sapp & wife -JJB
17 Jun 1855	Marcus David [Blubaugh] b 25 Dec 1854 s/o Joseph Blubaugh & Maria Anna Linebaugh. Sps: Jonathan Sapp & wife -JJB
25 Sep 1855	Anna Catherine Whisler b 24 Aug [1855] d/o Theodore Whisler & Barbara Allerding. Sps: John Nicholas & Catherine Allerding -JJB
21 Oct 1855	Maria Patience [Blubaugh] b 14 Aug [1855] d/o William Blubaugh & Ellen Emily Ann Jacobs. Sps: John Blubaugh & Rebecca Logsdon -JJB
12 Nov 1855	William Eugene [Durbin] b 24 Oct [1855] s/o John Durbin & Lucinda Sapp. Sps: Nathan Mattingly & wife -JJB
12 Nov 1855	Benjamin [Blubaugh] b 18 Jul [1855] s/o Benjamin Blubaugh & Charlotte Heckler. Sps: Simeon & Maria Anna Sapp -JJB
23 Dec 1855	Emma Celilia [Gardner] b 12 Nov 1855 d/o Anthony Gardner & Elizabeth Marshall. Sps: Victor Eifert & Matilda Gardner -JJB
03 Feb 1856	John Martin [Sapp] b 4 Nov [1855] s/o Charles Sapp & Winifred Porter. Sps: John & Maria Porter -JJB
03 Feb 1856	Anna Harriet [Hess] b 9 Jun 1855 d/o Samuel Hess & Sara Ann Eckenrode. Sps: John Blubaugh & wife -JJB

BAPTISMS

07 Feb 1856	Elizabeth [Walker] b 1 Jan [1856] d/o Samuel Walker & Margaret Kelly. Sps: Ben Durbin Sr. & Elizabeth Engle -JJB
25 Mar 1856	Alice [Porter] b 18 Jan [1856] d/o John Porter & Rachel Arnold. Sps: Jacob McKenzie & wife -JJB
25 Mar 1856	Manuel [Magers] b 19 Feb [1856] s/o Laurence Magers & Susanna McKenzie. Sps: Raphael Durbin & Maria Magers -JJB
25 Mar 1856	Catherine Christina [Gardner] b 13 Sep 1855 d/o Francis Gardner & Catherine Stuhlmiller. Sps: Francis & Christina Gardner -JJB
14 Apr 1856	Maria [Sapp] b 5 Feb [1856] d/o George Sapp & Delia Anna White. Sps: Benedict Magers & wife -JJB
14 Apr 1856	Catherine [Bricker] b 4 Dec 1855 d/o George Bricker & Catherine Buckingham. Sps: Basil Durbin & Sarah Buckingham -JJB
16 Apr 1856	Liguori [Engle] b 29 Mar [1856] s/o Joseph Engle & Susanna Durbin. Sps: Peter Durbin & Emma Brent -JJB
11 May 1856	Sarah Rebecca [Sapp] b 25 Jan [1856] d/o Levi Sapp [Jr.] & Matilda Arnold. Sps: Benedict Magers & wife -JJB
15 May 1856	Roman [Sapp] b 28 Jun 1855 adopted s/o Jonathan Sapp & wife_____ Simonis. Sps: J. & M. Sapp -JJB
22 May 1856	Jacob Michael [Hines] b 30 Apr [1856] s/o Thomas Hines & Catherine Stephens. Sps: M. B. Bigler & Elizabeth Stephens -JJB
01 Jun 1856	Thomas [Bradfield] b 20 Feb 1856 s/o James W. Bradfield & Sara Anna Sapp. Sps: Jacob Colopy & wife -JJB
01 Jun 1856	Francis [Robinson] b 29 Sep 1855 s/o Madison Robinson & Esther Jane White. Sps: George & Martha Frances Sapp -JJB
15 Jun 1856	Leo [Judson Arnold] b 27 Apr [1856] s/o Richard Arnold & Elizabeth Hardin. Sps: Benedict Magers & wife -JJB
15 Jun 1856	John [Klein] b 17 Mar [1856] s/o Martin Klein & Maria Stunner. Sps: Michael Milles & wife -JJB

29 Jun 1856	Joseph [King] b 10 May [1856] s/o Anthony King & Gertrude Keefer. Sps: Eberhart Buck & Catherine Bricker -JJB
13 Jul 1856	Jacob Leander _____ b 31 May [1856] s/o _____. Sps: Simon Hartley Sapp & wife -JJB
27 Jul 1856	John . [Shults] b 8 Nov 1848 s/o Jacob Schultz & Mary A. Breckler. Sps: Anthony Gimble & wife -JJB
27 Jul 1856	William Jacob [Duncan] b 14 Jun [1856] s/o William Duncan & Mary Jane Swarts. Sps: Jacob Swarts & wife [Margaret Breckler] -JJB
10 Aug 1856	Alice Joanna [Rice] b 27 Jun [1856] d/o Israel Rice & Elizabeth DeVore. Sps: George Payne & Sarah Ellen Bailes -JJB
10 Aug 1856	Lewis [Welker] b 18 Nov 1855 s/o [William Elliot] Welker & Rachel Durbin. Sps: William Walker & wife -JJB
09 Sep 1856	Hilary [Blubaugh] b 14 Oct 1855 s/o Zachary Blubaugh & Lydia Colglesser. Sps: Simon Sapp & wife -JJB
19 Oct 1856	Charles [Sapp] b 1 Sep [1856] s/o Simeon Sapp & Susanna Willis. Sps: Will Walker & wife -JJB
19 Oct 1856	John Henry [Mattingly] b 22 Sep [1856] s/o John Mattingly (dec'd) & Jane Durbin. Sps: John & Maria Anna Durbin -JJB
20 Dec 1856	Thomas Edgar [Hopwood] b 6 Oct [1856] s/o Samuel Hopwood & Nancy Jane Payne. Sps: John Porter & Eliza Jane Davidson -JJB
08 Feb 1857	Mary Ann [Blubaugh] b 27 Feb 1834 w/o Joseph Blubaugh. Sps: Jonathan Sapp & Frances Brent -JJB
09 Mar 1857	Sarah Elizabeth [Durbin] b 21 Nov [1856] d/o Solomon Durbin & Samantha Reynolds. Sps: Samuel Durbin & wife -JJB
22 Mar 1857	Basil [Blubaugh] b 19 Feb [1857] s/o John J. Blubaugh & Mary P. Dial. Sps: Samuel Durbin & wife -JJB

22 Mar 1857	Elizabeth Ellen [Arnold] b 30 Nov [1856] d/o Jonathan Arnold & Maria Blubaugh. Sps: Basil Durbin & W. Magers -JJB
22 Mar 1857	James Edward [Colopy] b 6 Dec [1856] s/o Jonathan A. Colopy & Sarah Jane Berry. Sps: Edward Colopy & Frances Sapp -JJB
24 Mar 1857	Rosa [Ashburn] b 3 Sep [1856] d/o Ellis Ashburn & Rebecca Durbin. Sps: Benjamin Durbin & wife -JJB
19 Apr 1857	John [Mumaw] b 23 Dec 1845 s/o Frederick Mumaw & Honora Logue. Sps: Stephen & Rebecca Blubaugh -JJB
03 May 1857	Rachel Josephine [Mumaw] b 21 Apr 1848 d/o Frederick Mumaw & Honora Logue. Sps: Ben Durbin & Sarah Blubaugh -JJB
07 May 1857	Mary Emma [Porter] b 25 Mar [1857] d/o Henry T. Porter & Elizabeth Headington Sps: Benjamin Durbin & wife -JJB
12 Jul 1857	Sara Agnes [Hess] b 16 May [1857] d/o Samuel Hess & Sara Ann Eckenrode. Sps: Benedict & Maria Magers -JJB
12 Jul 1857	James Roman [Blubaugh] b 25 Apr [1857] s/o Benjamin Blubaugh & Charlotte Heckler. Sps: Stephen Blubaugh & wife -JJB
12 Jul 1857	Sarah Jane Durbin b 1 Jun [1857] d/o John Durbin & Lucinda Sapp. Sps: Peter & Maria Anna Durbin -JJB
12 Jul 1857	Thomas [Algie Shapher/Shafer] b 18 Apr [1857] s/o [David] Jackson Shafer & Matilda Dial. Sps: J. Blubaugh & Rebecca McKenzie -JJB
29 Jul 1857	Anna [Brent] b 17 Jul [1857] d/o Edmund Brent & Frances Sapp. Sps: Samuel & Cecelia Brent -JJB
06 Sep 1857	Charles [Engle] b 9 Aug [1857] s/o Joseph Engle & Susanna Durbin. Sps: Simeon & Margaret Durbin -JJB
09 Sep 1857	Emma Jane [Parker] b 13 Jul [1857] d/o William Parker & Eliza Jane Pratt. Sps: Levi & Normanda Sapp -JJB
10 Sep 1857	Elizabeth Keziah [White nee Wade] b 14 Mar 1808 w/o Anthony White. Sps: A. & L. White -JJB

11 Oct 1857	Anna & Winifred White, Robert Alphonso Torman, Rebecca Joannna Durbin, Jacob Lewis Piar. -JJB
20 Dec 1857	Mary Margaret [Gardner] b 16 Nov [1857] d/o Anthony Gardner & Elizabeth Marshall. Sps: Margaret & Francis McNamara -JJB
20 Dec 1857	James Andrew [Blubaugh] b 30 Oct [1857] s/o Francis Blubaugh & Julie Anna Garland. Sps: Francis Durbin & Margaret Breckler -JJB
24 Jan 1858	William [Welker] b 16 Sep [1857] s/o [John B.] Jackson Welker & Miranda Dial. Sps: Laurence King & wife -JJB
25 Jan 1858	John Michael [Eifert] b 18 Dec [1857] s/o Victor Eifert & Matilda Gardner. Sps: John & Christina Gardner -JJB
04 Apr 1858	Jacob [Blie] b 3 Mar [1858] s/o George Blie & Catherine Zatpiller. Sps: Andreas Zimble & wife -JJB
18 Apr 1858	Maria Josephine [Walker] b 10 Mar 1858 d/o Samuel Walker & Margaret Kelly. Sps: William Walker & wife -JJB
18 Apr 1858	Dorothy [Sapp] b 27 Nov [1857] d/o Levi Sapp Jr. & Matilda Arnold. Sps: Benedict Magers & wife -JJB
09 May 1858	Zachary [Blubaugh] b 28 Jun 1857 s/o Zachary Blubaugh & Lydia Colglesser. Sps: John Blubaugh & wife -JJB
09 May 1858	Maria Elizabeth [Bradfield] b 27 Jan 1858 d/o James W. Bradfield & Sara Ann Sapp. Sps: Levi Sapp & wife -JJB
23 May 1858	Elias Theodore [Sapp] b 4 Mar [1858] s/o Charles Sapp & Winifred Porter. Sps: Benedict Magers & wife -JJB
06 Jun 1858	Maria [Samantha Mary Reynolds Durbin] b __ Mar 1832 w/o Solomon Durbin. Sps: G. Trullinger & Anna Bricker -JJB [Solomon Durbin md 20 Jan 1856 Samantha Reynolds.]
27 Jun 1858	Maria Agnes [Blubaugh] b 30 Mar [1858] d/o John Blubaugh & Harriet Eckenrode. Sps: G. Trullinger & Rachel Blubaugh -JJB
29 Jun 1858	Maria Matilda [Blubaugh] b 1 May [1858] d/o Joseph Blubaugh & Maria Anna Linebaugh. Sps: F. Blubaugh & Rachel Davidson -JJB

BAPTISMS

25 Jul 1858	Anthony [Robinson] b 14 May [1858] s/o Madison Robinson & Esther Jane White. Sps: Jonathan Colopy & Normanda Sapp -JJB
25 Jul 1858	Frances Josephine [Smithhisler] b 11 May [1858] d/o Michael Smithhisler & Mary Millis. Sps: Martin Homan & M. Mag. Shaff -JJB
05 Sep 1858	William Edward [Cummins] b 9 Aug [1858] s/o William Cummins & Maria Anna Cassidy. Sps: W. Lawler & Mrs. Caughlin -JJB
19 Sep 1858	Maria Caroline [Durbin] b 6 Aug [1858] d/o Solomon Durbin & Samantha Mary Reynolds. Sps: Benedict Magers & wife -JJB
17 Oct 1858	Susanna [Carpenter] b 22 Jan 1856 d/o _____ Carpenter & Margaret Coleman. Sps: George Payne & wife -JJB
17 Oct 1858	Michael Philip [Homan] b 21 Sep [1858] s/o Paul Homan & Elizabeth Smith. Sps: Michel Smithhisler & wife.
31 Oct 1858	Maria Josephine [Sapp] b 10 Sep [1858] d/o Simeon Sapp & Susan A. Willis Sps: William Walker & Maria Sapp -JJB
31 Oct 1858	Alice Anna [King] d/o Laurence King & Anna Draper. Sps: Benedict Magers & wife -JJB
03 Nov 1858	William Bernard [Durbin] b 10 Oct [1858] s/o Benjamin Durbin & Margaret McNamara. Sps: Peter & Sarah Durbin -JJB
12 Dec 1858	Julian [Sapp] b 6 Nov [1858] s/o George Sapp & Delia Anna White. Sps: Jos Colopy & Martha Frances Sapp -JJB
14 Dec 1858	Martin [Foley] b 24 Nov [1858] s/o Pat Foley & Anna Morton. Sps: Martin Homan & Marg Gessling -JJB
26 Dec 1858	James Baptist [Durbin] b 17 Nov [1858] s/o William Durbin & Margaret Sapp. Sps: John Durbin & Frances Brent -JJB
26 Dec 1858	Lucy [Colopy] d/o Jonathan A. Colopy & Sarah Jane Berry. Sps: Absalom Durbin & Deliah Colopy -JJB

71

27 Dec 1858   Martin [Pearl Hammond] b 17 Jun [1850] s/o Robert Hammond & Isabella Owens. Sps: Bapt Durbin -JJB

01 Jan 1859   Theodore Solomon [Blubaugh] b 11 Oct [1858] s/o William Blubaugh & [Emily] Ann Jacobs Sps: George Payne & wife.

23 Feb 1859   Julia Anna [Gagaghan] b 4 Jan [1859] d/o John Gagaghan & Julia Davis. Sps: Martin Walsh & Honora Joice -JJB

06 Mar 1859   Joseph Henry [Gardner] b 16 Jan [1859] s/o Anthony Gardner & Elizabeth Marshall. Sps: John & Christina Gardner -JJB

06 Mar 1859   Margaret Helen [Magers] b 22 Oct [1858] d/o Simeon Magers & Anna Theresa Logsdon. Sps: Francis Durbin & wife -JJB

30 Mar 1859   John Baptist [Durbin] b 16 Feb [1859] s/o John Durbin & Lucinda Sapp. Sps: Benedict Magers & wife -JJB

30 Mar 1859   Victoria [Arnold] b 20 Dec 1858 d/o Jonathan Arnold & Maria Blubaugh. Sps: William Dial & wife -JJB

03 Apr 1859   Thomas Solomon [Parker] b 29 Jan [1859] s/o [Robert] Selman Parker & Rebecca McKenzie. Sps: Benedict Magers & wife -JJB

03 Apr 1859   Clara Elizabeth [Tressel] b 29 Sep [1858] d/o Mathias Tressel & Wilhemina Smith. Sps: Mich Holler & Cath Smith -JJB

17 Apr 1859   Alexander [Welker] b 25 Jul 1858 s/o [William] Elliot Welker & Rachel Durbin. Sps: L. King & wife -JJB

17 Apr 1859   Sarah Catherine [Blubaugh] b 7 Mar 1859 d/o Francis Blubaugh & Julia Anna Garland. Sps: Stephen & Sarah Blubaugh -JJB

01 May 1859   Sarah Ellen [Blubaugh] b 29 Jun [1858] d/o John J. Blubaugh & Mary P. Dial. Sps: Stephen Blubaugh & wife -JJB

15 May 1859   Maria [Engle] b 4 Apr [1859] d/o Joseph Engle & Susanna Durbin. Sps: John & Maria Anna Durbin -JJB

29 May 1859	Henry [Carter] b 11 Mar [1859] s/o William Carter & Lydia Ann Barley. Sps: Ben Durbin & Rebecca Blubaugh -JJB
10 Jun 1859	Agnes [McKenzie] b 12 May [1859] d/o Aaron McKenzie & Sarah Dial. Sps: Isaac & Elizabeth Dial -JJB [See marriage letter dated 14 Sep 1909 St. Vincent (IN), md Albert King]
10 Jun 1859	Amanda Ellen [Dial], Emma Emila [Dial], Charles Jacob [Dial] relatives of Isaac Dial -JJB
12 Jun 1859	William Henry [Smithhisler] b 15 Feb [1859] s/o Philip Smithhisler & Magdalena Smith. Sps: William Shafer -JJB
23 Jun 1859	Elizabeth Ellen [Stevens] b 1 May [1859] d/o Cyrus Stevens & Mary Jane Smith. Sps: Laurence King & Maria Anna Durbin -JJB
23 Jun 1859	Elias Benedict [Sapp] b 21 May [1859] s/o Levi Sapp & Matilda Arnold. Sps: Benedict Magers & wife -JJB
23 Jun 1859	Aloysius [Engle] b 11 May [1859] s/o Martin Engle & Elizabeth Durbin. Sps: Ben Durbin & wife -JJB
23 Jun 1859	William [Hulse Porter] b 12 Jun [1859] s/o Henry T. Porter & Eliza Anna Headington. Sps: Levi Sapp & wife.
07 Aug 1859	John Rice b 25 Apr [1859] s/o Israel Rice & Elizabeth DeVore. Sps: Henry Porter & Maria Anna Bailes -JJB
01 Oct 1859	Liguori Benjamin [Durbin] b 29 Aug [1859] s/o Ben Durbin & Honora Blubaugh. Sps: Francis Blubaugh & wife -JJB
30 Oct 1859	Alice [Dial] b 9 Aug [1859] d/o Jonathan Dial & Elizabeth Sapp. Sps: Benedict Magers & wife -JJB
30 Oct 1859	Walter [Brent] b 15 Oct [1859] s/o Edmund Brent & Francis Sapp. Sps: William Walker & wife -JJB
06 Nov 1859	Henry Purcell [Smithhisler] b 14 Oct [1859] s/o Michael Smithhisler & Maria Millis. Sps: Henry Shaub & Elizabeth Homan -JJB

01 Jan 1860   William [Postlewait] b 27 Sep [1859] s/o Joseph Postlewait & Winifred White. Sps: G. Sapp & Cecelia Brent -JJB

29 Jan 1860   Cecilia Elizabeth [Durbin] b 15 Nov [1859] d/o Francis M. Durbin & Genevieve Henley. Sps: Peter Durbin & Penelope Bricker -JJB

29 Jan 1860   Joseph Anthony [Eifert] b 12 Dec [1859] s/o Victor [Eifert] & Gertrude Matilda Gardner. Sps: John & Catherine Gardner -JJB

29 Jan 1860   Elizabeth Ellen [Blubaugh] b 11 Nov [1859] d/o Joseph Blubaugh & Maria Anna Linebaugh. Sps: James Blubaugh & Rachel Dial -JJB

17 Mar 1860   Elias [   ] b 30 Mar 1856 & John [   ] b 16 Aug 1858 children of Ed Blubaugh's wife by a former husband & James Martin [Blubaugh] b 13 Jul 1859 s/o Ed Blubaugh [& wife Elizabeth Ann Stevens]. Sps: Benedict Magers & wife -JJB

08 Apr 1860   Michael [Walsh] b 23 Mar [1860] s/o Martin Walsh & Catherine Joice. Sps: Jacob Flarety & Anna Joice -JJB

26 Apr 1860   Francis Columbia [Sapp] b 2 Jan [1860] s/o Charles Sapp & Winifred Porter. Sps: L. Sapp & Mrs. John Porter -JJB

06 May 1860   Maria Anna [Branagan] b 25 Mar [1860] d/o Pat Branagan & Julia Broch. Sps: William Cummins & wife -JJB

20 May 1860   William Henry [Blubaugh] b 12 Jan [1860] s/o Zachary Blubaugh & Lydia Colglesser. Sps: Hilary Blubaugh & wife -JJB

07 Jun 1860   Basil [Durbin] b 7 Apr [1860] s/o Solomon Durbin & Samantha Mary Reynolds. Sps: Francis Durbin & wife -JJB

07 Jun 1860   Ignatius Lloyd [Logsdon] b 6 May [1860] s/o George Logsdon & Sarah Catherine Durbin. Sps: Ben Durbin & wife -JJB

BAPTISMS

26 Aug 1860	Sarah [Welker] b 6 Jul [1860] d/o [John B.] Jackson Welker & Sarah Miranda Dial. Sps: William Walker & wife -JJB
26 Aug 1860	Joseph [Clutz] b 25 Mar [1860] s/o Josiah Clutz & Eliza Welker. Sps: W. Walker & Marg. Durbin -JJB
07 Sep 1860	Samuel [Keefer] b 9 Oct [1860] s/o Henry Keefer & M. Keefer. Sps: Geo Payne & wife -JJB
20 Sep 1860	George [Carter] b 28 Aug [1860] s/o William Carter & Lydia Ann Barley. Sps: Geo Payne & wife -JJB
04 Nov 1860	Clement Eugene [Sapp] b 2 Sep [1860] s/o Simon Sapp & Susan Willis. Sps: Jonathan Colopy & Maria Anna Durbin -JJB
18 Nov 1860	Alice Isabella [Durbin] b 11 Oct [1860] d/o Ben Durbin & Margaret McNamara. Sps: Raphael Durbin & Joanna Mattingly -JJB
21 Nov 1860	Patience Ellen [Blubaugh] b 15 Oct [1860] d/o John Blubaugh & Harriet Eckenrode. Sps: Stephen Blubaugh & wife -JJB
19 Dec 1860	William Henry [McNamara] b 8 Nov [1860] s/o Francis McNamara & Sarah Elizabeth Porter. Sps: Jonathan Arnold & Eliz Porter -JJB
19 Dec 1860	Rachel Ellen [Parker] b 25 Sep [1860] d/o [Robert] Selman Parker & Rebecca A. McKenzie. Sps: Francis McNamara & wife -JJB
06 Jan 1861	Rebecca Elizabeth [Blubaugh] b 7 Nov [1860] d/o Francis Blubaugh & Julia Anna Garland. Sps: Steph Blubaugh & wife -JJB
03 Mar 1861	Barbara [Eifert] b 24 Jan [1861] d/o Victor Eifert & Matilda Gardner. Sps: Anthony & Christina Gardner -JJB
03 Mar 1861	Catharine Fritz b 2 Nov [1860] d/o John Fritz & Felicia Goodballer. Sps: Nicholas & Cath Hollet -JJB
17 Mar 1861	Rachel Ellen [Carter] b 6 Dec [1860] d/o Raphael Carter & Lydia Magers. Sps: Ben Eckenrode & Genevieve Durbin -JJB

25 Mar 1861	Eliza Ellen [Magers] b 29 Jan 1861 d/o Nathan Magers & Sarah Ann Headington. Sps: Francis Durbin & wife -JJB
28 Apr 1861	Honora Ellen [Durbin] b 14 Dec [1860] d/o Ben Durbin & Honora Blubaugh. Sps: Francis Durbin & wife -JJB
28 Apr 1861	Theodore [Durbin] b 1 Mar [1861] s/o John Durbin & Lucinda Sapp. Sps: Raphael Durbin & wife -JJB
28 Apr 1861	Margaret Frances [McGough] b 13 Oct [1860] d/o John McGough & Eliza Ann Losh. Sps: Christopher Bricker & wife -JJB
09 May 1861	John Julius [Gardner] b 21 Mar [1861] s/o Anthony Gardner & Elizabeth Marshall. Sps: Martin & Catherine Gardner -JJB
26 May 1861	Maria Alice [Magers] b 11 Apr [1861] d/o Simon Magers & Ann Theresa Logsdon. Sps: Jonathan Arnold & Maria Anna Durbin -JJB
10 Jun 1861	Rachel Emily [Blubaugh] b 19 Mar [1861] d/o William Blubaugh & Emily Jacobs. Sps: J. & Matilda Colopy -JJB
23 Jun 1861	Francis Marion [McKenzie] b 15 May [1861] s/o John McKenzie & Charlotte Critchfield. Sps: Elias Porter & wife -JJB
23 Jun 1861	Maria Alice [Shafer] b 15 May [1861] d/o [David] Jackson Shafer & Matilda Dial. Sps: Anthony White & wife -JJB
07 Jul 1861	Maria Isabella [Blubaugh] b 5 May 1861 d/o John J. Blubaugh & Mary P. Dial. Sps: Jonathan Arnold & wife -JJB
07 Jul 1861	Maria Frances [Snow] b 23 Apr [1861] d/o William D. Snow & Elizabeth A. Blubaugh. Sps: Ben Blubaugh & wife -JJB
18 Aug 1861	William Daniel [Hess] b 16 Jun [1861] s/o Samuel Hess & Sarah Anna Eckenrode. Sps: William Walker & wife -JJB
01 Sep 1861	Martha Ellen [Trullinger] b 13 Jun [1861] d/o James Trullinger & Mary Frasier. Sps: George Trullinger & wife -JJB

BAPTISMS

01 Sep 1861	Jacob [Cummins] b 5 Aug [1861] s/o William Cummins & Maria Anna Cassidy. Sps: Pat Branagan & wife -JJB
19 Sep 1861	Francis Albert [Trullinger] b 14 Aug [1861] s/o Michael Trullinger & Sarah M. Bricker. Sps: George Trullinger & wife -JJB
13 Oct 1861	Thomas Damian [King] b 31 Apr [1861] s/o Laurence King & Anna Draper. Sps: Jackson & Rachel Welker -JJB
13 Oct 1861	James Michael [Hollet] b 29 Jun [1861] s/o Nicholas Hollet & Catherine Eifert. Sps: Nicholas Hollet & wife -JJB
27 Oct 1861	Susan Willis Sapp aka Susan Anna w/o Simeon Sapp. Sps: Peter Durbin & Anna Walker -JJB
01 Nov 1861	James Thomas [Parker] b 31 Aug [1861] d/o William Parker & Eliza Joanna Pratt. Sps: Cristopher Bricker & wife -JJB
11 Nov 1861	Maria Hannah [White nee Dewitt] b 1815 w/o Joseph White. Sps: George Sapp & Maria Magers -JJB
08 Feb 1862	John [Rouse] b 8 Apr 1858 & Elinor [Rouse] b 8 Jan 1861 children of Benjamin Rouse & F. C. Critchfield. Sps: Levi Sapp & wife -JJB
06 Apr 1862	John Carter b 2 Feb [1862] s/o Raphael Carter & Lydia Magers. Sps: Hilary Blubaugh & wife -JJB
20 Apr 1862	Elizabeth Jane [Sapp] b 22 Feb [1862] d/o Charles Sapp & Winifred Porter. Sps: Francis McNamara & Mary Durbin -JJB
04 May 1862	Joseph [White] b 22 Nov [18__] s/o Joseph White & Hannah DeWitt. Sps: Jonathan Arnold & wife -JJB
04 May 1862	Thomas [Blubaugh] b 1 Mar [1862] s/o Zachary Blubaugh & Lydia [Colglesser]. Sps: Hilary Blubaugh & wife -JJB
04 May 1862	Margaret Ellen [Engle] b 4 Mar [1862] d/o Joseph Engle & Susanna Durbin. Sps: George & Margaret Durbin -JJB
04 May 1862	Cornelius Purcell [Durbin] b 21 Mar [1862] s/o Francis M. Durbin & Genevieve Henley. Sps: Abs. Durbin & Cath. Sapp -JJB

77

18 May 1862	Joseph E. Colopy b 19 Oct [1861] s/o [G.] Edward Colopy & Harriet Farquhar. Sps: Jos Colopy & Mary Jane Durbin -JJB
13 Jul 1862	Maria Elizabeth [Guenther] b 22 May [1862] d/o Jacob Guenther & Maria Anna Starner. Sps: Alexander & Dorothy Starner.
13 Jul 1862	Julius Peter [Durbin] b 11 Jun [1862] s/o Raphael Durbin & Barbara Buck. Sps: Peter Durbin & Emma Brent -JJB
27 Jul 1862	George Bernard [Blubaugh] b 13 Apr [1862] & Leo Bennet [Blubaugh] b 13 Apr [1862] twin sons of Joseph Blubaugh & Anna Linebaugh. Sps: Joseph, Levi, Delila, & Matilda Colopy -JJB
29 Jul 1862	Ellen Gertrude [Brent] age 20 w/o Edward Brent. Sps: Will O'Rouke & F. Brent -JJB
07 Sep 1862	Julian David [Sapp] b 30 May [1862] & Martina Isabella [Sapp] b 30 May [1862] twins of Levi Sapp Jr. & Matilda Arnold. Sps: Jonathan Arnold & wife W. Dial -JJB
21 Sep 1862	Frances Helen Sapp b 31 Aug [1862] d/o George Sapp & Delia Anna White. Sps: Peter Durbin & Louisa White -JJB
21 Sep 1862	Alphonso [Millis] b 26 Aug [1862] s/o Joseph Francis Millis & Elizabeth White. Sps: Anthony Smithhisler & Lorinda White.
02 Oct 1862	Martin Ischyrion [Porter] b 28 Aug [1862] s/o Elias P. Porter & Margaret Isabella Durbin. Sps: Peter Durbin & Francis Porter -JJB
19 Oct 1862	Maria Elizabeth [Durbin] b 19 Aug [1862] d/o Ben Durbin & Honora Blubaugh. Sps: Francis Blubaugh & Maria Breckler -JJB
19 Oct 1862	Ellen Artentia [Engle] b 20 Jul [1862] d/o Martin Engle & Elizabeth Durbin. Sps: Peter Durbin & Nancy [Anna Durbin] -JJB
16 Nov 1862	Francis [Smithhisler] b 22 Oct [1862] s/o Michael Smithhisler & Maria Millis. Sps: Francis Hess & Helen Shaub -JJB

78

17 Dec 1862	Stephen [Durbin] b 11 Nov [1862] s/o George Durbin & Amanda Workman. Sps: Raphael Durbin & wife -JJB
25 Jan 1863	Eliza Ellen [Snow] b 23 Dec [1862] d/o William [Darius] Snow & Elizabeth Blubaugh. Sps: Francis Blubaugh & Margaret Blubaugh -JJB
08 Feb 1863	Charles Rosecrans [Stevens] b 10 Nov [1862] d/o Cyrus Stevens & Mary Jane Smith. Sps: Jackson Welker & wife -JJB
22 Mar 1863	Frances Isabella [Durbin] b 24 Feb [1863] d/o John Durbin & Lucinda Sapp. Sps: Peter & Margaret Durbin -JJB
03 Apr 1863	William [Bradfield] b 19 Feb [1863] s/o James Bradfield & Sarah Ann Sapp. Sps: Levi Sapp & wife -JJB
19 Apr 1863	James Lewis Porter b 2 Jul 1854 s/o Thomas Porter & Phoebe Ann [Stull]. Sps: George Payne & wife -JJB
19 Apr 1863	Frances Maria [Blubaugh] b 7 Mar [1863] d/o Ben J. Blubaugh & Margaret Anna McNamara. Sps: Jonathan Arnold & wife -JJB
03 May 1863	Pauline Frances [King] b 7 Jan [1863] d/o Anthony King & Gertrude Keefer. Sps: Raphael Durbin & wife -JJB
17 May 1863	Frances Emily [Sapp] b 27 Mar [1863] d/o Simeon Sapp & Susan [Millis] Sapp. Sps: Peter Durbin & Nancy Walker -JJB
17 May 1863	Maria Elizabeth [Kline] b 30 Oct [1862] d/o Philip Kline & Emeline Sapp. Sps: Martin Kline & wife -JJB
31 May 1863	Hiram [Postlewait] b 17 Feb 1862 s/o Jos Postlewait & Winifred White. Sps: George Sapp & Kesiah White -JJB
14 Jun 1863	James David [Parker] b 11 Apr [1863] s/o [Robert] Selman Parker & Rebecca McKenzie. Sps: Absalom Durbin & Penelope Bricker -JJB
12 Jul 1863	Maria Ellen [Whisler] b 3 Jun [1863] d/o Anthony Whisler & Catherine Smith. Sps: Jacob Smith & Maria Anna Fisher -JJB

26 Jul 1863	Barbara Ellen [Gardner] b 24 Jun [1863] d/o Anthony Gardner & Elizabeth Marshall. Sps: Leo & Maria Gardner -JJB
18 Sep 1863	Sarah Ellen [Dial] b 26 Jul 1862 d/o Benjamin Dial & Sarah Grimes. Sps: Isaac Dial & wife -JJB
20 Sep 1863	Leon [Durbin] b 2 Jul [1863] s/o Solomon Durbin & Samantha Mary Reynolds. Sps: Jonathan Arnold & wife -JJB
20 Sep 1863	Clement Elmer [Durbin] b 16 Aug [1863] s/o Benjamin Durbin & Margaret McNamara. Sps: H. Durbin & Sarah Ellen Blubaugh -JJB
30 Sep 1863	Maria Teresa Frances [Durbin] b 31 Aug [1863] d/o Raphael & Barbara [Buck] Durbin. Sps: Margaret Durbin & Julius T. Tardaville -JJB
15 Nov 1863	James Roland [Trullinger] b 1 Jan 1863 s/o Jacob & Mary [Frasier] Trullinger. Sps: Jos Colopy & Martha Trullinger -JJB
16 Nov 1863	Rachel Susanna [McKenzie] b 23 Jul [1863] d/o John McKenzie & Charlotte Critchfield. Sps: Anthony White & Rebecca Parker -JJB
30 Nov 1863	Charles Richard [Garland] b 1860 s/o Jacob & Anna Garland. Sps: Martin Homan & Elizabeth Garland -JJB
13 Dec 1863	Camilla [Colopy] b 5 Jul [1863] d/o Edward Colopy & Harriet Farquhar. Sps: Henry Durbin & Deliah Colopy -JJB
02 Mar 1864	Barbara Jane [Durbin] b 9 Jan [1864] d/o Francis M. Durbin & Genevieve Henley. Sps: Henry & Catherine Durbin -JJB
27 Mar 1864	Rosa [Millis] b 1 Feb [1864] d/o Joseph Francis Millis & Elizabeth White. Sps: Peter Durbin & Anna Walker -JJB
24 Apr 1864	Agnes Emeline Hammond b 1845. -JJB
24 Apr 1864	James Clement [Gardner] b 13 Dec [1863] d/o Francis Gardner & Catherine Stuhlmiller. Sps: John Gardner & Mary Breckler -JJB

BAPTISMS

24 Apr 1864	Samuel Franklin [Payne] b 12 Jan [1864] s/o Laurence Payne & [Sarah] Anna Coleman. Sps: Mrs. Smithhisler & Elias Porter -JJB
05 May 1864	Lewis Franklin b 18 Dec [1863?], [privately] bapt. 24 Jan [1864]. Sps: Peter & Marianna Durbin -JJB
08 May 1864	Samuel [Rice] b 16 Jan [1864] s/o Israel Rice & Elizabeth DeVore. Sps: Hilary Blubaugh & wife -JJB
08 May 1864	Frances Lorraine [Shafer] b 17 Mar [1864] d/o [David] Jackson Shafer & Matilda Dial. Sps: Jos Millis & Maria Walsh -JJB
22 May 1864	Maria [McNamara] b 15 Apr [1864] d/o Francis McNamara & Sarah Elizabeth Porter. Sps: Peter Durbin & Joanna Porter -JJB
05 Jun 1864	Jacob Albert [Crowner] b 22 Feb [1864] s/o John Crowner & Margaret Whisler. Sps: Anthony Gardner & Catherine Allerding -JJB
05 Jun 1864	Mary Adele [Colopy] b 3 May [1864] d/o Jonathan A. Colopy & Sarah Jane Berry. Sps: Levi & Matilda Colopy -JJB
03 Jul 1864	Jacob Franklin [Postlewait] b 7 Jan [1864] s/o Jos Postlewait & Winifred White. Sps: Jonathan Colopy & Catherine Sapp -JJB
16 Jul 1864	Edward, Maria, Angela, & David Brewer, children of William Brewer & Mary Ann Sapp. Sps: Hartley Sapp & wife -JJB
30 Jul 1864	Maria Christina [Blubaugh] b 23 Jun [1864] d/o Ben Blubaugh & Margaret McNamara. Sps: J. Blubaugh & Christina McNamara -JJB
30 Jul 1864	Maria [O'Heren] b 6 Jul [1864] d/o Jacob O'Heren & Joanna _____. Sps: Dyonisuis (Dennis) Cerry & Cath Harris -JJB
23 Oct 1864	Regina Wilomena [Shaff] b 18 Aug [1864] d/o William Shaff & Margaret Fitzmyre. Sps: Francis Fitzmyre & wife -JJB

23 Oct 1864   Anthony [Smithhisler] b 5 Sep [1864] s/o Michael Smithhisler & Maria Millis. Sps: Anthony Smithhisler & 2nd wife -JJB

23 Oct 1864   Clement [King] b 10 Oct 1863 s/o Laurence King & Hanna Draper. Sps: Anthony & Catherine King.

20 Nov 1864   Henry Demetrius [Blubaugh] b 27 Oct [1864] s/o Hilary Blubaugh & Sarah Ellen Bailes. Sps: John Durbin & wife -JJB

04 Dec 1864   Selora Alphonsa [Durbin] b 20 Oct [1864] d/o Ben Durbin & Margaret McNamara. Sps: John Durbin & wife -JJB

01 Jan 1865   Ida Catherine [Hess] b 20 Oct [1864] d/o Samuel Hess & Sarah Anna Eckenrode. Sps: Ben Eckenrode & Mrs. Smith -JJB

02 Jan 1865   Giles Allen Butts b 15 Sep [1864] s/o Henry Butts & Anna Smith. Sps: Susan Sapp -JJB

15 Jan 1865   Edward Carpenter b 9 Oct [1864] s/o Ed Carpenter & Frances Sapp. Sps: Levi Colopy & Cath Sapp -JJB

29 Jan 1865   Genevieve [Sapp] b 13 Jan [1865] d/o George Sapp & Delia Anna White. Sps: John Durbin & wife Lucinda -JJB

01 Mar 1865   Charles William [Parker] b 29 Nov [1864] s/o [Robert] Selman Parker & Rebecca McKenzie. Sps: Samuel Durbin & wife -JJB

14 Apr 1865   John S. [White] b 11 Nov 1856 s/o Jacob White & Alice Smith. Sps: George Sapp & Louise White -JJB

25 May 1865   Barbara Elizabeth [McKenzie] b 28 Dec 1842 w/o Samuel McKenzie. Sps: Raphael & Margaret Durbin -JJB

25 May 1865   Anna Veronica [Durbin] b 21 Apr [1865] d/o Raphael Durbin & Barbara Buck. Sps: Simeon & Maria Anna Durbin -JJB

25 Jun 1865   John Francis [Gardner] b 1 Jun [1865] s/o Francis M. Gardner & Mary J. Allerding. Sps: John Gardner & Catherine Allerding -JJB

25 Jun 1865	James Anthony [Blubaugh] b 6 Apr [1865] s/o Jos Blubaugh & Maria Anna Linebaugh. Sps: Peter & Margaret Durbin -JJB
25 Jun 1865	Benjamin [Snow] b 26 Dec [1864] s/o William Darius Snow & Elizabeth Anna Blubaugh. Sps: Levi & Delila Colopy -JJB
09 Jul 1865	Charles [Welker] b 10 Jun [1865] s/o [John B.] Jackson Welker & Sarah Miranda Dial. Sps: Will Dial & Sarah Sapp -JJB
06 Aug 1865	Mary Catherine [Eckenrode] b 15 Jun [1865] d/o Benjamin Eckenrode & Margaret Shafer. Sps: Henry Durbin & S. E. McNamara -JJB
06 Aug 1865	Clement [McNamara] b 23 May [1865] s/o John McNamara & Emoline A. Hammond. Sps: Jos Colopy & Maria Welch -JJB
15 Aug 1865	Benjamin Franklin [Durbin] b 21 Jul [1865] s/o John Durbin & Lucinda Sapp. Sps: H. Durbin & Maria J. Durbin -JJB
15 Aug 1865	William Sherman [Blubaugh] b 28 Jun [1865] s/o John Blubaugh & Maria Dial. Sps: Peter & Maria Anna Durbin -JJB
01 Oct 1865	[Thomas] Bernard [Durbin] b 20 Aug [1865] s/o John L. Durbin & Margaret Colopy. Sps: George Durbin & Anna Colopy -JJB
01 Oct 1865	Benjamin Duncan b 1 Apr 1862 s/o William Duncan & Mary Jane Swarts. Sps: Jacob Swarts & Eliza (Ellen) McKenzie -JJB
15 Oct 1865	Rosella [Sapp] b 14 Aug [1865] d/o Simeon Sapp & Susan Willis. Sps: Jonathan Colopy & Eliz Engle -JJB
02 Nov 1865	Frances Ellen [Durbin] b 10 Oct [1865] d/o George Durbin & Normanda Workman. Sps: Francis & Maria Durbin -JJB
12 Nov 1865	Sarah Ellen [Durbin] b 15 Oct [1865] d/o Francis M. Durbin & Genevieve Henley. Sps: Gregory & Elizabeth Henley -JJB

12 Nov 1865	Martha Frances [Eckenrode] b 14 Aug [1865] d/o John Eckenrode & Mary Jane Forsythe. Sps: Benjamin & Agnes Eckenrode -JJB
12 Nov 1865	Francis [Piar] b 2 Apr [1865] s/o Vincent Piar & Rachel Blubaugh. Sps: Fr. Logsdon & Sarah Ellen Blubaugh -JJB
10 Dec 1865	Mary Catherine [Gardner] b 5 Nov [1865] d/o Anthony Gardner & Elizabeth Marshall. Sps: John Gardner & Charlotte Blubaugh -JJB
12 Feb 1866	Mary Anna Cath [McKenzie] b 28 Jan [1866] d/o Samuel P. McKenzie & B. E. Plucker. Sps: Julius P. Tardeville & Catherine King -JJB
08 Apr 1866	Charles Solomon [Sapp] b 8 Jan [1866] s/o Charles Sapp & Winifred Porter. Sps: Peter Durbin & W. E. McNamara -JJB
22 Apr 1866	Mary [Logsdon] b 24 May [1865] d/o George Logsdon & Sarah Catherine Durbin. Sps: Francis Logsdon & Maria L. Durbin -JJB
22 Apr 1866	James [Engle] b 21 Apr [1866] s/o Joseph Engle & Susanna Durbin. Sps: John (Rex) Durbin & wife -JJB
06 May 1866	Maria Matilda [Millis] b 5 Mar [1866] d/o Joseph Francis Millis & Elizabeth White. Sps: Jos Colopy & Maria White -JJB
31 May 1866	Julius [Arnold] b 27 Jan 1866 s/o Richard Arnold & Eliza Harden. Sps: Jonathan Arnold & wife -JJB
03 Jun 1866	Mary Barbara [Gardner] b 21 Mar [1866] d/o Francis M. Gardner & Catherine Stuhlmiller. Sps: J. N. Allerding & wife -JJB
26 Aug 1866	John [Colopy] b 26 Apr 1865 s/o Ed Colopy & Harriet Farquhar. Sps: Jacob & Matila Colopy-JJB
26 Aug 1866	John or Jane [Payne] b 11 Feb [1866] ?/o Lawrence Payne & Sarah Ann Ellen Coleman. Sps: Fr. Fitzmyre & wife -JJB

BAPTISMS

30 Sep 1866	Germain Elvry [Gardner] b 26 Aug [1866] s/o John Gardner & Mary Breckler. Sps: Stephen Blubaugh & wife -JJB
25 Oct 1866	Mary Alice [Houck] b 14 Aug [1866] d/o William Houck & Rachel Dial. Sps: Sam Durbin & wife -JJB
02 Dec 1866	Eliza Ellen [Swarts] b 16 Oct [1866] d/o Levi Swarts & Margaret McKenzie. Sps: Sam Durbin & wife -JJB
27 Jan 1867	Eliza Ellen [Blubaugh] b 21 Dec [1866] d/o Benjamin J. Blubaugh & Margaret McNamara. Sps: Jonathan Arnold & Eliza Blubaugh -JJB
10 Mar 1867	Francis Joseph [Durbin] b 29 Jan 1867 s/o John L. C. Durbin & Margaret Colopy Sps: Joseph Engle & wife -JJB
19 May 1867	William Wherle age 12. Sps: Ben J. Durbin & wife Rosa -JJB
05 Apr 1867	William Elias [Smithhisler] b 15 Mar [1867] s/o Michael Smithhisler & Maria Millis. Sps: Anthony Smithhisler & Rosa Homan -JJB
20 Apr 1867	James Walter [Bradfield] b 19 Jan 1866 s/o James W. Bradfield & Sarah Anna Sapp. Sps: Joseph H. & D. Anna Colopy -JJB
21 Apr 1867	Carl Edward [Durbin] b 20 May [1867] s/o Ralphael Durbin & Barbara Buck. Sps: Ben J. Durbin & Martha Buck -JJB
16 Jun 1867	Thomas L. [Arnold] b 5 May [1867] s/o Jonathan Arnold & Maria Blubaugh. Sps: Henry & Catherine Durbin -JJB
14 Jul 1867	Dennis [Durbin] b 1 Jul [1867] s/o Francis Durbin & Susanna Sapp. Sps: George Durbin & Catherine King -JJB.
18 Jul 1867	Mones Isaac Butts b 30 May [1867] s/o Henry A. Butts & Anna M. Smith. Sps: Maria Smith -JJB
25 Aug 1867	Theodora Jane [McNamara] b 15 Jul 1867 d/o Francis McNamara & Elizabeth Porter. Sps: Peter Durbin & Maria Weld -JJB

15 Sep 1867	Mary Matilda [Homan] b 14 Aug [1867] d/o Martin Homan & Catherine Miller. Sps: Charles Miller & Rosa Homan -JJB
29 Sep 1867	Ida Frances [Blubaugh] b 16 Aug [1867] d/o John J. Blubaugh & Mary P. Dial. Sps: William & Matilda Dial -JJB
29 Sep 1867	Maria O. [Shults] b 16 Aug [1867] d/o Henry Shults & Nora E. Blubaugh. Sps: Francis Durbin & wife -JJB
29 Sep 1867	Justin [Blubaugh] b 12 Aug [1867] s/o Joseph Blubaugh & Maria Anna Linebaugh Sps: Fr .Blubaugh & wife.
29 Sep 1867	Clement Aloysius [Blubaugh] b 28 Aug [1867] s/o Hilary Blubaugh & Sarah Ellen Bailes. Sps: Benjamin Blubaugh & wife -JJB
27 Oct 1867	Leo Raymond [Smithhisler] b 1 Oct 1867 s/o Anthony Smithhisler & Martha Eleanor Blubaugh. Sps: Philip J. Smithhisler & Cath Blubaugh -JJB
01 Dec 1867	Benjamin Raymond [Parker] b 2 Oct [1867] s/o Robert Selman Parker & Rebecca McKenzie. Sps: Sam Durbin & wife -JJB
12 Jan 1868	Honora Ellen [Durbin] b 15 Dec [1867] d/o John Durbin & Lucinda Sapp. Sps: Hilary Blubaugh & wife -JJB
26 Jan 1868	Charlotte [Logsdon] b 29 Dec [1867] d/o Francis Logsdon & Catherine Blubaugh. Sps: Anthony White & Ch. Blubaugh -JJB
08 Mar 1868	William H. Blubaugh b 31 Jan [1868] s/o Leo Blubaugh & Ellen Dial. Sps: Fr. Blubaugh & Matilda Dial -JJB
05 Apr 1868	John Baptist [Logsdon] b 15 Feb [1868] s/o George Logsdon & Sarah Durbin. Sps: Peter Durbin & Jane Bricker -JJB
19 Apr 1868	Mary Jane [Durbin] b 10 Feb [1868] d/o Benjamin & Margaret [McNamara] Durbin. Sps: Jos H. Colopy & Maria J. Durbin -JJB
03 May 1868	Veronica [Hess] b 5 Mar [1868] d/o Sam Hess & Sara Ann Eckenrode. Sps: Ch Durbin & wife -JJB

10 Jun 1868	John [Hess] b 10 Aug 1851 s/o Sam Hess & Sara Ann Eckenrode. Sps: Ch. Durbin & wife -JJB
10 Jun 1868	Margaret [Hess] b 2 Sep 1853 d/o Sam Hess & S. Anna Eckenrode. Sps: Ch. Durbin & wife -JJB
11 Jun 1868	James Edwin [Colopy] b 21 Aug 1867 s/o Edward Colopy & Harriet Farquhar. Sps: Levi & Matilda Colopy -JJB
28 Jun 1868	Agnes [Millis] b 29 May [1868] d/o [Joseph] Francis Millis & Elizabeth White. Sps: John Durbin & wife -JJB
26 Jul 1868	Joseph [Peters] b 30 May [1868] s/o Henry Peters & Anna Whisler. Sps: John Gardner & wife -JJB
27 Aug 1868	Francis Raymond [Durbin] b 12 Aug [1868] s/o Charles Durbin & Eleanor Frances Hess. Sps: Henry Durbin & wife Joanna -JJB
06 Sep 1868	Francis Benedict [Blubaugh] b 28 Jul [1868] s/o Ben J. Blubaugh & Margaret A. McNamara. Sps: Stephen Blubaugh & wife -JJB
04 Oct 1868	Elizabeth [Smithhisler] b 3 Sep [1868] d/o Philip Smithhisler & Mary H. White. Sps: Michael Smithhisler & Ellen White -JJB
18 Oct 1868	Gertrude [Durbin] b 7 Sep [1868] d/o Francis Durbin & Genevieve Henley. Sps: Lyman & Louisa J. Durbin -JJB
20 Oct 1868	S. Christina [Gardner] d/o Anthony Gardner & Elizabeth Marshall. Sps: John Beam & wife -JJB
08 Nov 1868	Rebecca Anna [Houck] b 18 Jul [1868] d/o William Houck & Rachel Dial. Sps: William Dial & Matilda Bailes -JJB
08 Nov 1868	Israel Wilson [Rice] b 22 Aug [1868] s/o Israel Rice & Elizabeth DeVore. Sps: Martin & Elizabeth Homan -JJB
22 Nov 1868	Mary Catherine [Blubaugh] b 14 Oct [1868] d/o Peter Blubaugh & Margaret Breckler. Sps: John Gardner & wife -JJB
22 Nov 1868	Charles Albert [Shults] b 2 Oct [1868] s/o Henry Shults & Nora E. Blubaugh. Sps: Stephen Blubaugh & wife -JJB

03 Jan 1869	Charles [Gardner] b 7 Nov [1868] s/o Francis M. Gardner & Mary J. Allerding. Sps: Charles & Caroline Henley -JJB
06 Jan 1869	Joseph Alphonse Liguori [Durbin] b 7 Dec [1868] s/o Raphael Durbin & B. [Barbara] Buck. Sps: Jos Engle & wife -JJB
21 Jan 1869	Oliva Josephine Durbin b 25 Oct [1868] d/o George Durbin & Normanda Workman. Sps: Fr. Durbin -JJB
31 Jan 1869	John H. [Marshall] b 18 Jan 1868 s/o John Marshall & Louise Trullinger. Sps: Hilary Blubaugh & Cath Marshall -JJB
11 Apr 1869	Dorothy [Durbin] b 15 Jan [1869] d/o Solomon Durbin & Samantha Mary Reynolds. Sps: Stephen Blubaugh & wife -JJB
11 Apr 1869	Anna E. [Laner] b 29 Nov 1868 d/o John Laner & M. A. Hammon. Sps: Adam Weber & wife -JJB
25 Apr 1869	George [Welker] b 29 Jan [1869] s/o [John B.] Jackson Welker & Sarah Miranda Dial. Sps: Sam Durbin & T. Shafer -JJB
25 Apr 1869	Joseph Franklin [Swarts] b 12 Jan [1869] s/o Levi Swarts & Margaret McKenzie. Sps: Will Dial & Rebecca Tanker -JJB
28 Apr 1869	Mary Isadora [Butts] b 22 Dec [1868] d/o Henry A. Butts & Anna Smith. Sps: G. Sapp & Hanna King -JJB
07 May 1869	Anthony Elias [Smithhisler] b 5 May [1869] s/o Anthony Smithhisler & Martha Eleanor Blubaugh. Sps: Adam Shaub & wife -JJB
20 Jun 1869	Mary Catherine [Durbin] b 18 May [1869] d/o John Durbin & Margaret Colopy. Sps: Peter & Eliz J. Durbin -JJB
20 Jun 1869	Flora Ellen [Swarts] b 1 Sep 1868 d/o X. [Christopher] Swarts & Eliza Cox. Sps: Jacob Swarts & wife -JJB
23 Jun 1869	Agnes Evelyn [Eckenrode] b 16 Feb [1869] d/o John Eckenrode & Mary J. Forsythe. Sps: Ben Eckenrode & H. Blubaugh -JJB

BAPTISMS

04 Jul 1869	Julius Jacob [Bailes] b 25 May [1869] s/o William J. Bailes & Matilda A. Dial. Sps: Will Dial & Rachel Durbin -JJB
04 Jul 1869	Peter Engle b 18 Oct 1830 s/o Homer [Engle]. Sps: Peter Durbin & S. [Susanna] Engle -JJB
04 Jul 1869	Flora Anna [Engle] b 18 Oct 1868 d/o [Joseph Engle] & Sara [Durbin] Engle. Sps: Peter Durbin & Susanna Engle -JJB
01 Aug 1869	Frances Catherine [Gardner] b 13 Jun [1869] d/o John Gardner & Mary Breckler. Sps: Anthony Gardner & wife -JJB
12 Sep 1869	Pius [Engle] b 6 Aug [1869] s/o Jos Engle & Susanna Durbin. Sps: Pius Durbin & Maria Welch -JJB
28 Sep 1869	Mary Aparilla [Durbin] b 28 Aug [1869] d/o Henry Durbin & Catherine Carpenter. Sps: Levi Colopy & Maria J. Durbin -JJB
03 Oct 1869	Rachel Ellen [Warner] b 27 Aug [1869] d/o Henry Warner & Sarah Dial. Sps: Jonathan Arnold & wife -JJB
30 Oct 1869	Liguori [Blubaugh] b 26 Sep [1869] s/o Leon Blubaugh & Ellen Dial. Sps: Fr. Logsdon & wife -JJB
28 Nov 1869	Cecilia [Frances Homan] b 10 Oct [1869] d/o Martin Homan & Catherine Miller. Sps: Mich Smithhisler & wife -JJB
01 Jan 1870	David William [Eckenrode] b 19 Oct [1869 s/o Ben Eckenrode & Margaret Shafer. Sps: Peter Durbin & wife -JJB
05 Jan 1870	Matilda Lybarger [Sapp] b 16 Nob 1851 w/o John Sapp. Sps: Fr. Durbin & wife -JJB
30 Feb 1870	Martina Louisa [Smithhisler] b 30 Jan [1870] d/o Philip Smithhisler & Mary H. White. Sps: George Smithhisler & Eliz Millis -JJB
24 Apr 1870	Paul Benjamin [Logsdon] b 15 Mar [1870] s/o George Logsdon & Sarah Durbin. Sps: John Durbin & wife -JJB

24 Apr 1870	Joseph James [Logsdon] b 15 Mar [1870] s/o G. L. & S. D. [George Logsdon & Sarah Durbin]. Sps: Ben Durbin & J. Mattingly -JJB
09 May 1870	Julia Jane Gardner b 6 Apr [1870] d/o Francis M. Gardner & Mary J. Allerding. Sps: Leo Gardner & Margaret Allerding -JJB
16 Jun 1870	Victoria Eliz [Blubaugh] b 4 May [1870] d/o John J. Blubaugh & Mary P. Dial Sps: Fr. Blubaugh & Margaret Blubaugh -JJB
03 Jul 1870	Lucy [Sapp] b 17 Jun [1870] d/o George Sapp & Delia White. Sps: Michael Smithhisler & wife -JJB
17 Jul 1870	Samuel Cornelius [Shults] b 2 Jun [1870] s/o Henry Shults & Nora E. Blubaugh. Sps: Ben Blubaugh & wife -JJB
17 Jul 1870	Julius Francis [Durbin] b 16 Jun [1870] s/o John Baptist Durbin & Angeline Shults. Sps: John Gardner & wife -JJB
17 Jul 1870	Leo Fidelis [Durbin] b 15 Jun [1870] s/o Francis M. Durbin & Genevieve Henley. Sps: Lewis & Caroline Henley -JJB
31 Jul 1870	C. Liguori [Blubaugh] b 3 Jul [1870] s/o Hilary Blubaugh & Sarah Bailes. Sps: Stephen Blubaugh & wife -JJB
18 Aug 1870	L. Francis Elias [Durbin] b 10 Aug [1870] s/o John S. Durbin & Mary Paul. Sps: Fr. Durbin & Barbara Powell -JJB
09 Oct 1870	Joanna [or John] [Welker] b 3 Aug [1870] ?/o [John B.] Jackson Welker & Sarah Miranda Dial. Sps: Samuel Durbin & wife -JJB
25 Oct 1870	Philina Joan Durbin b 13 Sep [1870] d/o George Durbin & Normanda Workman. Sps: Frances Durbin & wife -JJB
01 Nov 1870	Bernard [Parker] b 24 Sep [1870] s/o Robert Selman Parker & Rebecca McKenzie. Sps: Samuel Durbin & wife -JJB

04 Dec 1870	Victoria [Millis] b 27 Oct [1870] d/o Joseph Francis Millis & Elizabeth White. Sps: Pius & Margaret Durbin -JJB
04 Dec 1870	John Julius [Eckenrode] b 29 May [1870] s/o John Eckenrode & Margaret Forsythe. Sps: George Sapp & wife -JJB
01 Jan 1871	Stephen Lamy [Blubaugh] b 11 Nov 1870 s/o Peter Blubaugh & Margaret Breckler. Sps: Ben Eckenrode & Cath Blubaugh -JJB
29 Jan 1871	Aurelia [Logsdon] b 5 Dec 1870 d/o Francis Logsdon & Catherine Blubaugh. Sps: Jos Colopy & Emily Blubaugh -JJB
27 Feb 1871	Christina Jane [Blubaugh] b 24 Nov [1870] d/o Joseph Blubaugh & Maria Anna Linebaugh. Sps: Phil & Maria Smithhisler -JJB
26 Mar 1871	Martha Teresa [Gardner] b 10 Feb [1871] d/o Anthony Gardner & Elizabeth Marshall. Sps: John & Anna Fritz -JJB
29 Mar 1871	John Sylvester [Durbin] b 27 Feb [1871] s/o Raphael Durbin & Barbara Buck. Sps: Lyman Durbin & Cath Buck -JJB
23 Apr 1871	Cyril Robert [Smithhisler] b 21 Mar [1871] s/o Michael Smithhisler & Mary Millis. Sps: Jacob Millis & wife -JJB
18 May 1871	Edward [Critchfield]] b 9 Mar [1871] s/o [William] Thomas Critchfield & Isadora Smith. Sps: Pius Durbin & Anna Walker -JJB
04 Jun 1871	Mary Amelia [Beck] b 20 May [1871] d/o Xavier Beck & Amelia Schisler (dec'd in confinement). Sps: George Bliel & wife -JJB
08 Jun 1871	Emily Honora [Colopy] b 8 Jan 1870 d/o G. Edward Colopy & Harriet Farquhar. Sps: Levi Colopy -JJB
30 Jul 1871	Anna Louisa [Durbin] b 25 Jun [1871] d/o John Durbin & Lucinda Sapp. Sps: Ben J. Magers & M. Anna Durbin -JJB

30 Jul 1871	Thomas [Swarts] b 21 Nov 1870 s/o Levi Swarts & Margaret McKenzie. Sps: W. Dial & S. Warner -JJB
30 Jul 1871	Charles Edward [Smithhisler] b 10 Dec 1870 s/o Anthony Smithhisler & Martha Eleanor Blubaugh. Sps: E .Colopy & wife -JJB
03 Aug 1871	Elias Aloysius [Engle] b 11 Jul [1871] s/o Joseph Engle & Susanna Durbin. Sps: Benedict & M. Anna Durbin -JJB
13 Aug 1871	Fidelis E. [Sapp] b 28 Jun [1871] s/o George W. Sapp [Jr.] & Isabella Hess. Sps: Jacob Smith & wife -JJB
22 Oct 1871	Louisa Alice [Smithhisler] b 20 Feb 1870 d/o Philip Smithhisler & Margaret Smith. Sps: Maria & Michael Smithhisler -JJB
22 Oct 1871	Elizabeth Bertha [Durbin] b 3 Oct [1871] d/o John Durbin & Margaret Colopy. Sps: Pius Durbin & Joanna Engle -JJB
22 Oct 1871	Mary Ellen [Blubaugh] b 19 Sep [1871] d/o Leon Blubaugh & Ellen Dial. Sps: Leo Gardner & wife -JJB
04 Nov 1871	Mary L. [Sapp] b 21 Sep [1871] d/o John Sapp & Matilda S. Lybarger. Sps: Roman Sapp & M. Walker -JJB
10 Dec 1871	Olive Bertha [Durbin] b 30 Nov [1871] d/o Ben Durbin & Margaret McNamara. Sps: Will & Maria Durbin -JJB
28 Jan 1872	Mary Constance [Welker] b 28 Nov [1871] d/o Andrew D. Welker & Louisa White. Sps: John Breckler & wife -JJB
11 Feb 1872	Edward [Blubaugh] b 20 Jul 1867 s/o David Blubaugh & Henrietta Hibbets. Sps: Ben Blubaugh & R. Hopkins -JJB
11 Feb 1872	Camilla [Blubaugh] b 12 Apr 1871 [d/o David Blubaugh & Henrietta Hibbets]. Sps: Jos Blubaugh & wife -JJB
12 Feb 1872	Sara Zimmerman [Gardner] w/o Francis Gardner. -JJB
09 Mar 1872	Barbara Jane [Durbin] b 1 Feb [1872] d/o John S. Durbin & Mary Paul. Sps: Fr. Logsdon & Maria Durbin -JJB
09 Mar 1872	Julius Augustus [Smith] b 5 Feb [1872] s/o James Smith & Maria E. Blubaugh. Sps: George Sapp & wife -JJB

09 Mar 1872	Rosa Elizabeth [Homan] b 24 Jan [1872] d/o Martin Homan & Cath Miller. Sps: Paul Homan & E. Miller -JJB.
24 Mar 1872	Joseph Zimmerman. Sps: Jacob Colopy & N. Walker -JJB
05 May 1872	Cyril Francis [Butts] b 13 Jan [1872] s/o Henry A. Butts & Anna M. Smith Sps: Ralph Durbin & wife -JJB
05 May 1872	Gertrude [Smithhisler] b 10 Mar [1872] d/o George Smithhisler & Sarah Bradfield. Sps: Michael Smithhisler & wife -JJB
05 May 1872	Rosa Eileen [Smithhisler] b 30 Mar [1872] d/o Philip J. Smithhisler & Mary H. White. Sps: Jos Colopy -JJB
19 May 1872	Barbara Jane [Gardner] b 11 Apr [1872] d/o John Gardner & Mary Breckler. Sps: Bapt Durbin & wife -JJB
19 May 1872	Barbara Agatha [Swingle] b 13 Apr [1872] d/o Christopher Swingle & Florence J Blubaugh. Sps: J. Blubaugh & Sarah Warner -JJB
19 May 1872	Mary Isabella [Durbin] b 17 Apr [1872] d/o Baptist Durbin & Angeline Shults. Sps: John Durbin & wife -JJB
16 Jun 1872	Julius Bernard [Smithhisler] b 8 May [1872] s/o Anthony Smithhisler & Martha [Eleanor] Blubaugh. Sps: George & Maria Smithhisler -JJB
30 Jun 1872	Maria Alice & Margaret Frances Swarts & Bertha [Swarts?] Sapp. -JJB
22 Sep 1872	Emma Cecila [Sapp] b 11 Aug [1872] d/o Francis Sapp & Mary Ann Carney. Sps: Peter Durbin & Ann Walker -JJB
22 Sep 1872	John Joseph [Fesler] b 6 Aug [1872] s/o Joseph Fesler Jr. & Barbara Paul. Sps: John Durbin & wife -JJB
22 Sep 1872	Henry Albert [Fesler] b 15 Aug [1872] s/o Jacob Feslar & Katherine Paul. Sps: Peter Paul & wife -JJB
06 Oct 1872	Cletus [Blubaugh] b 13 Jul [1872] s/o Francis Blubaugh & Elizabeth A. Sapp. Sps: Christopher Swingle & wife -JJB

01 Nov 1872	Catherine Philomena [Shults] b 26 Aug [1872] d/o Henry Shults & Nora E. Blubaugh. Sps: J. J. Blubaugh & wife -JJB
15 Dec 1872	Emily [Bailes] b 21 Oct [1872] d/o William J. Bailes & Matilda A. Dial. Sps: John Blubaugh & S. Warner -JJB
15 Dec 1872	Francis Albert [Sapp] b 14 Oct [1872] s/o George W. Sapp [Jr.] & Isabella Hess. Sps: Solomon Durbin & Fr. Carpenter -JJB
15 Dec 1872	Victoria Letitia [McNamara] b 24 Oct [1872] d/o Francis McNamara & Sarah Elizabeth Porter. Sps: Joseph Colopy & wife -JJB
15 Dec 1872	Margaret E. [Sapp] b 18 Sep [1872] d/o Simeon Sapp & Susan Millis. Sps: John & Margaret Durbin -JJB
12 Jan 1873	Julius Alphonse [Logsdon] b 15 Nov [1872] s/o Francis Logsdon & Catherine Blubaugh. Sps: Lyman Durbin & Mag. Shults -JJB
12 Jan 1873	Gertrude Margaret [Durbin] b 3 Dec [1872] d/o Raphael Durbin & Barbara Buck. Sps: George Durbin & Kate King -JJB
26 Jan 1873	John Benedict [Gardner] b 16 Dec [1872] s/o Leo J. Gardner & Catherine Blubaugh. Sps: John Blubaugh & wife -JJB
09 Feb 1873	Thomas Bernard [Logsdon] b 2 Jan [1873] s/o George Logsdon & Sarah Catherine Durbin. Sps: Phil Smithhisler & wife -JJB
17 Mar 1873	William Simon [Mattingly] b 14 Mar [1873] s/o John B. Mattingly & Mary D. Engle. Sps: John & Margaret Durbin -JSC
05 Apr 1873	Bertha Maria [Henley] b 22 Jan [1873] d/o Charles Henley & [Frances Helen] Ellen Giffin. Sps: Francis & Genevieve Durbin -JJB
06 Apr 1873	Charles W. [Bricker] b 18 Jan [1873] s/o [John] Baptist Bricker & Rosa Hyatt. Sps: Dan & Ellen Bricker -JJB
11 May 1873	Sarah Elizabeth [Welker] b 16 Jan [1873] d/o Andrew Welker & Louisa White. Sps: Joseph Colopy & wife -JJB

BAPTISMS

12 Jun 1873	Mary Agnes [Durbin] b 14 Jan [1873] d/o George Durbin & Normanda Workman. Sps: Fr. Durbin & wife -JJB
20 Jul 1873	Bernard Levi [Colopy] b 11 Apr 1872 & Julius (Leander) [Colopy], twins, s/o Edward Colopy & Harriet Farquhar. Sps: Levi & Delila Colopy -JJB
20 Jul 1873	Leo J. [Gardner] b 30 Oct 1872 s/o Francis A. Gardner & Sarah Zimmerman. Sps: Stephen Blubaugh & wife -JJB
17 Aug 1873	Anna E. Butts b 26 May [1873] d/o Henry A. Butts & Anna M. [Smith] Butts. Sps: J. C. Durbin & Anna Walker -JJB
18 Sep 1873	Edward Mark [Eckenrode] b 14 Dec 1872 s/o John Eckenrode & Margaret Forsyth. Sps: Agnes Eckenrode -JJB
28 Sep 1873	Charles [Smithhisler] b 7 Mar [1873] s/o Philip Smithhisler & Margaret Smith. Sps: Michael Smithhisler & wife -JJB
28 Sep 1873	William Bazil [Smith] b 28 Aug [1873] s/o Jacob Smith & Maria Elizabeth Blubaugh. Sps: Will Dial & Sarah Dial -JJB
28 Sep 1873	Lewis P. [Smithhisler] b 1 Aug [1873] s/o Anthony Smithhisler & Martha Eleanor Blubaugh. Sps: Francis Logsdon & wife -JJB
28 Sep 1873	Rose Elizabeth [Colopy] b 30 Aug [1873] d/o Joseph Colopy & Mary Jane Durbin. Sps: Levi & Delila Colopy -JJB
28 Sep 1873	Emma Josephine [Durbin] b 1 Sep [1873] d/o John Durbin & Lucinda Sapp. Sps: Bapt Durbin & wife -JJB
26 Oct 1873	Bernadette [Durbin] b 26 Sep [1873] d/o Henry Durbin & [Catherine] Kate Carpenter. Sps: Lyman Durbin & Penelope Bricker -JJB
26 Oct 1873	Peter Michael [Durbin] b 29 Sep [1873] s/o John Durbin & Margaret Colopy. Sps: Peter & Margaret Durbin -JJB
02 Nov 1873	Callis Edward [Sapp] b 15 Oct [1873] s/o John Sapp & Matilda Lybarger. Sps: Peter & Marg Durbin -JJB

95

ST. LUKE'S RECORDS

14 Dec 1873	Agnes R. [Blubaugh] b 3 Nov [1873] d/o John J. Blubaugh & Mary P. Dial. Sps: Jonathan Arnold & wife -JJB
18 Jan 1874	John Emmett [Blubaugh] b 18 Dec 1873 s/o Joseph Blubaugh & Maria Anna Linebaugh. Sps: Francis & Emma McKenzie-TJB
01 Feb 1874	William Thomas [Engle] b 2 Jan 1874 s/o Joseph Engle & Susanna Durbin. Sps: Simeon Durbin & Anna Walker -TJB
02 Feb 1874	Emily Gertrude [Blubaugh] b 11 Dec 1873 d/o Leo Blubaugh & Ellen Dial. Sps: Benjamin Eckenrode & Sarah Warner -TJB
05 Mar 1874	Elizabeth [Fesler] b Jun 1873 d/o Joseph Fesler & Alice Starner. Sps: Peter Paul & _____ Starner -TJB
13 Mar 1874	Charles Clinton [Welker] b 12 Feb [1874] s/o Ambrose Welker & Agnes Metzger. Sps: Jackson Welker & wife -JJB
29 Mar 1874	Julius Edward [Miller] b Oct [1873] s/o Peter Miller & Isabella Morrison (non cath). Sps: Joseph Zimmerman & Matilda Connelly -TJB
29 Mar 1874	Clara May [Blubaugh] b 23 Nov 1873 d/o Francis Blubaugh & Elizabeth A. Sapp. Sps: Levi Colopy & Frances Carpenter -TJB
29 Mar 1874	Charlotte Bertha [Swingle] b 8 Jan 1874 d/o Christopher Swingle & Florence I. Blubaugh. Sps: Hilary Blubaugh & Sara E. Blubaugh -TJB
05 Apr 1874	Mary Frances Weaver b 26 Jan [1874] d/o John [Weaver] & Anna Losh. Sps: Michael Homan & wife -JJB
26 Apr 1874	Anna Frances [Fesler] b 14 Feb [1874] d/o Jacob Fesler & Katherine Paul. Sps: Jos Fesler & wife -JJB
10 May 1874	Rachel May [Logsdon] b 15 Mar [1874] d/o Francis Logsdon & Catherine Blubaugh. Sps: Lyman Durbin & Maria Blubaugh -JJB

BAPTISMS

10 May 1874	Mary Elizabeth [Gardner] b 9 Apr [1874] d/o Leo J. Gardner & Mary Catherine Blubaugh. Sps: John Gardner & wife -JJB
10 May 1874	John Joseph [Durbin] b 27 Nov [1873] s/o John S. Durbin & Mary Paul. Sps: Joseph Fesler & wife -JJB
24 May 1874	Laura Isadora [Lybarger] b 16 May 1870 d/o Jacob Lybarger & Rosanna Grub. Sps: Jonathan Colopy & T. Colopy -JJB
24 May 1874	Amelia Agnes Zimmerman b 21 Apr [1874] d/o Joseph Zimmerman & Maria [Helen] Miller. Sps: Ellen Miller & Ch Miller -JJB
14 Jun 1874	Mary Inez [Bradfield] b 4 Dec 1873 d/o Jacob Bradfield & Sara Sapp. Sps: Jonathan Sapp & Maria Sapp -TJB
14 Jun 1874	Mary Frances [Sapp] b 21 Jan [1874] d/o Francis Sapp & Mary Ann Carney. Sps: Pius Durbin & Mary Sapp -TJB
21 Jun 1874	Thomas Bulger Durbin b 25 May [1874] s/o Francis Durbin & Susanna Sapp. Sps: Ben Durbin & Anna Walton -TJB (He married 23 Nov 1908 at Des Moines Iowa, Lucy Steinmetz bapt. 18 Dec 1887 at St. Vincents, Mt. Vernon).
13 Sep 1874	Maria Cecilia [McKenzie] b 13 Aug 1873 d/o Francis McKenzie & Emma Blubaugh. Sps: Joseph Blubaugh & Maria Anna Blubaugh -TJB
11 Oct 1874	Rachel Lucinda [Carter] b 27 Aug 1873 d/o Richard Carter & Mary E. Phifer. Sps: Peter Miller & Helena Zimmerman -TJB
11 Oct 1874	Maria Elizabeth [Cox] d/o Michael Cox & Sara Jane Cox (non cath). -TJB
11 Oct 1874	John Snow s/o William D. Snow (non cath) & Elizabeth Blubaugh. Sps: Francis Logsdon & Martha Smithhisler -TJB
18 Oct 1874	William [Homan] b 28 Aug 1873 s/o James Homan & Margaret Kaylor. Sps: Frederick Rice & Louisa Homan -TJB

25 Oct 1874	Louisa Isabella [Blubaugh] d/o David Blubaugh & Henrietta Hibbetts (non cath). Sps: Francis & wife Catherine Logsdon -TJB
01 Nov 1874	Rebecca [Butts] b 27 Aug 1874 d/o Henry Butts & Anna Smith. Sps: Martin Engle & Elizabeth Engle -TJB
08 Nov 1874	Raymond Monterville [Sapp] b 16 Oct 1874 s/o George W. Sapp [Jr.] & Isabella Hess. Sps: Francis & wife Genevieve Durbin -TJB
08 Nov 1874	Lewis [or Louise] Green by conversion. Sps: John L. Durbin & Henrietta Porter -TJB
10 Nov 1874	Elizabeth Angela [Houck] b 15 Dec 1873 d/o William Houck & Rachel Dial. Sps: William Dial & Sara Warner -TJB
28 Nov 1874	Henrietta [Hibbetts] Blubaugh b 23 Jan 1849 (was Methodist) d/o Jacob Hibbetts & Elizabeth Hibbetts (non-cath), w/o David Blubaugh. -TJB
16 Feb 1875	Charles [Waggoner] b 18 Dec 1874 s/o Sylvester Waggoner & Margaret Sapp. Sps: Samuel Durbin & Rachel Durbin -TJB
16 Feb 1875	John [Waggoner] b 3 Oct 1869 s/o Sylvester Waggoner & Margaret Sapp. Sps: Samuel Durbin & Rachel Durbin -TJB
10 Mar 1875	William Eberhard [Durbin] b 22 Feb 1875 s/o Raphael Durbin & Barbara Anna Buck. Sps: John Durbin & Margaret Durbin -MA
12 Mar 1875	David [Wilder] b 18 Mar 1845 s/o Chester Wilder (non cath) & Maria Anna McGrath. -TJB
29 Mar 1875	Robert S. Parker b 11 Mar 1828 (1827 in family bible) -TJB
24 Apr 1875	David Robert [Swarts] b 12 Jan 1875 (in Jefferson twp) s/o Levi Swarts & Margaret McKenzie. Sps: Thomas McKenzie & Sara Warner -MA
06 May 1875	Louisa Emma [Shafer] b 12 Feb 1875 d/o [David] Jackson Shafer & Matilda Dial. Sps: Samuel & wife Rachel Durbin -TJB

BAPTISMS

16 May 1875	Charles Alfred [Gardner] b 1 Apr 1875 s/o John Gardner & Maria Breckler. Sps: Francis Gardner & Margaret Blubaugh -TJB
16 May 1875	Cornelius Blubaugh b 8 Mar 1875 s/o Francis Blubaugh & Elizabeth A. Sapp. Sps: Stephen Blubaugh & Charlotte Blubaugh -TJB
27 May 1875	William Marcellus [McKenzie] b 26 Mar 1875 s/o John W. McKenzie & Barbara (Charlotte) Critchfield. Sps: Levi Colopy & Maria McGough -TJB
13 Jun 1875	Agnes Louisa [Simpkins] b 22 Feb 1875 d/o George Simpkins & Anastasia Maria McKenzie. Sps: William Dial & Miranda Welker -MA
20 Jun 1875	Angela Cecilia [Shults] b 1 May 1875 d/o Henry Shults & Nora E. Blubaugh. Sps: John Gardner & Angeline Durbin -MA (notation: married Michael Grow 14 Oct 1915 at Gambier OH)
01 Jul 1875	Louise Larribey b 3 Aug 1859 d/o Lyman Larribey & Maria Engle (non cath). -TJB
01 Jul 1875	Catherine [Stonebaugh] age 11 d/o Philip Stonebaugh & Lovina Stonebaugh (non cath). Sps: Richard Arnold & Lewis Arnold -TJB
26 Jul 1875	Badelia Jane [Swingle] b 9 Jul 1875 d/o Christopher Swingle & Florence J. Blubaugh. Sps: Benjamin Blubaugh & Charlotte Blubaugh -MA
26 Jul 1875	Mark Durbin b 28 May 1875 s/o George Durbin & Normanda Workman. Sps: Francis Durbin & Susanna Durbin -MA

The following was in tabular form, we have continued it in the previous format.

08 Aug 1875	James Alfred [Durbin] b 25 Jul 1875 s/o George Durbin & Catherine Buck. Sps: Peter Durbin & Catherine Durbin -HJM

08 Aug 1875	Levi Aloysius [Lucas] b 25 Jul 1874 s/o Samuel Lucas & Amanda E. Lore. Sps: Levi Colopy & Martha Power -HJM
29 Aug 1875	William [Welker] b 16 Aug 1875 s/o Ambrose Welker & Agnes Metzger. Sps: William Dial & Sarah Warner -HJM
26 Sep 1875	Helena Elizabeth "Lena" [Fesler] b 21 Aug 1875 d/o Jacob Fesler & Katherine Paul. Sps: Paul Homan & Eliz Smith -ESM
03 Oct 1875	Anna Blubaugh b 12 Sep 1875 d/o Leo Blubaugh & Ellen Dial. Sps: John L. Durbin & Delila Porter -ESM
03 Oct 1875	Charles Bernard Durbin b 29 Aug 1875 s/o John Sylvester Durbin & Mary Paul. Sps: Peter Paul & Barbara Zink -ESM
06 Oct 1875	Ann Elizabeth [Porter] b 6 Feb 1866 d/o Michael Porter & Anna Ward. Sps: John Sapp & Victoria Arnold -HJM
06 Oct 1875	Sarah [Porter] b 14 Sep 1870 d/o Michael Porter & Anna Ward. Sps: Peter Durbin & Penelope Bricker -HJM
06 Oct 1875	Mary Luella [Porter] b 12 Jun 1874 d/o Michael Porter & Anna Ward. Sps: Samuel Durbin & Rachel Durbin -HJM
07 Oct 1875	Martha Jane [Porter] b 19 Mar 1863 d/o Michael Porter & Anna Ward. Sps: Michael Smithhisler & Julia Gunther -ESM
04 Nov 1875	Laura Ann [Elliott] b __ Feb 1853 d/o Jacob Elliott & Dorcas Sprague. Sps: Thomas Critchfield & Isadora Critchfield -HJM
16 Nov 1875	Wesley Joseph [Shaw] b 22 Jun 1848 s/o John Shaw & Charlotte Porter. Sps: Dan Bricker & Penelope Bricker -HJM
21 Nov 1875	William Dennis [Gardner] b 10 Oct [1875] s/o Leo J. Gardner & Catherine Blubaugh. Sps: Samuel Durbin & Rachel Durbin -HJM
29 Nov 1875	William Edmund [Hunt] b 16 Nov [1875] s/o Mary McGarry. Sps: Edmund Hunt & Mary Hunt -HJM

BAPTISMS

26 Dec 1875	David Stephen [Smithhisler] b 14 Sep 1875 s/o Anthony Smithhisler & Martha Eleanor Blubaugh. Sps: Michael Smithhisler & Mary Smithhisler -HJM
06 Jan 1876	James Thomas [Durbin] b 3 Jan 1876 s/o John Durbin & Lucinda Sapp. Sps: George Sapp & Delia Sapp -HJM
05 Mar 1876	Emma Rosa [Carter] b 31 Aug 1875 d/o Raphael Carter & Lydia Magers. Sps: John & Maria Arnold -JBE
12 Mar 1876	Amelia Agnes Smith ....?.... Mt.Holly. Sps: Jacob & Maria Smith -JBE
02 Apr 1876	Francis Aledo [Parker] b 20 Feb [1876] s/o Robert S. Parker & Rebecca A. McKenzie. Sps: John Lyman Durbin & Alice Porter -JBE
09 Apr 1876	Francis Bernard [McNamara] b 28 Nov 1874 s/o Francis McNamara & Maria Sailor. Sps: Christina McNamara -JBE
09 Apr 1876	Margaret Edith [McNamara] b 20 Feb 1876 d/o Francis McNamara & Maria Sailor. Sps: Margaret Anna Blubaugh -JBE
23 Apr 1876	John Ludger [Durbin] b 25 Mar [1876] s/o John Durbin & Margaret Colopy. Sps: Raphael & Barbara Durbin -FM
23 Apr 1876	Maria Lucy [Durbin] b 13 Mar [1876] s/o Francis M. Durbin & Genevieve Henley. Sps: Jonathan Arnold & Maria Arnold -FM
30 Apr 1876	Charles Joseph [Beck] b 15 Mar [1876] s/o Xavier Beck & Mary Fesler. Sps: Joseph Fesler & Elizabeth Homan -FM
07 May 1876	Irene Elizabeth [Weaver] b 24 Mar [1876] d/o John Weaver & Mary Anna Losh. Sps: Adam Weaver & Elizabeth Weaver -FM
07 May 1876	Francis Anthony [Durbin] b 2 Apr [1876] s/o Pius Durbin & Maria Magdalena Smithhisler. Sps: A. Smithhisler & Margaret Durbin -FM
14 May 1876	Curtis Ligouri [Sapp] b 29 Mar [1876] s/o John [George W.] & Isabella [Hess] Sapp. Sps: Pius Durbin & Elizabeth Homan -FM

101

14 May 1876	Charles Francis [Blubaugh] b 20 Jan [1876] s/o Joseph Blubaugh & Mary Ann [Linebaugh]. Sps: John & Maria Blubaugh -FM
25 May 1876	Edwin Stephen [Homan] b 31 Mar [1876] s/o Michael Homan & Elizabeth Losh. Sps: Joseph Losh & Frances Losh -FM
__ Jun 1876	William Everett [Rice] b 10 Dec 1875 s/o Israel Rice & Elizabeth [Devore]. Sps: Charles Durbin & Matilda Bailes -FM
16 Jul 1876	Bertha [Quinn] b 4 Aug 1875 d/o Cicero Quinn & Matilda Quinn. Sps: R. S. Parker & Margaret _____ -FM
16 Jul 1876	Henrietta Green b 21 Apr 1864 d/o John & Rachel Green. Sps: Richard Arnold & Sarah Warner -FM
16 Jul 1876	Charles [Green] b 17 Aug 1875 s/o John Green & Rachel Green. Sps: John McKenzie & Rebecca Parker -FM
16 Jul 1876	Agnes [Welsh] b 19 Jun [1876] d/o Michael Welsh & Ellen Bricker. Sps: D. Bricker & Maria Bricker -FM
23 Jul 1876	Anna [Miller] b 18 Oct [1876] d/o Vincent Miller & Margaret [Stillinger]. Sps: F. M. & Martha Buck -FM
02 Sep 1876	Mark [Encell] b 27 Jul [1876] s/o Alex Encell & Helena White. Sps: Jerome George Durbin & Catherine Durbin -FM
02 Sep 1876	Frederick [Penhorwood] b 1 Sep [1876] s/o Jacob & Helena Penhorwood. Sps: George Sapp & Deliah Sapp -FM
09 Oct 1876	Mary Ann [Fesler] b 9 Sep 1876 d/o Joseph Fesler Jr. & Barbara Paul. Sps Xavier Beck & M. Warner -FM
22 Oct 1876	George Michael [Ernest] b 13 Sep 1876 s/o Michael Ernest & Margaret Reigle. Sps: George Reigle & Eugena Piar -FM
__ Dec 1876	Elizabeth [Paul] b 7 Nov [1876] d/o Casper Paul & Martha Piar. Sps: Jack Piar & Eugena Piar -FM
18 Jan 1877	Maria Virginia Murphy age 21 (adult). Sps: Francis Moitrier & Maria Smithhisler -FM

28 Jan 1877	Jacob Monty [Gaume] b 11 Nov 1877 s/o Augustus Gaume & Mary Matilda [Colopy]. Sps: Jacob Colopy & Math Connelly -FM
18 Feb 1877	Rose Katherine [Fesler] b 9 Dec 1876 d/o Jacob Fesler & Katherine [Paul]. Sps: John & Maria Durbin -FM
08 Apr 1877	Mary Frances [Swingle] b 23 Feb [1877] d/o Christopher Swingle & Florence [J. Blubaugh] Sps: C. Durbin & Frances Durbin -FM
08 Apr 1877	Lucy Hammond b 12 Mar 1877 d/o Martin P. Hammond & Mary Keziah Sapp. Sps: John & Flora [Sapp] Breckler -FM
10 May 1877	Francis Raphael [Durbin] b 19 Apr [1877] s/o Raphael Durbin & Barbara Anna Buck. Sps: Francis Moitrier & Josephine Diamond -FM
10 May 1877	Maria Louisa [Durbin] b 7 Apr 1877 d/o Benedict ~~Pius~~ Durbin & Josephine Smithhisler. Sps: Michael Smithhisler & Maria Anna Durbin -FM
10 May 1877	Ameda Gertrude [Gaume] b 12 Apr [1877] d/o Eugene Gaume & Sara [Eugenia Durbin]. Sps: William Durbin & Catherine Durbin -FM
13 May 1877	Charles Francis [Bailes] b 5 Apr [1877] s/o William J. Bailes & Matilda [A. Dial]. Sps: Ben Durbin & S. E. Blubaugh -FM
13 May 1877	Rachel Philomena [Weaver] b 29 Apr [1877] d/o Adam Weaver & Eva [Doneck]. Sps: John Lower & Maria Lower -FM
20 May 1877	Bertha Frances [McKenzie] b 16 Mar [1877] d/o John W. McKenzie & Charlotte Critchfield. Sps: Lyman Durbin & Ella Arnold -FM
04 Aug 1877	John [Henley] b 9 May [1877] s/o Charles Henley & Frances Helen [Giffen]. Sps: Solomon Durbin & wife -FM
15 Aug 1877	Francis Augustus [Metzger] b 15 Jul [1877] s/o Ambrose & Agnes Elizabeth Metzger. Sps: Leo Blubaugh & Fannie Diamond -FM

09 Sep 1877	Joseph Harvey [Weaver] b 9 Aug [1877] s/o John Weaver & Mary Anna [Losh]. Sps: Joseph Losh & wife -FM
14 Oct 1877	Mark [Colopy] b 5 Feb [1877] s/o Edward Colopy & Harriet [Farquhar]. Sps: Joseph Colopy & wife -FM
12 Nov 1877	Charles Michael [Durbin] b 17 Oct [1877] s/o William E. Durbin & Catherine Smithhisler. Sps: Daniel Bricker & wife -FM
25 Nov 1877	Maria Agnes [Alexander] b 18 Sep [1877] d/o John William Alexander & Theodora Jane Blubaugh. Sps: John Blubaugh & Maria Arnold -FM
25 Nov 1877	Margaret Monica [Durbin] b 13 Nov [1877] d/o Gregory Pius Durbin & Mary [Magdalena Smithhisler]. Sps: Peter & Maria Anna Durbin -FM
23 Dec 1877	Margaret Ellen (Elizabeth) Smithhisler b 5 Oct [1877] d/o Anthony Smithhisler & Martha Eleanor Blubaugh. Sps: James Milles & wife -FM
23 Dec 1877	Edward Moitrier[Durbin] b 13 Oct [1877] s/o John Durbin & Mary Paul. Sps: Charles Durbin & wife -FM
23 Dec 1877	Bernard [Blubaugh] b 8 Dec [1877] s/o Leo Blubaugh & Ellen Dial. Sps: John Blubaugh & Sarah Warner -FM
28 Dec 1877	Frances Gertrude [Smith] b 8 Nov [1877] d/o James Smith & Maria Ellen Blubaugh. Sps: August Blubaugh & Ella Blubaugh -FM
10 Mar 1878	Maria Eliza [Swarts] b 15 Dec [1877] d/o Levi Swarts & Margaret McKenzie. Sps: Sol Parker & Sarah Warner -FM
24 Mar 1878	James Roland [Smithhisler] b 15 Jan [1878] s/o John Smithhisler & Maria Murphy. Sps: M^l [Michael] Smithhisler & wife -FM
25 Mar 1878	Emma Cecilia [Sapp] b 22 Jan [1878] d/o Timothy Sapp & Mary Blubaugh. Sps: William Welker & Josephine Diamond -FM
13 Apr 1878	Edward Fulton [Stevens] b 7 Nov [1877] s/o Isaac Stevens & Laura Elliott. Sps: Thomas Critchfield & wife -FM

BAPTISMS

18 Apr 1878	Stephen Francis [Logsdon] b 11 Mar [1878] s/o Francis Logsdon & Katherine Blubaugh. Sps: Stephen Blubaugh & Flora Breckler -FM
05 May 1878	Rose [Welsh] b 31 Mar [1878] d/o William Welsh & Helena Bricker. Sps: Daniel Bricker & Penelope Bricker -PK
26 May 1878	John Sylvester [Hunt] b 22 May [1878] s/o John Hunt & Mary McGarry. Sps: Francis A. Durbin & Susanna Durbin -PK
26 May 1878	Cletus Andrew [King] b 21 Apr 1878 s/o Peter King & Anna Miller. Sps: Andrew & Frances King -PK
07 Jul 1878	Henry Thomas [Bricker] b 11 Jun 1878 s/o Daniel Bricker & Josephine Smithhisler. Sps: Henry Smithhisler -PK
14 Jul 1878	Thomas Bernard [Sapp] b 13 Jun [1878] s/o John Baptist [Sapp] & Matilda Lybarger. Sps: Levi Colopy -PK
21 Jul 1878	Mary Charlotte [Gardner] b 16 Jun [1878] d/o John Gardner & Mary Breckler. Sps: John Breckler & Catherine Blubaugh -PK
04 Aug 1878	Lucy Ellen [Shults] b 2 Jul [1878] d/o Henry Shults & Nora E. Blubaugh. Sps: Martin Reigle & Ellen Blubaugh -FM.
11 Aug 1878	Walter Henry [Smithhisler] b 20 Jun [1878] s/o George Smithhisler & Sarah Bradfield. Sps: Jacob Milles & wife -FM
15 Oct 1878	Lucy Maude [Miller] b 23 Sep [1878] d/o Charles H. Miller & Della J. Engle. Sps: Peter & Margarita Durbin -FM
17 Oct 1878	Mary Eloise [Smithhisler] b 18 Sep [1878] s/o Philip J. Smithhisler & Mary H. [White]. Sps: Francis & Maria Smithhisler -FM
03 Nov 1878	Julius Albert [Durbin] b 4 Oct [1878] s/o Francis M. Durbin & Genevieve Henley. Sps: Solomon Durbin & wife -FM
27 Nov 1878	Francis [Reigle] b 26 Apr [1878] s/o Martin Reigle & Angela [Durbin]. Sps: Jacob Shults & wife -FM

01 Dec 1878	Mary Margaret [Durbin] b 1 Nov [1878] d/o Benedict [Durbin] & Josephine Smithhisler. Sps: Peter & Margarita Durbin -FM
__ Mar 1879	Maude Ellen [Breckler] & Claude [Breckler] children of Michael & Matilda Breckler. Sps: Michael Smithhisler & wife & Francis Moitrier & _____ Breckler -FM
16 Mar 1879	Martha Rosa [Weaver] b 8 Jan [1879] d/ John Weaver & Anna Losh. Sps: Joseph Losh & wife. -FM (She married 9 Jun 1915 William W. Fletcher, non cath,.at Coshoctin, OH).
28 May 1879	M. Catherine [Arnold] b 29 Jan [1879] d/o Leo Judson Arnold & Lydia Ann [McCleary]. Sps: Samuel Durbin & wife -FM
29 Jun 1879	Louisa Lucy [Smithhisler] b 19 May [1879] d/o John Smithhisler & Mary [Murphy]. Sps Henry & Maria Smithhisler -FM
13 Jul 1879	Charles Raymond Basil [Durbin] b 14 Jun [1879] s/o John Durbin & Margaret [Colopy]. Sps: Simeon Durbin & Maria Anna Durbin -FM
13 Jul 1879	Elizabeth [Durbin] b 3 Jun [1879] d/o George & Normanda Durbin. Sps: Francis Durbin & wife -FM
24 Aug 1879	Dorothy Aurelia [Blubaugh] b 14 Jul [1879] d/o James R. Blubaugh & Victoria [F. Smith]. Sps: Stephen & Charlotte Blubaugh -FM
24 Aug 1879	Justina Matilda [Smithhisler] b 2 Aug [1879] d/o William & Catharine Smithhisler. Sps: Francis Smithhisler & F. Durbin -FM (She married 21 Apr 1921 Jacob C. Miller.)
31 Aug 1879	Mary Ann [Boner] b 4 Aug [1879] d/o Hubert Boner & Margaret [Blubaugh]. Sps: Stephen Blubaugh & wife -FM
07 Sep 1879	Frances Eugenia [or Francis Eugene King] b 30 Jul [1879] ?/o Peter King & Anna Miller. Sps: Raphael Durbin & wife -FM
14 Sep 1879	Maria [Jackson] b 1871 d/o Lafayette Jackson & Sylvia Jackson. Sps: Jackson Welker & wife -FM

12 Oct 1879	Maria Helen Elizabeth [Rice] b 23 Jul [1879] d/o Israel Rice & Elizabeth [Devore]. Sps: Henry & Sarah Ellen Blubaugh -FM
16 Nov 1879	Ellen Celilla [Sapp] b 7 Oct [1879] d/o George W. Sapp [Jr.] & Isabella [Hess]. Sps: Charles Durbin & wife -FM
08 Dec 1879	Leo Selman [Durbin] b 26 Nov [1879] d/o Raphael Durbin & Barbara Buck. Sps: Pius Durbin & wife -FM
14 Dec 1879	Charles Francis [Durbin] b 24 Oct [1879] s/o Francis Durbin & Susanna Sapp. Sps: George & Margaret Durbin -FM
21 Dec 1879	Francis Roland [Gaume] b 2 Nov [1879] s/o Augustus Gaume & Matilda Colopy. -FM
05 Jan 1880	Monica [Stevens] b 3 [Jan 1880] d/o Isaac Stevens & Laura Elliott. Sps: Francis Moitier & Rachel Welker -FM
21 Jan 1880	Maria [Banbury] b 6 Dec 1878 d/o John R. Banbury & Deliah A. Colopy. Sps: F. Moitier & ____ Colopy -FM
08 Feb 1880	Lucy Josephine [Weaver] b 11 Jun [1880] d/o Adam & Eva Weaver. Sps: Andrew King & Sarah Gertrude Weaver -FM (She married Jun 1933 Augustus Kiefer at Coshocton, OH.)
26 Feb 1880	Joseph Demetrius [Sapp] b 20 Dec 1879 s/o Timothy Sapp & Mary [Blubaugh] . Sps: Rosa Sapp -FM
29 Feb 1880	Rose Hammond b 30 Jan [1880] d/o Martin Hammond & Mary Keziah Sapp. Sps: George Sapp & wife -FM
21 Mar 1880	Lewis Purcell [Smithhisler] b 22 Feb [1880] s/o Michael & Matilda Smithhisler. Sps: Jacob Millis & wife -FM
25 Mar 1880	Rebecca Alice [Bailes] b 14 Dec [1879] d/o William J. Bailes & Matilda [A. Dial]. Sps: Rich Arnold & Eliz McNamara -FM (She married 17 Sep 1918 Harvey Arnold - non cath.)
04 Apr 1880	Edna Veronica [Blubaugh] b 23 Nov [1879] d/o Joseph F. Blubaugh & Lillis Jane Smith. Sps: Charles Durbin & wife -FM (She married 13 Nov 1914 John O'Neill.)

18 Apr 1880	Clarence Edward [Swingle] b 6 Jan [1880] s/o Christopher Swingle & Florence J. Blubaugh Sps: Francis Logsdon & wife -FM (He married 1 Jun 1909 Maria Miller bpt 2 May 1909 at St Vincent; Wit: Cosmos Blubaugh & wife Lucille.)
18 Apr 1880	Benjamin Walter [Logsdon] b 19 Jan [1880] s/o Francis Logsdon & Catherine Blubaugh. Sps: Christopher Swingle & wife -FM
02 May 1880	Mary Honora [Durbin] b 20 Feb [1880] d/o John S. Durbin & Mary [Paul]. Sps: George Sapp & wife -FM
05 May 1880	Josephine Maria [Sapp] b 21 Feb [1880] d/o John Sapp & Matilda [Lybarger]. Sps: William Durbin & wife -FM
16 May 1880	Catherine May [Blubaugh] b 1 May [1880] d/o Leo Blubaugh & Ellen [Dial]. Sps: Jonathan Arnold & wife -FM
13 Jun 1880	Mary Penelope [Welsh] b 20 Apr [1880] d/o William Welsh & Helen Bricker Sps: Levi Colopy & Maria Smithhisler.
04 Jul 1880	Matilda Amelia [Fesler] b 15 Apr [1880] d/o Jacob Fesler & Katherine Paul. Sps: John & Maria Durbin -FM
04 Jul 1880	Mary Angela [Durbin] b 29 May [1880] d/o Benedict Durbin & Josephine Smithhisler. Sps: Anthony Smithhisler & wife -FM
13 Jul 1880	Mary Catherine [Welker] b 16 Jun [1880] d/o Ambrose Welker & Agnes Metzger. Sps: Phillip Smithhisler & wife -FM
18 Jul 1880	Mary Isabel "Belle" [Parker] b 14 Jun [1880] d/o Robert Selman Parker & Rebecca McKenzie. Sps: George Sapp & wife -FM
__ Aug 1880	Maria Gertrude McMahon b 7 May [1880] d/o John McMahon & Victoria Snow. Sps: Charles Durbin & wife -FM
06 Sep 1880	George Harrison [Smithhisler] b 30 Jul [1880] s/o George Smithhisler & Sarah F. Smithhisler. Sps: Phillip & Matilda Smithhisler -FM

BAPTISMS

06 Sep 1880	Charles Bernard [Henley] b 2 Jul [1880] s/o Charles Henley & Frances H. Ellen [Giffen]. Sps: Albert Henley & Josephine Durbin -FM
27 Sep 1880	Maria Elizabeth _____ b 2 Nov 1856 adult. Sps: F. Moitier & Lucy Colopy.
03 Oct 1880	Sylvester Aloysius Durbin b 24 Sep [1880] s/o John Durbin & Margaret [Colopy]. Sps: Benedict Durbin & wife. -FM (He married first 28 Oct 1910 Mabel Jones bapt. 30 Sep 1910 at St. Joseph in Columbus, OH; he married second 27 Apr 1921 Justina Matilda Durbin.)
14 Nov 1880	James Clifford [Miller] b 28 Sep [1880] s/o Charles H. Miller & Della J. Engle. Sps: Benedict Durbin & wife -FM
05 Dec 1880	Jacob Raymond [Shults] b 9 Aug [1880] s/o Henry Shults & Nora Ellen [Blubaugh]. Sps: Christopher Swingle & Helena Blubaugh -FM
26 Dec 1880	Stephen Marcus (John) [Gardner] b 3 Nov [1880] s/o John Gardner & Mary Breckler. Sps: John Breckler & wife -FM (He married 6 Apr 1910 at Cleveland, OH Edith Teslik bpt 10 Jun 1890; Wit: Hugh Gardner & Genevieve Teslik.)
09 Jan 1881	Mary Alice Maude [Blubaugh] b 4 Dec 1880 d/o Zachary Blubaugh & Margaret Helen Engle. Sps: Robert Engle & H. Engle -FM
20 Jan 1881	Marcus J. [Arnold] b 5 Oct [1880] s/o [Benjamin] Oliver Arnold & Emma Gaines. Sps: Michael Smithhisler & wife -FM
24 Apr 1881	George Franklin [King] b 5 Mar [1881] s/o Peter King & Anna Miller. Sps: Jacob Smith & wife -FM. (He married 25 Apr 1936 at Dayton, OH Nellie Kieffer.)
22 May 1881	Lamy Jacob [Smithhisler] b 6 Dec 1880 s/o Michael J. Smithhisler & Victoria B. Arnold. Sps: Jonathan Arnold & wife -FM

29 May 1881	Elsa Helen [McKenzie] b 21 Jan [1881] d/o John W. McKenzie & Charlotte (Charity) Critchfield. Sps: Joseph Colopy & wife -FM
12 Jun 1881	Maria Domitila [Bricker] b 10 May [1881 - d 13 Sep 1882] d/o Daniel Bricker & Josephine Smithhisler. Sps: Phillip Smithhisler & Miranda Bricker -FM
14 Aug 1881	Ann Louisa [Durbin] b 20 Jul [1881] d/o William E. Durbin & Catharine Smithhisler. Sps: Eugene Gaume & wife -FM
21 Aug 1881	Charles Raymond [Davis] b 27 Jul [1881] s/o Samuel F. Davis & Elizabeth Blubaugh. Sps: Maria Engle -FM
18 Sep 1881	Amelia Estelle [Durbin] b 4 Aug [1881] d/o Francis Durbin & Susan Sapp. Sps: Simeon & Anna Durbin -FM
30 Oct 1881	Henry Walter [Blubaugh] b 7 Sep [1881] s/o James R. Blubaugh & Victoria F. Smith. Sps: Hubert & Margaret Boner -FM
30 Oct 1881	Cordelia Mildred [Sapp] b 4 Aug [1881] d/o George W. Sapp [Jr.] & Isabella Hess. Sps: Levi & Melissa Colopy -FM
05 Nov 1881	Mary Elizabeth [Bailes] b 3 Oct [1881] d/o William J. Bailes & Matilda A. [Dial]. Sps: Charles Durbin & wife -FM
23 Nov 1881	Henry Vincent [Welker] b 6 Oct [1881] s/o William Welker & Sadie Winifred Parker. Sps: Helen Blubaugh -FM
02 Dec 1881	Maria Louisa [Sheneberger] b 21 Nov [1881] d/o Anna Sheneberger. Sps: M. Sheneberger -FM
25 Dec 1881	Alice [Welker] b 6 Nov [1881] d/o Lewis G. Welker & Lucy Colopy. Sps: Jacob & Alice Colopy -FM
01 Jan 1882	Jonathan Lamy [Logsdon] b 6 Nov 1881 s/o Francis Logsdon & Katherine Blubaugh. Sps: Leo Blubaugh & wife -FM
26 Feb 1882	John Ferrel Lavern [Durbin] b 8 Jan [1882] s/o Gregory Pius Durbin & Mary Magdalena Smithhisler. Sps: Simeon & Anna Durbin -FM

BAPTISMS

26 Mar 1882	Charles Gregory [Sapp] b 27 Nov 1881 s/o Clement Sapp & Frances King. Sps: Charles Durbin & wife -FM
16 Apr 1882	Mark [Miller] b 5 Feb [1882] s/o Charles H. Miller & Della J. Engle. Sps: George Durbin & Maria Anna Durbin -FM
08 Jun 1882	William Claude [Blubaugh] b 8 May [1882] s/o Zachary Blubaugh & Margaret Helen Engle. Sps: Charles Miller & wife -FM
25 Jun 1882	Mary Ellen [Smithhisler] b 4 May [1882] d/o Michael J. Smithhisler & Victoria B. Arnold. Sps: Jonathan Arnold & wife -FM
25 Jun 1882	Francis Orville [Parker] b 30 Jan [1882] s/o [Thomas] Solomon Parker & Mary Victoria Burris. Sps: Rich Arnold & wife -FM
02 Jul 1882	George Benjamin [Swingle] b 8 Jun [1882] s/o Christopher Swingle & Florence Blubaugh. Sps: Jacob Smith & Maria Smith -FM
09 Jul 1882	Charlotte Estelle [Boner] b 12 Jun [1882] d/o Hubert Boner & Margaret Blubaugh. Sps: John Breckler & S. E. Blubaugh -FM
16 Jul 1882	Maria Pauline [Durbin] b 29 Jun [1882] d/o Benedict Durbin & Josephine Smithhisler. Sps: Pius Durbin & Maria Durbin -FM
03 Sep 1882	Leah Maria [Arnold] b 29 Jun [1882] d/o [Benjamin] Oliver Arnold & Emma Gaines. Sps: Michael Smithhisler & Helena Arnold -FM
03 Sep 1882	Nancy Catherine [Welsh] b 3 Jul [1882] d/o William Welsh & Helen Bricker. Sps: Thomas Durbin & wife -FM
08 Oct 1882	Charles [Simpkins] b 7 Apr [1882] s/o Jacob Aron & Frances Simpkins. Sps: Charles Howard & Maria Simpkins -FM
22 Oct 1882	George [Hammond] b 26 Sep [1882] s/o Martin Hammond & Mary Keziah Sapp. Sps: George Logsdon & wife -FM

12 Nov 1882	Rose Estelle [Sapp] b 24 Aug [1882] d/o John Sapp & Matilda [Lybarger]. Sps: Charles Parker & Maria Blubaugh -FM
19 Nov 1882	John Lamy [Durbin] b 21 Oct [1882] s/o John Durbin & Mary Blubaugh. Sps: Joseph Engle & wife -FM
26 Nov 1882	Frances Estelle [Blubaugh] b 15 Oct [1882] d/o Joseph F. Blubaugh & Lillis [Jane] Smith. Sps: Francis Logsdon & wife -FM
27 Nov 1882	Leo Francis [Shults] b 18 Oct [1882] s/o Henry Shults & Nora Ellen Blubaugh. Sps: Leo Blubaugh & Helen Blubaugh -FM
07 Jan 1883	Leo Raymond [Blubaugh] b 23 Dec [1882] s/o Leo Blubaugh & Elizabeth Helena Blubaugh. Sps: Raymond Arnold & Helen Blubaugh -FM
26 Feb 1883	John J. Lamy [Smith] b 12 Feb [1883] s/o Jacob Smith & Maria E. Blubaugh. Sps: Aloysius Smith & M. Blubaugh -FM
06 May 1883	Elizabeth Alice [Weaver] b 3 Apr [1883] d/o Adam Weaver & Eva Doneck. Sps: George Logsdon & wife -FM
14 Mar 1883	Mary Ann [Durbin] b 4 Feb [1883] d/o Thomas Durbin & Susanna Hattie Porter. Sps: Joseph Colopy & Eliz McNamara -FM (She married 25 Jun 1913 Charles Boeshart at Washington, DC.)
18 Mar 1883	Sarah Elizabeth [Smithhisler] b 25 Jan [1883] d/o John Smithhisler & Mary Murphy. Sps: Daniel Bricker & wife -FM
18 Mar 1883	Margaret [Swarts] b 6 Jan [1883] d/o Levi Swarts & Rebecca McKenzie. Sps: R. S. Parker & wife -FM
06 May 1883	Rosa Helen [Blubaugh] b 20 Mar [1883] d/o J. Augustine Blubaugh & Sarah Agnes Hess. Sps: Henry Blubaugh & Helen Blubaugh -FM
27 May 1883	Clarence Damian [Sapp] b 27 Apr [1883] s/o George W. Sapp [Jr.] & Isabella Hess. Sps: Jonathan Colopy & wife -FM

17 Jun 1883	John Watterson [Swarts] b 29 Jan [1883] s/o Christopher Swarts & Elizabeth Cox. Sps: J. J. Blubaugh & wife -FM
17 Jun 1883	Sarah Eugenia [Swarts] b 20 Jan 1881 d/o Christopher Swarts & Elizabeth Cox. Sps: J. J. Blubaugh & wife -FM
17 Jun 1883	Charles Franklin [Swarts] b 4 Jun 1879 s/o Christopher Swarts & Elizabeth Cox. Sps: J. J. Blubaugh & wife -FM
01 Jul 1883	Michael Henry [Piar] b 20 May [1883] s/o Jacob Piar & Rebecca Hoglin. Sps: Jacob Colopy & wife -FM
15 Jul 1883	Margaret [Bricker] b 14 Jun [1883] d/o Daniel Bricker & Josephine Smithhisler. Sps: William Durbin & wife -FM
23 Sep 1883	Frances Margaret [Losh] b 18 Aug [1883] d/o John Losh & Sarah Breckler. Sps: Joseph Losh & wife -FM
23 Sep 1883	Leo Mirgon bapt. at St. Joseph, married 26 May 1909 Ann Maria Engle bapt. 26 May 1885 St. Luke, Danville, OH, d/o Ligouri Engle -FM [See her baptism below.]
04 Nov 1883	Michael Charles [Smithhisler] b 5 Oct [1883] s/o Philip J. Smithhisler & Mary H. White. Sps: Jacob Miller & wife -FM
25 Dec 1883	Theodore Raymond [Logsdon] b 1 Nov [1883] s/o Francis Logsdon & Sara Catherine Blubaugh. Sps: Hubert Boner & wife -FM
06 Apr 1884	Raymond Rollin [Durbin] b 20 Mar [1884] s/o Francis Durbin & Susanna Sapp. Sps: Jonathan Colopy & wife -FM
06 Apr 1884	Mary Helen [Arnold] b 30 Jan 1884 d/o B. Oliver Arnold & Emma Gaines. Sps: Jonathan Arnold & wife -FM
03 May 1884	William [Henley] b 25 Jan [1884] s/o Charles Henley & Frances Helen Giffin. Sps: Eugenia Durbin -FM
04 May 1884	Mary Vesta [Durbin] b 7 Apr [1884] d/o John B. Durbin & Mary A. Blubaugh. Sps: Lloyd Logsdon & Harriet Blubaugh -FM
06 Jun 1884	Helen [Gardner] b 8 May [1884] d/o John Gardner & Mary Breckler. Sps: Francis Gardner & wife -FM

06 Jun 1884	Maria [Baker] b 11 Jan 1878 d/o Adam Baker & Amanda _____ . Sps: Margaret Durbin -FM
06 Jul 1884	Christopher Francis [Swingle] b 11 Jun [1884] s/o Christopher Swingle & Florence J. Blubaugh. Sps: William Bailes & wife -FM. (He married 21 Oct 1914 Pauline Caecilia Durbin).
30 Aug 1884	Maude Elizabeth [Durbin] b 30 Aug [1884] d/o Thomas Durbin & Susanna Porter. Sps: John & Marg Durbin -FM
14 Sep 1884	Purcell Henry [Smithhisler] b 2 Sep [1884] s/o Henry Smithhisler & Catherine Henegan. Sps: Jacob Colopy & Maria Berry Sps: Samuel Durbin & Maria Arnold.
24 Oct 1884	Thomas J. [Colopy] b 26 Jul [1884] s/o Levi F. Colopy & Melissa A. Durbin. Sps: Clement Durbin & Selora Durbin -FM
02 Nov 1884	Maria Estelle [Miller] b 6 Oct [1884] d/o Charles H. Miller & Della J. Engle. Sps: Margaret Durbin -FM
16 Nov 1884	Rosa Elizabeth [Smith] b 9 Oct [1884] d/o James Smith & Maria E. Blubaugh. Sps: Phillip & Elizabeth Homan -FM (She married 21 Apr 1915 Charles G. Strasbaugh.)
28 Dec 1884	Helen Maude [Alexander] b 31 Oct [1884] d/o John William Alexander & Phedora Jane Blubaugh. Sps: William Bailes & wife -FM
11 Jan 1885	Mary Louisa [Gardner] b 2 Nov 1884 d/o Thomas Gardner & Emma Peters. Sps: John Gardner & Louisa Gardner -FM
04 Feb 1885	Lucy Agnes [Losh] b 13 Dec [1884] d/o John Losh & Sarah Breckler. Sps: Michael Homan & Elizabeth Homan -FM
08 Feb 1885	Catherine Sapp b 1822 (adult) w/o Julian Sapp. Sps: John Breckler & wife -FM
15 Feb 1885	Odo [Sapp] b 1 Jan [1885] s/o George W. Sapp [Jr.] & Isabella Hess. Sps: Edward Carpenter & Maria Engle -FM

12 Apr 1885	John [Hammond] b 11 Apr [1885] s/o Martin Hammond & Mary Keziah Sapp. Sps: John Walsh & Margaret Durbin -FM
19 Apr 1885	Mary Clara [Durbin] b 9 Mar [1885] d/o William E. Durbin & Catherine Smithhisler. Sps: Benedict & Helena Durbin -FM
24 Apr 1885	Joseph Francis [Logsdon] b 19 Mar [1885] s/o Lloyd Logsdon & Frances Diamond. Sps: F. Moitrier & Ella Vance -FM
26 Apr 1885	Damian (Cosmos) [Blubaugh] b 3 Mar [1885] s/o James Augustine Blubaugh & Sarah Agnes Hess. Sps: Sherman Blubaugh & Victoria Blubaugh -FM (He married 1 Jun 1909 at St. Vincent, Akron, OH, Lucille Swingle; Wit: Edward Swingle & Maria Miller.)
03 May 1885	[Harry] Francis [Magers] b 17 Oct 1884 s/o Calvin Magers & Helen Ellen Arnold. Sps: Samuel Durbin & Maria Arnold -FM. (He contracted marriage 20 Jul 1945 with Mary Conklin at St. Anne, Rochester, NY, his first wife is dead.)
21 May 1885	Charles Francis [Blubaugh] b 31 Mar [1885] s/o Leo Blubaugh & Helena Dial. Sps: George Henley & Helen Blubaugh -FM
05 Aug 1885	Anna Maria [Engle] b 8 Jul [1885] d/o Liguori Engle & Eugenia Colopy. Sps: John C. Durbin & wife -FM
18 Oct 1885	William [Bricker] b 10 Sep [1885] s/o Daniel Bricker & Josephine Smithhisler. Sps: William Welsh & Helena Welsh -FM
22 Nov 1885	William Austin [Blubaugh] b 19 Oct [1885] s/o Basil Blubaugh & Florence McKenzie. Sps: Phillip & Elizabeth Homan -FM
25 Dec 1885	Joseph Henry [Durbin] b 27 Nov [1885] s/o John B. Durbin & Mary A. Blubaugh. Sps: Francis Sapp & Maria Sapp -FM
07 Mar 1886	George Emmett [Weaver] b 7 Feb [1886] s/o Adam Weaver & Eva [Doneck]. Sps: J. S. Durbin & wife -FM

28 Mar 1886	Joseph Edward [Gardner] b 11 Feb [1886] s/o Thomas Gardner & Emma Peters. Sps: Nicholas Whisler & Frances Whisler -FM
11 Apr 1886	Thomas Joseph [Gainor] b 8 Jul [1886] s/o Patrick Gainor & Elizabeth Mani. Sps: Joseph Colopy & Maria Anna Colopy -FM
11 Apr 1886	Peter [Gainor] b 3 Jan [1886] s/o Patrick Gainor & Elizabeth Mani. Sps: Francis Logsdon & wife -FM
02 May 1886	Orium Purcel [Bailes] b 1 Apr [1886] s/o William J. Bailes & Matilda [A. Dial]. Sps: Sherman Blubaugh & Ida Blubaugh -FM
02 May 1886	Charles Colopy s/o James Edward Colopy & Margaret J. McMahon]. Sps: Mrs. Alice Rightmire -FM
09 May 1886	Henry Dallas [Smith] b 15 Oct [1885] s/o J. W. Smith & M. A. Fisher. Sps: D. Smith & Martha Smith -FM
30 May 1886	Martha Evelyn [Blubaugh] b 23 Feb [1886] d/o James R. Blubaugh & Victoria F. Smith. Sps: Christopher Swingle & wife -FM
30 May 1886	Ida Cecila [Blubaugh] b 28 Mar [1886] d/o Joseph F. Blubaugh & [Lillis Jane] Melissa Smith. Sps: D. Smith & wife -FM (She married 6 May 1914 Thomas Lamy Arnold.)
13 Jun 1886	Francis Walter [Davis] b 7 Dec 1883 s/o Samuel F. Davis (non cath) [& Elizabeth Blubaugh]. Sps: Francis Gardner & wife -FM
13 Jun 1886	Francis Henry [Davis] b 27 Oct 1885 s/o Samuel F. Davis (non cath) [& Elizabeth Blubaugh]. Sps: John Breckler & wife -FM
18 Jul 1886	Elizabeth [McGough] b 7 Feb 1877 d/o John McGough & Mary Burris. Sps: Jacob Parker & Alice Porter -FM
18 Jul 1886	Henry [McGough] b 18 Mar 1880 s/o John McGough & Mary Burris. -FM
25 Jul 1886	Charles [Hammond] b 27 Jun [1886] s/o Martin Hammond & Maria Sapp. Sps: Julius Sapp & wife -FM

05 Sep 1886	Cletus [Sapp] b 27 Jun [1886] s/o Timothy Sapp & Maria Blubaugh. Sps: Julian Arnold & R. Logsdon -FM
14 Sep 1886	Charles Edward [Blubaugh] b 13 Aug [1886] s/o Francis Blubaugh & Elizabeth A. Sapp. Sps: Charles Durbin & wife -FM
24 Sep 1886	Hans Smith adult. -FM
03 Oct 1886	Levi Claude [Colopy] b 20 Aug [1886] s/o Levi F. Colopy & Melissa A. Durbin. Sps: Edward Carpenter & Charlotte Logsdon -FM
10 Oct 1886	Lucy Clara [Sapp] b 30 Aug [1886] d/o Clement Sapp & Frances King. Sps: Clement Blubaugh & Alice King -FM
10 Oct 1886	James [Durbin] b ___ Jul [1886] s/o Francis Durbin & Susanna Sapp. Sps: George Durbin & Frances Logsdon -FM
12 Oct 1886	Victoria Florence [Smith] Blubaugh b 26 Dec 1856 (adult). -FM [w/o James R. Blubaugh.]
12 Oct 1886	Maria Smith b 27 Sep 1863. -FM
14 Oct 1886	Elizabeth McGough. -FM
17 Oct 1886	George Lewis [Piar] b 17 Aug [1886] s/o Jacob Piar & Rebecca Hoglin. Sps: James Blubaugh -FM
17 Oct 1886	Corretta Cecilia [Smithhisler] b 13 Aug [1886] d/o Philip J. Smithhisler & Mary H. White Sps: Michael Smithhisler & wife -FM (She contracted marriage 27 Apr 1922 with Otto C. Young -non cath- at Columbus OH.)
28 Nov 1886	Cyril [Millis] b 20 Oct [1886] s/o Phillip Millis & Josephine Weaver. Sps: Adam Weaver & Margaret Miller -FM
24 Jan 1887	Lucy Armantha [Swingle] b 17 Nov [1886] d/o Christopher Swingle & Florence J. Blubaugh. Sps: Jacob Blubaugh & Armita Logsdon. -FM (She contracted marriage 7 Jun 1909 with Cosmos Blubaugh bapt. St. Luke; Wit: Edward Swingle & Maria Miller.)

117

30 Jan 1887	Rosalie Elizabeth [Durbin] b 10 Dec [1886] d/o William E. Durbin & Catherine Smithhisler. Sps: William Smithhisler & Maria Smithhisler -FM (She married 1 May 1816 Lewis Smith.)
13 Mar 1887	Ida Bertha [Alexander] b 4 Feb [1887] d/o John William Alexander & Phedora Jane Blubaugh. Sps: Sherman Blubaugh & Victoria Blubaugh -FM
13 Mar 1887	Isadora [King] b 4 Dec [1886] d/o Julius King & Olive Josephine Durbin. Sps: Clement Blubaugh & Anna Durbin -FM
27 Mar 1887	Mary Margaret [Losh] b 26 Jan [1887] d/o John Losh & Sarah Breckler. Sps: Francis Gessling & Thorina Breckler -FM
08 May 1887	Ansel Lyman [Shults] b 18 Mar [1887] s/o Henry Shults & Nora Blubaugh. Sps: Jacob Smith & wife -FM (Frederick Ansel Lyman Shults married 14 Oct 1915 Anna Maria Kollian).
10 May 1887	Maria McArtor. Sps: M. Butts & ____ Butts -FM
19 May 1887	Clara Gertrude [Homan] b 19 Apr [1887] d/o Phillip Homan & Catharine Sheneberger. Sps: Jacob Homan & Elizabeth Homan -FM
26 Jun 1887	Mary Agnes [Purcell] b 1 Jun [1887] d/o Patrick Purcell & Ellen Sapp. Sps: John Breckler & wife -FM. (She married 27 May 1925 Francis E. Town at Mt. Vernon.)
10 Jul 1887	Maria Rosalie [Engle] b 24 Jun [1887] d/o Ligouri Engle & Eugenia Colopy. Sps: Joseph Engle & Susan Engle -FM
17 Jul 1887	Jacob Bernard [Blubaugh] b 30 May [1887] s/o James A. Blubaugh & Sarah Agnes Hess. Sps: Sherman & Victoria Blubaugh.
17 Jul 1887	Maria Elizabeth [Sapp] b 25 Jun [1887] d/o Julian Sapp & Catherine Sapp. Sps: Patrick & Helena Purcell -FM
23 Jul 1887	Festus Bernard [Loney] b 24 Apr [1887] s/o Festus Loney & Flora McKenzie. Sps: John McGough & Margaret McGough -FM

BAPTISMS

24 Jul 1887	Lita Margaret [Sapp] b 10 Jul [1887] d/o George W. Sapp [Jr.] & Isabella Hess. Sps: Frank Durbin & Eddie Hess -FM
31 Jul 1887	Charles Lamy [Gardner] b 3 Jul [1887] s/o Thomas Gardner & Emma Peters. Sps: Jerome Gardner & Frances Gardner -FM
07 Aug 1887	Louisa Beatrice [Albaugh] age 18 adult. Sps: Francis Moitrier & Anna Colopy -FM
14 Aug 1887	Charles Bernard [Blubaugh] b 25 Jun [1887] s/o James R. Blubaugh & Victoria F. Smith. Sps: Charles Durbin & Frances Durbin -FM
28 Aug 1887	Elizabeth Edna [Connelly] b 22 Oct 1886 d/o Hubert Connelly & Elizabeth Hixon. Sps: Jacob Colopy & wife -FM
28 Aug 1887	Christopher [Mattingly] b 7 Aug [1887] s/o Bernard J. Mattingly & Eugenia Sapp. Sps: George Sapp & Eudie -FM
28 Aug 1887	Charles [Arnold] b 20 Jun [1887] s/o Francis Arnold & Frances [Slusser]. Sps: John McGough & Margaret McGough -FM
02 Oct 1887	Mary Monica [Logsdon] b 5 Jul [1887] d/o Lloyd Logsdon & Frances Diamond. Sps: Francis Smithhisler & Maria Smithhisler -FM
01 Nov 1887	Maria Maude [Welker] b 28 Sep 1886 d/o William Welker & Barbara Krout. Sps: Stephen Blubaugh & Elizabeth Homan -FM
13 Nov 1887	Anna Rosalie [Durbin] b 8 Oct [1887] d/o John B. Durbin & Mary A. Blubaugh. Sps: Clement Durbin & Frances Durbin -FM
18 Mar 1888	Thomas Lamy [Arnold] b 17 Oct [1887] s/o [Benjamin] Oliver Arnold & Emma Gaines. Sps: John McKenzie & Margaret McGough -FM (He married 26 May 1914 Ida Caecilia Blubaugh.)

01 Apr 1888	Frances Jane [Bricker] b 1 Feb [1888] d/o Daniel Bricker & Josephine Smithhisler. Sps: George Smith & Maria Smithhisler -FM
08 Apr 1888	Lewis Raymond [Carpenter] b 26 Jan [1888] s/o Edward Carpenter & Frances Homan. Sps: Charles Durbin & Francis Durbin -FM
01 May 1888	Eleanor (Musie Ellen) [Arnold] b 4 Aug 1880 s/o Leo Judson Arnold & Lydia Anna McClerry. Sps: Sara Elizabeth Durbin -JW
27 May 1888	Jacob Charles [Millis] b 20 Apr 1888 s/o Phillip Millis & Josephine Elizabeth Sarah Weaver. -FM
27 May 1888	Lucy Leona [Colopy] b 30 Apr [1888] d/o James Edward Colopy & Margaret J. McMahon. Sps: Jonathan Colopy & Maria Anna Colopy -FM
10 Jun 1888	Thomas Bernard [McGough] b 23 May [1888] s/o John McGough & Elizabeth Burris. Sps: Patrick Thomas Durbin & Lottie McGough -FM
22 Jul 1888	Delia Helen [Mickley] b 19 Jun [1888] d/o Lewis A. Mickley & Charlotte A. Logsdon. Sps: Francis Logsdon & Catherine Logsdon -FM
25 Aug 1888	Rosalie [Butts] b 10 Jul [1888] d/o Giles A. Butts & Eva M. McCarter. Sps James Breckler & wife -FM
25 Aug 1888	Rosalie Margaret [Logsdon] b 16 Jun [1888] d/o Albert Logsdon & Selora Durbin. Sps: Benjamin Durbin & wife -FM
23 Sep 1888	Raymond Alphonso [Blubaugh] b 18 Aug [1888] s/o Basil Blubaugh & Florence McKenzie. Sps: Sherman Blubaugh & Victoria Blubaugh -FM
23 Sep 1888	Germanus Stanton [Colopy] b 24 Aug [1888] s/o Francis John Colopy & Frances Catherine Gardner. Sps: Stephen Blubaugh & Charlotte Blubaugh -FM
30 Sep 1888	Charles Francis [Smith] b 26 Aug [1888] s/o James Smith and Maria E. Blubaugh. Sps: Stephen Blubaugh & Charlotte Blubaugh -FM

30 Sep 1888	Stella Gertrude [Blubaugh] b 29 Sep [1888] d/o Henry D. Blubaugh & Anna V. Durbin. Sps: Edw. Durbin & Gertrude Durbin -FM (Stella md 25 Jan 1910 L. Guy Buckingham at St Vincent de Paul in Mt. Vernon, OH; Wit: Leo Omler & Lucy Sapp.)
13 Dec 1888	Hugh Urban [Gardner] b 12 Oct 1888 s/o John Gardner & Mary Breckler. Sps: John Colopy & Joan Gardner Mt. Vernon, OH -LM
13 Dec 1888	Robert Eugene [Hammond] b 27 Oct 1888 s/o Martin P. Hammond & Mary K. Sapp. Sps: Francis Sapp & Maria Sapp at Mt. Vernon, OH -LM
25 Feb 1889	Elizabeth Agnes [Sapp] b 16 Dec 1888 d/o George W. Sapp [Jr.] & Isabella Hess. Sps: Francis N. Durbin & Jenifer Durbin -TJO
28 Apr 1889	Charles Thomas [King] b 4 Jan 1889 s/o Clement King & Martina Smithhisler. Sps: Michael Smithhisler & Maria Smithhisler -TJO
28 Apr 1889	Blanche Lavina Durbin b 27 Feb 1889 d/o Benjamin Franklin Durbin & Theodora Jane McNamara. Sps: Theodore Durbin & Frances Durbin -TJO
29 Apr 1889	Clara Louise [Losh] b 27 Mar 1889 d/o John J. Losh & Sara Breckler. Sps: John Breckler & Florence Breckler -TJO
10 Jun 1889	Clement [Paul Durbin] b 14 May 1889 s/o John B. Durbin & Mary A. Blubaugh. Sps: John Weaver & Barbara Parker at Mt.Vernon, OH -LM
02 Jul 1889	Blanche [Smithhisler] b 5 Jun 1889 d/o Henry Smithhisler & Catherine Henegan. Sps: Robert Hudson & Helen Vance -LM (Blanche md 6 Feb 1917 Raymond E. Haclett at Cathedral St. James, Seattle, WA.)

"A few others who were baptized by Rev. L. Mulhane between Oct 1888 and Aug 1889 are recorded in the register in Mt.Vernon, Ohio."

18 Aug 1889	Julius M. Blubaugh b 27 Jun 1889 s/o James Blubaugh & Sara Agnes Hess. Sps: Julius Augustine Smith & Ida Blubaugh -WM (Julius md 20 Oct 1915 Agatha Maria Butts.)
25 Aug 1889	Joseph Levi Colopy b 21 Sep 1888 s/o Joseph H. Colopy & Eliza aka Porter. Sps: Levi Colopy & Elizabeth Colopy - WM (Joseph md 29 Aug 1918 Donna Emerick non-cath.)
29 Sep 1889	____ Alphonso [Smithhisler] b 8 Aug 1889 s/o George Smithhisler & Sara Murray Sps: Francis Smithhisler & Alice Murray.
06 Oct 1889	Arthur Urban [O'Hearn] b 7 Sep 1889 s/o Jacob O'Hearn & Frances Peters. Sps: Wilburn Harris & Clara Peters -WM (Arthur md 29 ____ 1922 Rosalin Horing at St. Steffan, Cleveland, OH.)
09 Oct 1889	Emmanual [Gilbert] b 15 Aug 1889 s/o Francis Gilbert (non-cath) & Helen Carter. Sps: Peter Burns & Lydia Carter -WM
10 Oct 1889	S. Veronica Blubaugh b 2 Sep 1889 d/o Leo Blubaugh & Ellen Dial. Sps: Henry Blubaugh & Anna Blubaugh -WM (Veronica md 18 May 1914 Charles Jewell, mixed religion, at Mt. Vernon, OH.)
24 Nov 1889	Benjamin Aloysius [Logsdon] b 14 Nov 1889 s/o Albert Logsdon & [Selora] Durbin. Sps: Clement & Catherine Durbin -WM
24 Nov 1889	Hubert Lamar [Connelly] b 5 May 1889 s/o Hubert Connelly & Elizabeth Hixon (non-cath). Sps: Levi Colopy & Della Miller -WM
29 Jan 1890	Levi Carl [Durbin] b 28 Nov 1889 s/o [John] Thomas Durbin & Susanna Porter. Sps: Levi Colopy & Melissa Colopy -WM
09 Feb 1890	William Dyonisus [Shults] b 11 Nov 1889 s/o Henry Shults & Nora E. Blubaugh. Sps: Augustine Blubaugh & Sarah Warner -WM

23 Mar 1890	Ethel Lucy [Durbin] b 16 Feb 1890 d/o William E. Durbin & Catherine Smithhisler. Sps: John Gardner & Amelia Buck -WM
23 Mar 1890	Bertha Catherine Lower d/o Jacob [Lower] & Mary Shults, his wife at St. Elizabeths in Killbuck, OH. Sps: John M. Lower & Mary P. Lower -WM (Bertha md 15 Oct 1910 Wm Henry Blubaugh, bpt 22 Feb 1891 Sacred Heart, at Coshocton, OH.)
26 Mar 1890	Alice Gwendolyn Durbin b 20 Mar 1890 d/o Clement Durbin & Mary Catherine [Durbin-3rd cousin]. Sps: John C. Durbin & wife -WM
02 Apr 1890	Mary Cecilia [or Caroline Mickley] b 21 Feb 1890 d/o Lewis A. Mickley (non-cath) & Charlotte A. Logsdon. Sps: Jacob Blubaugh & Ida Blubaugh -WM
20 Apr 1890	Anna Gertrude Bricker b 22 Mar 1890 d/o Daniel Bricker & Josephine Smithhisler. Sps: Francis & Irene Smithhisler -WM
10 May 1890	Mary [Carter] b 10 Jan 1869 d/o Raphael Carter & Lydia Magers. Sps: Rev. G. McDermott & Agnes Blubaugh -WM
15 May 1890	Theodora Burris b 24 Dec 1873 (new convert) d/o Josiah Burris & Rebecca _____ (non-cath). Sps: Sherman Blubaugh & Rena Smithhisler -WM
06 Jul 1890	George Dickeson [Browne] b 7 Mar 1890 s/o George Browne & Helen _____. Sps: Francis Durbin & Rilla Logsdon -WM
06 Jul 1890	Jane Selora [Arnold] b 19 Feb 1890 d/o Benjamin Oliver Arnold & Emma J. [Gaines] (non-cath). Sps: William Bailes & Matilda Bailes -WM
06 Jul 1890	Agnes Bertilla [Bailes] b 15 May 1890 d/o William Bailes & Matilda Dial. Sps: Jacob Smith & Maria Smith -WM
13 Jul 1890	Mary Agnes [Butts] b 17 Jun 1890 d/o Giles A. Butts & Eva Mary McCarter. Sps: Henry Blubaugh & Anna Blubaugh -WM (Maria md 20 Oct 1915 Julian W. Blubaugh.)

20 Jul 1890	James Barry Colopy b 11 Jun 1890 s/o James Edward Colopy & Margaret J. McMahon. Sps: Levi Colopy & Melissa Colopy-WM
27 Jul 1890	Isabel Pauline [Finneran] b 11 Jul 1890 d/o Patrick Finneran & Isabelle Henegan. Sps: Benjamin Parker & Lucy Sapp-WM
21 Sep 1890	[Dwight] Jonathan [Magers] b 2 Jul 1890 s/o Calvin Magers (non-cath) and Ellen Arnold. Sps: John Blubaugh & Mary Blubaugh-WM
21 Sep 1890	Helen Bertilla [Durbin] b 26 Aug 1890 d/o John B. Durbin & Mary A. Blubaugh. Sps: Thomas Durbin & Josephine Durbin-WM
06 Oct 1890	Lucy Florence [Blubaugh] b 30 Sep 1890 d/o Clement A. Blubaugh & Ella Welker. Sps: Henry & Anna Blubaugh. -WM
25 Nov 1891	Thomas Edward [Sapp] b 29 Sep 1890 s/o Clement Sapp & Frances King. Sps: Henry Blubaugh & Isabella Sapp -WM
__ __ 1891	William Alexander [Losh] b 28 Nov 1890 s/o John Losh & Sara Breckler. Sps: John Hosfelt & Clara Breckler -WM
03 Feb 1891	Fenton Fidelis [Durbin] b 2 Feb 1891 s/o Benjamin F. Durbin & Theodora [Jane McNamara]. Sps: Rev. Wm McDermott & Eliz Durbin -WM. (Fenton md 15 Sep 1914 Ethel Maria Logsdon.)
14 Feb 1891	Leo[n] Earl Blanchard b 20 Dec 1890 s/o Lawrence V. Blanchard & Florence A. Engle (non-cath). Sps: Pius & Alberta Engle -WM. (Leon md 17 Oct 1916 Mary King.)
15 Feb 1891	Frances Donna (Shults] b 18 Nov 1890 d/o John Taylor Shults & Alice J. Rice. Sps: John & Mary Gardner -WM (Frances md 26 Apr 1917 Bernard Hammond.)
20 Feb 1891	Bernard Leonard [Hammond] b 11 Jan 1891 s/o Martin Hammond & Mary [Keziah] Sapp. Sps: Henry Blubaugh & Lucy Sapp -WM. (Bernard md 26 Apr 1917 Donna Shults, see above.)

BAPTISMS

22 Feb 1891	William Henry Blubaugh b 6 Jan 1891 s/o Thomas Blubaugh & Margaret S. Shuman (non-cath). Sps: Chris & Florence Swingle -WM
29 Mar 1891	Bertha [Sapp] b 19 Mar 1891 d/o Julian Sapp & Catherine [Wiggins]. Sps: ____- & Albertha Sapp -WM (Bertha md 24 Feb 1916 Walter H. Gillmore at St. John, Cleveland, OH.)
05 Apr 1891	Clarence Augustus [Austin Carpenter] b 5 Feb 1891 s/o Edward Carpenter & Frances Homan. Sps: Rev. Wm McDermott & Elizabeth Strapp -WM (Austin md 16 Sep 1913 Anna Metzger at Sacred Heart of Mary, Shelby OH; Wit: Jacob Metzger & Mary Carpenter.)
10 May 1891	Mary Frances [Blubaugh] b 3 May 1891 d/o Henry D. Blubaugh & Anna V. Durbin. Sps: Joseph Durbin & Maria Blubaugh. -WM
14 Jun 1891	Bertha Agnes [Blubaugh] b 14 May 1891 d/o Charles Blubaugh & Emma Guenther. Sps: Charles & Deliah Guenther -WM
14 Jun 1891	Lucy [King] b 13 Apr 1891 d/o Clement King & Martina Smithhisler. Sps: George Smithhisler & Maria Smithhisler -WM. (Lucy md 29 Oct 1912 at St. Luke John Sheedy (bapt. 23 Jun 1887 at St. Vincent de Paul Mt. Vernon, OH) s/o Nicholas.)
05 Jul 1891	William Mark [King] s/o Julius King & Olive J. Durbin Sps: Edward Durbin & Philena Durbin -WM
10 Jul 1891	Francis [Gilbert] b 31 Nov 1855 s/o George Gilbert & Hulda Barnes. Sps: Francis Sapp & Catherine Devan -WM
19 Jul 1891	William Bernard [Piar] b 7 May 1891 s/o Hillery D. Piar & Mary E. Whistler. Sps: Jacob Smith & Maria Smith -WM. (William md 22 Sep 1920 Gertrude Vaughn at Altoona, PA.)
02 Aug 1891	Bertha Cecelia [Logsdon] b 18 ___ 1891 d/o Albert Logsdon & Selora Durbin. Sps: Thomas Durbin & Joanna Durbin -WM

04 Oct 1891   Rosa Veronica [Gilbert] b 6 Sep 1891 d/o Francis Gilbert & Helen Carter. Sps: Francis & Maria Smithhisler -WM

15 Oct 1891   Ada Helen [Durbin] b 3 Sep 1891 d/o Francis Durbin & Eve Asher. Sps: Charles Durbin & Frances Durbin -WM

07 Nov 1891   Florence Joan [Connelly] b 10 May 1891 d/o Hubert Connelly & Elizabeth Hixon. Sps: Levi Colopy & Melissa Colopy -WM

30 Nov 1891   Pauline Cecelia [Durbin] b 23 Nov 1891 d/o Clement E. Durbin & Mary Catherine Durbin. Sps: Albert Logsdon & Selora Logsdon -WM (Pauline md 21 Oct 1914 Christopher Swingle.)

06 Dec 1891   George William [Blubaugh] b 28 Oct 1891 s/o Sherman William Blubaugh & Lorena G. [Lena] Smithhisler. Sps: George & Maria Smithhisler -WM. (George md 28 oct 1914 Mabel Easterday.)

03 Jan 1892   Eva Pruly [O'Hearn] b 6 Dec 1891 d/o James O'Hearn & Frances Peters. Sps: Lamy Blubaugh & Maria Blubaugh -WM

06 Mar 1892   Agatha Cecelia [Durbin] b 24 Jan 1892 d/o John B. Durbin & Mary A. Blubaugh Sps: Thomas Durbin & Joan Durbin -WM

17 Apr 1892   Robert Emmett [Colopy] b 20 Feb 1892 s/o James [Edward] Colopy & Margaret J. McMahon. Sps: Rev. Wm McDermott & Lucy Welker -WM. (Robert md 30 Jun 1920 Gertrude W. Wadigan at St. Augustine, Barbarton, OH.)

21 Apr 1892   Stephen Joseph [Breckler] b 14 Apr 1892 s/o John P. Breckler & Flora Sapp. Sps: George Sapp & Delila Sapp -WM. (Stephen md 17 Oct 1913 Jessie Annabell Prill at St. Francis, Columbus, OH.)

08 May 1892   Catherine [Sapp ?] b 18 Sep 18__ d/o George Sapp non cath) & Maria Butts "not married". Sps: Jonathan Colopy & wife -WM

BAPTISMS

08 May 1892	Lawrence [Church] b 8 Mar 1892 s/o Ulysses G. Church (non-cath) and Martha Homan. Sps: Michael Homan & wife -WM
05 Jun 1892	Agnes [Bricker] b 28 Apr 189_ d/o Daniel Bricker & Josephine Smithhisler. Sps: Robert S. Parker & wife -WM
06 Jun 1892	Ethel Maria [Sapp ?] b 12 Mar 189_ d/o William Sapp & Aurelia "Rilla" Logsdon, "not married". Sps: Francis Logsdon & wife -WM. (Ethel md 15 Sep 1914 Fenton F. Durbin of Akron, OH.)
26 Jun 1892	Anthony Raymond [Blubaugh] b 7 May 1892 s/o James R. Blubaugh & Victoria F. Smith. Sps: Francis Logsdon & wife -WM. (Anthony md 4 Jun 1913 Edna Victoria Blubaugh.)
10 Jul 1892	Maria Helen [Parker] b 7 Nov 1891 d/o George W. Parker & Artensia E. Engle Sps: Charles Durbin & Carita McKenzie -WM
10 Jul 1892	Daniel Ray [Longstretch] b 1 Jul 1892 s/o Alexander Longstretch & Alice Fatler. Sps: William Longstretch & Ida Fatler -WM
07 Aug 1892	John Aloysius [Blubaugh] b 19 Jun 1892 s/o James A. Blubaugh & Sara Agnes Hess. Sps: Francis Sapp & Helen Blubaugh -WM. (John md 12 May 1917 Elizabeth Butts.)
04 Sep 1892	John Thomas [Losh] b 6 Aug 1892 s/o John Losh & Sara Breckler. Sps: Thomas B. Durbin & Joan Durbin -WM. (John md 2 May 1917 Anna Cecila Smith at St. Mary, Tiffin, OH.)
07 Sep 1892	Sylvester Raymond [Blubaugh] b 1 Sep 1892 s/o Clement A. Blubaugh & Ellen Welker. Sps: Charles R. & Isabel Sapp -WM
12 Oct 1892	Mary Esther [Smithhisler] b 3 Oct 1892 d/o Francis Smithhisler & Monica Diamond. Sps: John Mumaw (per proxy) & wife -WM

127

23 Oct 1892	Francis Jerome [Mickley] b 4 Aug 1892 s/o Lewis A. Mickley (non-cath) & Charlotte A. Logsdon. Sps: Charles Logsdon & wife -WM
08 Dec 1892	Lucy Mary [Homan] b 26 Oct 1892 d/o Philip Homan & Sara Catherine Sheneberger. Sps: Jacob Smith & wife -WM
08 Jan 1893	Judson Cletus [Durbin] b 20 Nov 1892 s/o John Thomas Durbin & Susanna "Hattie" Porter. Sps: Charles Logsdon & wife -WM. (Judson md 19 Oct 1921 Drusilla Simpson.)
02 Feb 1893	Edith Ethel Maria [Arnold] b 16 Nov 1892 d/o B. Oliver Arnold & Emma J. Gaines (non-cath). Sps: Jonathan Arnold & wife Maria -WM. (Edith md 17 Apr 1926 Jacob P. Weller (non-cath) at St. Francis, Columbus, OH.)
02 Feb 1893	Bernice Edna [Arnold] b 16 Nov 1892 d/o B. Oliver Arnold & Emma J. Gaines (non-cath). Sps: Jonathan & Maria Arnold -WM
03 Feb 1893	Lewis Grover Cleveland [Durbin] b 20 Jan 1893 s/o William E. Durbin & Catherine Smithhisler. Sps: Rev. Wm McDermott & Josephine Durbin -WM. (Lewis md 1 May 1816 Rhea Smith.)
17 Mar 1893	Helen Josephine [Durbin] b 15 Mar 1893 d/o Benjamin F. Durbin & Theodora J. McNamara. Sps: William Durbin & wife -WM
16 Apr 1893	Mary Catherine [Blubaugh] b 9 Jan 1893 d/o Thomas Blubaugh & Margaret Sophia Shuman (non-cath). Sps: Jacob A. Blubaugh & wife -WM
19 Apr 1893	John Thomas Blubaugh b 26 Mar [1893], [twin], s/o Basil Blubaugh & Florence McKenzie. Sps: Jacob Smith & wife -WM. (John md1 22 Oct 1919 Charlotte Rebecca Blubaugh; he md2 27 Dec 1960 Verna Snyder.)
19 Apr 1893	Mary Ellen [Blubaugh] b 26 Mar [1893], (twin), d/o Basil Blubaugh & Florence McKenzie. Sps: John & Helena Blubaugh-WM

BAPTISMS

23 Apr 1893	Raymond Cletus [Butts] b 4 Mar 1893 s/o Giles A. Butts & Eva Mary McCarter. Sps: Clement Blubaugh & wife -WM
30 Apr 1893	Dorotha Cecelia Piar b 4 Mar 1893 d/o Hillery D. Piar & Mary E. Whistler Sps: John Beam & wife -WM
30 Apr 1893	Mary Selora [Logsdon] b 14 Apr 1893 d/o Albert Logsdon & Selora Durbin. Sps: Edward & Bertha Durbin -WM
11 May 1893	Raymond Theodore [Parker] b 3 May 1893 s/o Benjamin R. Parker & Frances Baker. Sps:Edward & Bertha Durbin -WM. (Raymond md 5 Jan 1964 Mildred Nelson at Washington, DC.)
11 May 1893	Jacob Frederick [Church] b 23 Feb 1893 s/o Ulysses G. Church (non-cath) and Martha Homan. Sps: John Weaver & wife-WM
11 May 1893	Walter Ambrose [Blubaugh] b 17 Apr 1893 s/o Charles Blubaugh & Emma Guenther. Sps: Henry Blubaugh & wife -WM
14 May 1893	Rilla Agnes [Swingle] b 25 Jan 1893 d/o Christopher Swingle & Florence J. Blubaugh. Sps: Francis Sapp & wife -WM
11 Jun 1893	Francis Charles [King] b 10 Apr 1893 s/o Clement King & Martina Smithhisler. Sps: Francis Smithhisler & wife -WM. (Francis md 15 Jul 1918 Mabel McMahon.)
04 Aug 1893	Maria Angeline [Librado] b 1 Aug 1893 d/o John Librado & Elizabeth Amicome. Sps: Murachin Anthony & Florence Amicome -WM
27 Aug 1893	Edna Veronica [Blubaugh] b 13 Aug 1893 d/o Sherman William Blubaugh & Lorena G. Smithhisler. Sps: Henry Smithhisler & Victoria Blubaugh -WM. (Edna md 4 Jun 1913 Anthony R. Blubaugh.)
01 Oct 1893	Mary Alice [King] b 26 Aug 1893 d/o Julius King & Olive J. Durbin. Sps: Henry Blubaugh & Helen Blubaugh-WM (Maria md 17 Oct 1916 Earl Blanchard.)

15 Oct 1893   Maria Teresa [Coleman] (non-cath) b 12 Sep 1869 d/o
                John Coleman & Anna Liffer. Sps: John Durbin & Maria
                Helen Blubaugh -WM

02 Nov 1893   Celestine Corwin [Blanchard] b 26 Sep 1893 s/o
                Lawrence V. Blanchard & Florence A. Engle (non-cath)
                Sps: Rev. Wm McDermott & Susanna Engle-WM
                (Celestine md 12 Nov 1918 Sara Agnes Lower.)

19 Nov 1893   William McDermott Smithhisler b 8 Nov 1893 s/o Henry
                Smithhisler & Catherine Henegan. Sps: Patrick & Isabel
                Nenegan -WM. (William md 12 Jun 1917 Clara Ziegler at
                St. Joseph, Monroeville, OH (previous month in civil
                ceremony.)

19 Nov 1893   Maria Antonia [Smithhisler] b 11 Nov 1893 d/o Francis
                Smithhisler & Monica Diamond. Sps: Charles Durbin &
                Maria Smithhisler -WM. (Maria md 19 Jun 1926 Joseph
                Thomas Judge.)

28 Nov 1893   Amanda Helen [South] b 1837 (new convert) d/o
                Abraham McNamee and Elizabeth Hawn (non-cath). Sps:
                Rev. Wm McDermott & Susan Engle -WM

14 Jan 1894   Henry Sanford [Hammond] b 14 Dec 1893 s/o Martin P.
                Hammond & Mary Keziah Sapp. Sps: Benjamin Parker
                & Frances Parker-WM (Henry md 7 Aug 1919 Eva
                Verna Frase at St. Augustine, Barbarton, OH.)

22 Jan 1894   Bernadette Agnes [Durbin] b 15 Jan 1894 d/o Clement E.
                Durbin & Mary Catherine Durbin. Sps: Benjamin Durbin
                & Elizabeth Durbin -WM

22 Mar 1894   Samuel Shrimplin age 80 yrs Sps: Charles Sapp -WM.

15 Apr 1894   William Edward [Gilbert] b 16 Oct 1893 s/o Francis
                Gilbert & Helena Carter. Sps: Clement Blubaugh & wife
                -WM. (William md 5 Apr 1920 Viola Banberry, non-cath,
                at Mt. Vernon.)

19 May 1894   Anna Lulu [Purcell] (new convert) b 5 Apr 1872 d/o
                Charles Purcell & Sarah M. Duvall (non-cath). Sps:
                Francis Gaines & wife -WM

BAPTISMS

24 May 1894	William [Collins] b 11 Feb 1859 (new convert) s/o Jacob Collins & Delilah Butler. Sps: John C. Durbin & wife -WM
27 May 1894	Charles Cleophus [Breckler] b 17 May 1894 s/o John P. Breckler & Flora Sapp. Sps: Lamy Blubaugh & Maria Sapp -WM (Charles md 12 Feb 1918 Maria W. Stull at Steubenville.)
27 May 1894	Daniel Levi (Donald) [Colopy] b 14 Apr 1894 s/o James Edward Colopy & Margaret J. McMohan. Sps: Levi Colopy & wife -WM. (Daniel md 16 Apr 1918 Florence Blanchard.)
27 May 1894	Agnes Anastasia [Blubaugh] b 25 May 1894 d/o Henry D. Blubaugh & Anna V. Durbin. Sps: Clement Blubaugh & wife -WM
23 Sep 1894	Alice [Blubaugh] b 12 Sep 1894 d/o Clement A. Blubaugh & Ella Welker. Sps: Charles & Emma Blubaugh -WM
30 Sep 1894	Stephen Henry [Losh] b 24 Aug 1894 s/o John Losh & Sara Breckler. Sps: Stephen & Carol Blubaugh -WM
14 Oct 1894	Florine Matilda [Wells] b 11 Jun 1894 d/o Pearl Wells & Rebecca Logsdon. Sps: Benjamin & Maria Logsdon -WM (Flora md 14 Apr 1920 Francis Riepenhoft at St. John, Lima, OH.)
15 Oct 1894	Mary Almeda [McFadden] b 4 Jul 1894 (new convert) d/o Harrison McFadden & Martha Boyd (non-cath). Sps: Rev. Wm McDermott & Elizabeth Strapp -WM
28 Oct 1894	Ann Martella [O'Hearn] b 2 Oct 1894 d/o James O'Hearn & Frances Peters. Sps: Charles Logsdon & Alice Logsdon -WM
01 Nov 1894	Robert Owen [Parker] b 9 Aug 1894 s/o Benjamin R. Parker & Frances Baker. Sps: Robert & Rebecca Parker -WM. (Robert md 22 Jan 1924 [who?] at Mt. Vernon.)
04 Nov 1894	Agnes Isabel [Blubaugh] b 11 Sep 1894 d/o James Aug. Blubaugh & Sara Agnes Hess. Sps: Jacob Smith & Maria Smith -WM (Agnes md 12 May 1920 Francis W. Blubaugh.)

18 Nov 1894   Louis Arthur [Smith] b 11 Oct 1894 s/o Julius A. Smith & Rose Elizabeth Colopy. Sps: Joseph Colopy & Maria Smith -WM (Louis md 1 May 1916 Rosann Durbin.)

25 Nov 1894   Edward Marion [Singer] b 9 Jun 1874 s/o Andrew Singer & Amanda Parsons (non-cath). Sps: Benjamin & Eizabeth Durbin -WM

09 Dec 1894   Vincent Piar b 3 Aug 1828 (new convert) s/o Samuel Piar & Catherine Dumbaugh (non-cath.) Sps: Jacob & Maria Smith -WM

11 Dec 1894   Margaret Sophia [Shuman Blubaugh] b 7 Sep 1871 (new convert) d/o John Shuman & Catherine Shuman (non-cath) & w/o Thomas Blubaugh . Sps: Rev. Wm. McDermott & Elizabeth Strapp -WM

10 Jan 1895   Lucy Anastasia [Blubaugh] b 13 Dec 1894 d/o Liguori Blubaugh & Mary Coleman. Sps: Leo Blubaugh & wife -WM. (Lucy md 23 Nov 1915 Sylvester Highman (non-cath).)

24 Feb 1895   Albert Jackson [King] b 24 Nov 11894 s/o Clement King & Martina Smithhisler. Sps: Charles Sapp & Alice King -WM

14 Apr 1895   Barbara Esther [Durbin] b 29 Mar 1895 d/o Edward C. Durbin & Mary E. Blubaugh. Sps: William & Metta Blubaugh -WM

21 Apr 1895   Sara Isabel [Blubaugh] b 17 Feb 1895 d/o Sherman W. Blubaugh & Lorena Smithhisler. Sps: William Smithhisler & wife -WM

21 Apr 1895   Margaret Isabel [Durbin] b 28 Feb [1895] d/o Frederick Durbin & Martha Eckenrode. Sps:George W. Sapp & wife -WM (Margaret's marriage 4 May 1921 registered in St. Peter, Mansfield, OH.)

28 Apr 1895   Hubert Purcell [Butts] b 10 Mar 1895 s/o Giles A. Butts & Eva Mary McCarter. Sps: John C. Durbin & wife -WM. (Hubert md April 1895 reg. 18 Jun 1919 Rosina Weber at Warington, OH.)

05 May 1895	Maria Ursula [Shuff] b 5 May 1893 d/o Francis Shuff (non cath) & Aurelia Logsdon (not married). Sps: Charles Durbin & wife -WM
12 May 1895	Maria Ethel [Phillips] b 16 Apr 1895 d/o Edward Phillips & Joan Neil. Sps: Joseph Phillips & Maria Phillips -WM
13 Jun 1895	Bernard Marcellus [Durbin] b 3 Jun 1895 s/o Thomas B. Durbin & Mary Jane Durbin. Sps: John Durbin & wife -WM. (Bernard md 19 Jun 1928 Hilda Siebewalter at St. Conifas, New Rigal, OH.)
28 Jun 1895	Paul Marion [Smithhisler] b 14 Jun 1895 s/o Francis L. Smithhisler & Monica Diamond. Sps: Patrick McGann & Amelia Buck -WM
28 Jun 1895	Frederick [Critchfield] b 9 Nov 1886 s/o Jacob Critchfield & Joanna Weaver. Sps: Rev. Wm McDermott & Alice Logsdon -WM
21 Jul 1895	Robert Clarence [Logsdon] b 21 May 1895 s/o George Logsdon & Almeda McFadden. Sps: Charles Durbin & Frances Durbin -WM
15 Aug 1895	Ann Blanche Logsdon b 9 Aug 1895 d/o Albert Logsdon & Selora Durbin. Sps: Raymond Arnold & Maria Arnold -WM
18 Aug 1895	Theodora Isabel [Bricker] b 28 Jun 1895 d/o Daniel Bricker & Josephine Smithhisler. Sps: William Smithhisler & wife -WM. (Thedora md 17 Jan 1913 at Barbarton, OH.)
25 Aug 1895	Ethel Lutila [Gaum] b 1 Aug 1895 d/o Francis Roland Gaum & Frances Isabel Durbin. Sps: Theodore Durbin & Louisa Durbin -WM. (Ethel md 23 Sep 1918 Lewis Maday at St. Vincent, Akron, OH.)
28 Sep 1895	Mary Margaret [Blubaugh] b 20 Sep 1895 d/o Stephen Lamy Blubaugh & Isabella Sapp. Sps: Francis Sapp & Charlotte Blubaugh -WM
03 Nov 1895	John Julius Smithhisler b 2 Oct 1895 s/o Henry Smithhisler & Catherine Henegan. Sps: Rollin Henegan & Lucy Welker -WM

08 Dec 1895	Martha Helen Blubaugh b 24 Nov 1895 d/o Charles Blubaugh & Emma Guenther. Sps: Clement & Helen Blubaugh -WM
08 Dec 1895	Alva Burton Joseph [Kemp] b 14 Feb 1874 (new convert) s/o Andrew J. Kemp & Elizabeth Mikesell (Protestant). Sps: Peter & Honora Peters -WM
05 Apr 1896	Helen Victoria [Lower] b 24 Dec 1895 d/o John M. Lower & Mary Py. -WM (Helen md 28 Nov 1918 John Roman Weber at Spring Mountain, OH.)
07 Apr 1896	Jonathan Gaines [Arnold] b 22 Oct 1895 s/o B. Oliver Arnold & Emma J. Gaines. Sps: Rev. Wm McDermott & Elizabeth Strapp -WM (Jonathan md 7 Oct 1919 Maria Virgilia Gardner.)
12 Apr 1896	Albert Oscar Piar b 21 Feb 1896 s/o Hillery D. Piar & Mary Whistler. -WM (Albert md 25 Oct 1922 Maria Alta Frazee.)
19 Apr 1896	Thomas Andrew [Blubaugh] b 23 Jan 1896 s/o Thomas Blubaugh & Margaret S. Shuman. Sps: Phillip Homan & wife -WM
19 Apr 1896	Mary Agnes [Engle] b 3 Mar 1896 d/o Lewis D. Engle & Isabel Myers. -WM
19 Apr 1896	Justin Leo [Durbin] b 14 Apr 1896 s/o Clement E. Durbin & Mary Catherine Durbin. Sps: Thomas B. Durbin & wife -WM (Justin md 27 Oct 1856 Marie A. Dresen at St. Luke, Riverfort, IL.)
26 Apr 1896	Charles Roland [Peterson] b 11 May 1895 s/o Desilva Peterson & Aurelia Blubaugh. Sps: Samuel & Margaret Shults -WM
26 Apr 1896	Helen Cecelia [Parker] b 1 Apr 1896 d/o Benjamin R. Parker & Frances Baker. Sps: Elmer Parker & Esther Parker -WM
10 May 1896	James Ferdinand [Logsdon] b 31 Mar 1896 s/o James Logsdon & Margaret Homan. Sps: George Logsdon & wife -WM (Jacob md 17 Jun 1919 Mary Pauline Hammond.)

BAPTISMS

08 Jun 1896	Mary Margaret [Colopy] b 1 Apr 1896 d/o James Edward Colopy & Margaret J. McMahon. Sps: Julius Sapp & wife -WM
28 Jun 1896	Benjamin Francis [Losh] b 3 Jun 1896 s/o John Losh & Sara Breckler. Sps: Benjamin Durbin -WM
29 Jun 1896	Clarence Edward [Hammond] b 21 May 1896 s/o Martin P. Hammond & Mary Keziah Sapp. Sps: Thomas B. Durbin & wife -WM (Clarence md 29 Jun 1922 Amelia B. Partridge at St. Augustine, Barbarton, OH.)
12 Sep 1896	Aloysius Marion [Durbin] b 8 Sep 1896 s/o Edward C. Durbin & Mary E. Blubaugh Sps: Henry Blubaugh & wife.
12 Sep 1896	Mary Helen [Mickley] b 3 Jul 1896 d/o Wm Mickley & Aurelia Logsdon. Sps: Jacob Smith & Frances Logsdon -WM
04 Oct 1896	Francis William Aloysius [Blubaugh] b 25 Sep 1896 s/o Clement A. Blubaugh & Ella Welker. Sps: John Durbin & Gertrude Durbin -WM (Francis md 12 May 1920 Agnes Blubaugh.)
04 Oct 1896	Paul Beck [Welker] b 27 Sep 1896 s/o Paul Welker & Mary Amelia Beck. Sps: Francis Smithhisler & wife -WM
18 Oct 1896	Bertha Agnes [Homan] b 3 Sep 1896 d/o Philip Homan & Sara Catherine Sheneberger. Sps: Charles Durbin & wife -WM
01 Nov 1896	Marie [Magers] b 29 Aug 1896 d/o Calvin Magers & Ellen Arnold. Sps: Ben Oliver & Maria Arnold -WM
13 Dec 1896	William Edward [Blubaugh] b 15 Nov 1896 s/o Liguori Blubaugh & Mary Coleman. Sps: Edward Durbin & Maria Durbin -WM
13 Dec 1896	Clarence Joseph [Kemp] b 13 Nov 1896 s/o Alva Burton Joseph Kemp & Helena B. Peters. Sps: Rev. Wm McDermott & Clara Peters -WM

135

22 Dec 1896	Albinus Joseph [Singer] b 1 Oct 1878 (new convert) s/o John Singer & Jane Parsons. Sps: Jacob McDermott & Margaret McDermott -WM
25 Dec 1896	Gertrude Rosetta [Durbin] b 11 Nov 1896 d/o John B. Durbin & Mary A. Blubaugh. Sps: Francis Gaum & Frances Gaum -WM
01 Jan 1897	Mary Jane [Smith] b 5 Dec 1896 d/o Julius Smith & Rose Elizabeth Colopy. Sps: Levi Colopy & wife -WM. (Maria (Rhea) md 1 May 1916 Lewis Durbin.)
31 Jan 1897	Virginia Anastasia [Blubaugh] b 22 Jan 1897 d/o Stephen Lamy Blubaugh & Isabel Sapp. Sps: Raymond Sapp & Joanna Gardner -WM
03 Feb 1897	Edna Mary Magdalena [Logsdon] b 27 Jan 1897 d/o Albert Logsdon & Selora Durbin. Sps: John Durbin & wife Margaret -WM
21 Mar 1897	Edna Frances [Kelly] b 18 Feb 1897 d/o John Kelly & Emma Beam. Sps: John & Maria Beam -WM
17 Apr 1897	David Heiple (new convert). Sps: Clement Durbin & Lillian Sapp -WM
09 May 1897	Lucy Agnes [Bailes] b 12 Apr 1897 d/o Julius Bailes & Philena J. Durbin Sps: Julius King & wife Olive -WM
09 May 1897	Harold Ambrose [Sapp] b 10 Apr 1897 s/o Fidelius Sapp & Mary Dete. Sps: William Durbin & Lucy Dete -WM. (Harley md 14 Sep 1926 Marion L. "Goldie" Martin at St. Aloysius, Columbus, OH; Wit: Raymond J. Sapp & Isabel Julia Sapp. Marion was d/o Thomas & Maria Catherine Martin.)
23 May 1897	Ethel Maria [Dial] b 14 May 1890 d/o Jacob Dial & Henrietta Hess. (case of invalid marriage, dead & invalid). Sps: George Sapp & wife Isabella -WM
23 May 1897	Raymond Sylvester [Dial] b 4 Oct 1891 Jacob Dial & Henrietta Hess. (case of invalid marriage, dead & invalid). Sps: George Sapp & wife Isabella -WM

BAPTISMS

23 May 1897	Evelyn Neole Teresa [Dial] b 8 Nov 1893 Jacob Dial & Henrietta Hess. (case of invalid marriage, dead & invalid) Sps: George Sapp & wife Isabella-WM
27 May 1897	William Henry [Welker] b 8 Feb 1892 s/o George Welker & Eva Mae Stull Sps: Lewis Welker & wife Elizabeth.
27 May 1897	Charles Franklin Welker b 14 Mar 1894 s/o George Welker & Eva Mae Stall. Sps: Lewis Welker & wife Elizabeth -WM
27 Jul 1897	Julius Webster [Peterson] b 8 Dec 1892 s/o Desilva Peterson & Aurelia Blubaugh. Sps: Levi Colopy & wife Melissa -WM
08 Aug 1897	Mary Monica Martha [Smithhisler] b 23 Jul 1897 d/o Francis L. Smithhisler & Monica Diamond. Sps: Rev. Wm McDermott & Monica Logsdon -WM
15 Aug 1897	William Henry [O'Hearn] b 22 Jul 1897 s/o James O'Hearn & Frances Peters. Sps: Raymond Arnold & Maria Arnold -WM
15 Aug 1897	Hilda Maria [Gardner] b 11 Mar 1897 d/o John F. Gardner & Emma Josephine Durbin. Sps: Francis Gardner & Maria Gardner -WM. (Hilda md 24 Oct 1917 Edward Mickley.)
18 Aug 1897	Eva Mae [Stall Welker] b 10 Mar 1871 (new convert) d/o Samuel Stall & Maria Sara Smith non-cath), [& w/o George Welker]. Sps: Earnest Welker & Elizabeth Strapp -WM
29 Aug 1897	Joseph Francis [Smithhisler] b 9 Aug 1897 s/o Henry Smithhisler & Catherine Henegan. Sps: Joseph Killdoff & Maria Henegan -WM
29 Aug 1897	Daniel Carter Sps: Albert King. -WM
26 Sep 1897	Florence Esther [Blanchard] b 10 Jun 1897 d/o Lawrence V. Blanchard & Florence A. Engle. Sps: Jacob Miller & Lucy Miller -WM. (Florence md 16 Apr 1918 Donald Colopy.)

03 Oct 1897	Ethel Maria [Lower] b 4 Aug 1897 d/o Henry Lower & Louella Moore. Sps: John Lower & wife -WM (Ethel md 30 Oct 1926 Daniel P. Conroy at St. Vincent, Akron, OH; Wit: Howard Conroy & Mrs. Carl Mitchell.)
15 Oct 1897	Rosa Anna [Weigard] b 18 Aug 1897 d/o Edward Weigard & Clara Urban. Sps: Rev. Wm McDermott & Maria Weigard -WM
17 Oct 1897	Laura Isabella [Blubaugh] b 29 Aug 1897 d/o Charles Blubaugh & Emma Guenter. Sps: Clement Sapp & Lillian Sapp -WM
31 Oct 1897	Maria Bernadette [Purcell] b 21 Oct 1897 d/o John Purcell & Maria Ray. Sps: Rev. Wm McDermott & Anna Purcell -WM
01 Nov 1897	Rebecca Elizabeth [Butts] b 10 Sep 1897 d/o Giles A. Butts & Eva Mary McCarter. Sps: Jonathan Colopy -WM (Rebecca md 10 May 1917 John A. Blubaugh.)
21 Nov 1897	Monica [Blubaugh] b 22 Sep 1897 d/o James Augustine Blubaugh & Sara Agnes Hess. Sps: William S. Blubaugh & wife Laurina -WM
22 Dec 1897	Helen Catherine [Wells] b 11 Nov 1897 d/o Pearl Wells (non-cath) & Rebecca Logsdon. Sps: Rev. Wm McDermott & Lucinda Dick -WM
06 Feb 1898	Theodore [Durbin] b 14 Jan 1898 s/o Benjamin F. Durbin & Theodora Jane McNamara. Sps: John Gardner & wife Josephine -WM (Theodore md 6 Oct 1927 Maria A. Dyer at St. Mary, Marietta, OH.)
20 Mar 1898	Herman Sylvester [Blubaugh] b 24 Jan 1898 s/o Thomas Blubaugh & Margaret S. Shuman. Sps: George W. Sapp & wife -WM. (Herman md 20 Jan 1929 Charlotte _____.)
27 Mar 1898	Mary Pauline [Hammond] b 15 Feb 1898 d/o Martin P. Hammond & Mary Keziah Sapp. Sps: Jacob Smith & Frances Logsdon -WM. (Mary md 17 Jun 1919 James Ferdinand Logsdon.)

17 Apr 1898	Mary Magdalena [King] b 4 Mar 1898 d/o Julius King & Olive J. Durbin. Sps: Rev. Wm McDermott & Elizabeth Strapp -WM
17 Apr 1898	James Leo [Colopy] b 8 Feb 1898 s/o James Colopy & Margaret J. McMahon. Sps: Julius Sapp & wife -WM
01 May 1898	Cornelius Gregory [Henley] b 4 Mar 1898 s/o Gregory Henley & Honora Peters. Sps: William Peters & wife -WM
04 May 1898	John Henry [Durbin] b 30 Mar 1898 s/o Frederick Durbin & Martha Eckenrode. Sps: William Grassbaugh & wife -WM. (John md 19 Sep 1922 Caroline E. Tilly at St. Ann, Freemont City, OH.)
04 May 1898	James Michael [Durbin] b 30 Mar 1898 s/o Frederick Durbin & Martha Eckenrode. Sps: William Grassbaugh & wife -WM
28 May 1898	Maria Velma Virgillia [Gardner] b 20 May 1898 d/o Edward L. Gardner & Mary F. Weaver. Sps: Francis Gardner & wife -WM. (Maria md 7 Oct 1919 Jonathan Gaines Arnold.)
12 Jun 1898	Cora Agnes Lower b __ May 1898 d/o John M. Lower & Maria Py. Sps: Clement Durbin & Catherine Durbin -WM. (Cora md 12 Nov 1918 Celestine Corwin Blanchard.)
09 Jul 1898	James William [Gaines] b 10 May 1877 (new convert) s/o Uriah Gaines & Ellen Bradfield. Sps:Lloyd Logsdon & Frances [Diamond] Logsdon -WM
10 Jul 1898	Gertrude Cecilia [Welker] b 14 May 1898 d/o George Welker & Eva Mae Stall. Sps: Lewis & Elizabeth Welker.
10 Jul 1898	Maria Ocia [Blubaugh] b 28 Jun 1898 d/o William Henry Blubaugh & Clara Peters (non-cath). Sps: Rev. Wm McDermott & Elizabeth Strapp -WM
11 Jul 1898	Mary Audrey Payne b 16 Aug 1886 d/o William E. [Elias] Payne & Caroline Parrish (not cath, not bapt.). Sps: Rev. Wm McDermott & Elizabeth Strapp -WM

07 Aug 1898	Mary Charlotte [Peters] b 28 Jul 1898 d/o William Peters & Joan Gardner. Sps: John & Maria Gardner -WM
11 Aug 1898	Catherine [Arnold] b 5 Mar 1894 d/o Julius Arnold & Lydia Berkheimer. Sps: Raymond & Maria Arnold -WM
28 Aug 1898	Beatrice Theresa [Durbin] b 25 Aug 1898 d/o Clement E. Durbin & Mary Catherine Durbin. Sps: Frances & Agatha Durbin -WM
05 Sep 1898	Constance Maria [Durbin] b 26 Aug 1898 d/o Thomas B. Durbin & Mary Jane Durbin. Sps: Albert & Selora Logsdon -WM. (Constance md 21 Jun 1922 John C. Halsema of Minster, OH.)
29 Sep 1898	Ethel Maria [Arnold] b 2 May 1893 d/o Francis Arnold & Frances Slusser. Sps: Rev. Wm McDermott & Maria Arnold -WM
29 Sep 1898	Rowena Frances [Arnold] b 24 May 1898 d/o Frances Arnold & Frances Slusser. Sps: Rev. Wm McDermott & Maria Arnold -WM. (Rowena md 29 May 1915 Nicholas A. Engle at St. Vincent, Akron, OH.)
07 Oct 1898	William Alphonso Liguori [Durbin] b 30 Aug 1898 s/o John B. Durbin & Mary A. Blubaugh. Sps: Theodore Durbin & Maria Arnold -WM
07 Oct 1898	Peter Francis [Blubaugh] b 30 Sep 1898 s/o Stephen Lamy Blubaugh & Isabella Sapp. Sps: John Breckler & wife -WM. (Peter md Grace Swaid at St. Sebastian, Akron, OH.)
09 Oct 1898	Lucy Hildegard [Sapp] b 2 oct 1898 d/o Julian Sapp & Catherine Wiggins. Sps: Augustine Gardner & Lucy Sapp -WM
09 Oct 1898	Mary Agnes [King] b 14 Sep 1898 d/o Thomas D. King & Agnes E. Eckenrode. Sps: Joseph Grassbaugh & Emma Eckenrode -WM
16 Oct 1898	Mary Florence [Blubaugh] b 20 Jan 1898 d/o James R. Blubaugh & Victoria F. Smith. Sps: Joseph Blubaugh & wife -WM. (Mary md 11 Jan 1916 John Ralph Colopy.)

27 Nov 1898	Hilary David [Blubaugh] b 18 Nov 1898 s/o Clement A. Blubaugh & Ellen Welker. Sps: William Durbin & Rosa Sapp -WM. (Hilary md 10 Jun 1925 Henrietta Schlaselt at Mt. Vernon, OH.)
15 Jan 1899	Stephen Callistus [Colopy] b 21 Dec 1898 s/o John Colopy & Frances Gardner. Sps: John & Maria Gardner -WM. (Stephen md Mary Eileen Hanna at St. Vincent de Paul, Logensport, IN.)
15 Jan 1899	Francis Joseph [McElroy] b 17 Jan 1875 (new convert) s/o Cornelius McElroy & Maria Thomas. Sps: Benjamin & Elizabeth Durbin -WM
06 Feb 1899	Cyril Ambrose [Smithhisler] b 13 Jan 1899 s/o Henry Smithhisler & Catherine Henegan. Sps: Rev. Wm McDermott & Elizabeth Strapp -WM
09 Apr 1899	Theodora Helena Blubaugh b 18 Feb 1899 d/o Liguori Blubaugh & Mary Coleman. Sps: William Henry & Martella Blubaugh -WM
12 Apr 1899	Joseph Rollin [Sapp] b 19 Mar 1899 s/o Fidelis Sapp & Mary Dete. Sps: Rev. Wm McDermott & Julia Buason; -WM. (md 11 Jun 1924 Frances Condon at St. Vincent de Paul, Mt. Vernon, OH; she was d/o Patrick Condon & Cunta Firmack; Wit: Ambrose Sapp & Sarah Condon.)
13 Apr 1899	Mabel Frances [Parker] b 10 Mar 1899 d/o Benjamin R. Parker & Frances Baker. Sps: Charles Durbin & Isabella Parker -WM
13 Apr 1899	Marie [Parker] b 4 Oct 1887 d/o [Thomas] Solomon Parker & [Mary] Victoria Burris. Sps: Rev. Wm McDermott & Frances Parker -WM
28 May 1899	Charles Francis [Durbin] b 1 May 1899 s/o Frederick Durbin & Martha Eckenrode. Sps: Julius Bailes & Philina Bailes -WM. (Charles md 20 Jun 1951 Ann Bacus at Holy Cross, Cleveland, OH.; Wit: Ralph Durbin & Gertrude Durbin.)
28 May 1899	Ethel Gertrude [Piar] b 2 Mar 1899 d/o Hillery D. Piar & Mary Whistler. Sps: Henry Lower & wife -WM

25 Jun 1899	Aloysius Benedict [Logsdon] b 22 Jun 1899 s/o Albert Logsdon & Selora Durbin. Sps: Sylvester Durbin & Emma Logsdon -WM
06 Aug 1899	Mary Frances [Blubaugh] b 23 Jul 1899 d/o William Henry Blubaugh & Clara Peters. Sps: Edward Durbin & Metta [Armetta] Blubaugh -WM
08 Sep 1899	James Donald [Durbin] b 7 Aug 1899 s/o Edward C. Durbin & Mary E. Blubaugh. Sps: Joseph & Gertrude Durbin -WM
10 Sep 1899	Levi Joseph [Smith] b 13 Aug 1899 s/o Julius A. Smith & Rose Elizabeth Colopy. Sps: Levi Colopy & wife -WM (Levi J. md 1 Sep 1920 Georgia Hazelene Shaw.)
24 Sep 1899	Claude Edward [Blubaugh] b 29 Aug 1899 s/o Sherman William Blubaugh & Lorena G. Smithhisler. Sps: Cosmos & Anna Blubaugh -WM. (Claude md 3 Aug 1919 Flossie Pearl Singer (non-cath).)
01 Oct 1899	Mary Elizabeth [Blubaugh] b 10 Sep 1899 d/o Charles L. Blubaugh & Emma Guenther. Sps: John & Agnes Durbin -WM
12 Oct 1899	Mary Elizabeth [Peterson] b 27 Aug 1899 d/o Decilva Peterson & Aurelia Blubaugh. Sps: Rev. Wm McDermott & Lillian Blubaugh -WM
30 Oct 1899	Desilva Sylvester [Peterson] b 25 Oct 1871 s/o Shadrack Peterson & Rachel Mackey. Sps: George Earnest & Agnes Durbin -WM
19 Nov 1899	Martha Evelyn [Mickley] b 30 May 1899 d/o William Mickley & Aurelia Logsdon. Sps: Henry Blubaugh & Agnes Durbin -WM
09 Dec 1899	Helen Margaret [Basch] b 16 Aug 1899 d/o John Basch & Lucy Gruner. Sps: Francis Dronhard & wife-WM. (Helena md Thomas Bassett at St. Peter, Loudenville, OH.)
21 Dec 1899	Paul [McMahon] b 11 May 1899 s/o Lloyd McMahon & Alberta Baker. Sps: Lawrence Blanchard & Susanna Engle -WM

BAPTISMS

08 Apr 1900   Helena Beatrice Peters b 16 Mar 1900 d/o William Peters
                & Jane Gardner. Sps: Stephen Blubaugh & wife -WM.
                (Helena md 26 Dec 1942 Edward Krout at St. Mary,
                Akron, OH.)

This ends the baptismal records copied.

The records at St. Lukes continue after this date. In concurrence with good
genealogical practice we chose to end our baptismal transcription at this
date to protect the privacy of anyone who might still be living.

MARRIAGES

18 Mar 1830	John [Alton] Arnold md Christina Sapp. [Late entry]
14 May 1832	Patrick McGough md Ellen/Helen Durbin. [Late entry]
10 Apr 1833	James McKenzie md Elsie Arnold. [Late entry]
30 Jul 1837	Thomas White md Agnes Durbin. [Late entry]
30 Jul 1837	James Logue md Mrs. Mary [Dial] McKenzie. [Later entry]
08 Aug 1837	Joseph Sapp md [widow Mrs. Margaret McKenzie. [Late entry]
20 May 1839	Thomas McGough md Druscilla Losh, having formerly been married by the squire.
30 May 1840	Michael Sheneberger (s/o Michael [Sheneberger] & Magdalena Boeshart) md Margaret Richman (d/o Martin Richman & Catherine Anchler); Wit: Martin Richman, Henry Shenenberger, Martin Ambrouche.
23 Sep 1840	James Sapp (s/o George [Sapp] and Margaret Log [Logsdon]) md Winifred Blubaugh (d/o Benjamin [Blubaugh] & Honora Logsdon); Wit: William Carter & John Log [Logue].
15 Oct 1840	Benjamin Blubaugh (s/o [Benjamin Blubaugh] & Rebecca Sapp) md Charlotte Heckler; Wit: George Sapp & Benjamin Draper.
22 Nov 1840	Thomas Garety md Elizabeth McKenzie; Wit: Gabriel McKenzie & Henry Porter.
13 Dec 1840	Jacob Holler md Catharine Swendal; Wit: George Sapp.
14 Dec 1840	John Collins md Honora Durbin; Wit: Elijah Durbin & Benjamin Durbin.
14 Feb 1841	Daniel Horn md Jane Rose Durbin Wit: Benjamin Durbin & Baptist Durbin.
22 Apr 1841	Benjamin Draper md Martha Sapp; Wit: George Sapp & Levi Sapp.

ST. LUKE'S RECORDS

02 Jan 1842	Gaspard Kehler md Maria Arnold.
27 Jan 1842	David Garret md Brigetta Breunon; Wit: George Dunn & John Martin.
11 Apr 1842	Andrew Kronenberger md Apolla Ulm; Wit: Robert Fitzgerald & Joan Marot.
12 Apr 1842	William Zach Logsdon md Sara Buckingham; Wit: Absalom Buckingham & Daniel Buckingham.

===

23 Jan 1844	Elias McKenzie md Mary Blubaugh.
15 Apr 1844	William Kelley md Eliza Welker.
06 Jun 1844	Gaspar Sheneberger md Apollonia Fritz.
15 Sep 1844	James Welsh md Catharine McNamara; Wit: Michael Welsh & Edgar Brent.
__ Oct 1844	Jacob McKenzie md Esther Sapp.
20 Oct 1844	Michael Smithhisler md Mary A. Millis.
21 Nov 1844	J. Colglesser md Elizabeth Blubaugh (Sapp).
13 Jul 1845	James W. Bradfield md Sara Ann Sapp.
05 Sep 1845	Washington Welker md Phebe Ann Kreakbaum.
18 Sep 1845	Richard Arnold md Eliza Harden.
28 Sep 1845	Michael Welsh md Elizabeth Crawford.
27 Nov 1845	Cyrus Stevens md Mary Jane Smith.
27 Nov 1845	Ellis Ashburn md Rebecca Durbin.
01 Jan 1846	Benedict Magers md Mary Trullinger.
08 Jan 1846	[William Elliot] Welker md Rachel Durbin.
19 Feb 1846	Benjamin Magers md Lucinda Porter.
22 Feb 1846	Michael Grim md Phebe Weoperzaum.
19 Jul 1846	Abraham C. Black md Sarah Catherine Colopy.
07 Aug 1846	George B. Parker md Henrietta Magers.
27 Sep 1846	Joseph Bechtel md Maria Brophy.
18 Oct 1846	Jacob Milless md Margaret Mowery.
30 Oct 1846	Jacob/John Boeshart md Catherine Schmidtt.

MARRIAGES

01 Nov 1846	Zachary Blubaugh md Lydia Colglesser.
25 Nov 1846	Vincent Haverick md Hester Ann Magers.
11 Jan 1847	Levi Sapp md Matilda Arnold.
09 Feb 1847	Raphael Magers md Margaret Welker.
11 Feb 1847	Samuel Hopwood md Nancy Jane Payne.
15 Feb 1847	Henry Ridgely md M. Larany.
01 Mar 1847	Peter Ferenbaugh md Barbara Wiggand ?
31 May 1847	Elias Arnold md Ann Lovina Logsdon.
20 Jun 1847	John Blair md Anna Handland [Hanlin ?].
23 Jun 1847	Conrad Brodin md Catarina Aberly [Eberly ?].
27 Aug 1847	Jacob Welsh/Walsh & Bridget Welsh.
12 Oct 1847	Jacob McVay md Margaret Anna Crowner.
08 Nov 1847	John Baptist (Jackson) Welker md Sarah Miranda Dial.
18 Jan 1848	Jacob Smith (non cath) md Elizabeth Morton/Martin.
__ Feb 1848	James White md Anna Sapp; Wit: Jackson Shaffer & Maria Teresa Boulger.
__ Feb 1848	Jonathan Arnold md Maria Blubaugh; Wit: Laurence Magers & Jane Buckingham.
29 Feb 1848	John Hamer md Margaret Whisler.
29 Feb 1848	Lawrence King md Hannah Draper.
29 Feb 1848	Laurence Magers md Susanna McKenzie.
15 Jul 1848	John Bechtel md Catherine King.
15 Jul 1848	Lewis C. Frinier/Frazier md Martha Walsh.

01 Jan 1852	Andy Kemmerer md Ablonia Schop; Wit: F. Fitzmyre & wife.
16 Feb 1852	Hannibal Bernard Leonard md Catherine A. Holden; Wit: William Leonard & Catherine Cassidy.
17 Feb 1852	Andrew Henley md Margaret Reed; Wit: Peter & Maria Walsh.

18 Feb 1852	Patrick Dial md Margaret Kinney; Wit: Patrick Murphy & Elizabeth McKenzie.
01 Nov 1852	Jacob Downs md Maria Marshall.
02 Nov 1852	James J. Skilling md Caroline Allerding; Wit: J. Crowner & J. Brent.
09 Jan 1853	Joseph Blubaugh md Maria Anna Linebaugh; Wit: Jonathan Colopy & Rachel Blubaugh.
06 Feb 1853	Joseph Reuben Cook md Sarah Arnold; Wit: Jacob Henry Porter & Maria Dial.
21 Feb 1853	Casper Weil md Catherine Armbrust; Wit: H. Hosfeld & J. Armbrust.
02 Apr 1853	Clement Hosfeld md Maria Anna Armbrust; Wit: John Witman & Elizabeth Marshall.
18 Apr 1853	John Durbin md Lucinda Sapp; Wit: George Sapp & Delila White.
04 Sep 1853	Joseph Engle md Susanna Durbin; Wit: Benjamin & Maria Anna Durbin.
06 Oct 1853	Martin Bowman md Maria Porter; Wit: John Porter & Elias Arnold.
13 Oct 1853	Francis Payne md Samantha Clark; Wit: Levi Clark & Harriet Critchfield.
13 Oct 1853	Levi Clark md Harriet Critchfield; Wit: Francis Payne & wife.
10 Nov 1853	John Mattingly md Jane Durbin: Wit: Jacob Mattingly & Emma Brent.
10 Nov 1853	Christopher Mattingly md Teresa Durbin; Wit: Joseph Mattingly & Joanna Buckingham.
06 Jan 1854	Vincent Piar md Rachel Blubaugh; Wit: Francis Fitzmyre & Mag. Fitz.

==

28 Sep 1855	Simon Sapp md Susan Willis; Wit: Levi Sapp & Anna Walker.

22 Oct 1855	Ignatius McKenzie md Susanna Sapp; Wit: John Blubaugh & Margaret Logue.
02 Jan 1856	John Blubaugh md Harriet Eckenrode; Wit: Stephen Blubaugh & Agnes Eckenrode.
20 Jan 1856	Solomon Durbin md Samantha [Mary] Reynolds; Wit: Hiram Trullinger & Sarah McGough.
05 Feb 1856	Jonathan Dial md Elizabeth Sapp; Wit: Edward Blubaugh & Maria Bowman.
20 Feb 1856	Jonathan A. Colopy md Sarah Jane Berry; Wit: Edward Colopy & Martha Blubaugh.
13 Jul 1856	Peter Magers md Mrs. Sarah Logsdon; Wit: Jacob McGough & wife.
16 Jul 1856	David J. [Jackson] Shaffer md Matilda Dial; Wit: Harrison Jacobs & Eliza Sloan.
29 Jul 1856	Joseph Clutz md Eliza Kelly; Wit: Catharine Welker & Maria Anna Durbin.
25 Aug 1856	Francis Blubaugh md Julia Anna Garland; Wit: Stephen & Martha Blubaugh.
26 Aug 1856	Edward Blubaugh md Elizabeth Ann Stevens; Wit: Jos. Hosfeld & wife Genevieve Henley.
08 Jan 1857	Joseph Postlewait md Winifred White; Wit: Laurence White & W. Morton.
08 Feb 1857	Victor Eifert md Matilda Gardner Wit: Joseph & Martha Eifert.
23 Feb 1857	Stephen Blubaugh md Mary C. Breckler; Jos Colopy & Martha Blubaugh.
29 Jun 1857	William Durbin md Margaret Sapp; Levi & Maria Sapp.
08 Sep 1857	William Brewer md Mary Anna Sapp; Wit: Simeon Sapp & J. Brent.
19 Jan 1858	Benjamin Durbin md Margaret McNamara; Wit: Francis McNamara & Sarah Porter at Mt. Vernon.
24 Jan 1858	Mathias Tressel md (first) Wilhemina Smith; Wit: Nicholas Hollet & Catharine Smith.

09 May 1858	Patrick Lowery md Anna Branagan; Wit: Chris Branagan & Theresa Dial.
27 Jun 1858	William Dermody md Anna Dolan; Wit: Michael Dolan & Maria Barley.
27 Jun 1858	William Carter md Lydia Ann Barley.
05 Sep 1858	Frederick Bumpus md Elizabeth Allerding; Wit: <u>Sap</u> Blubaugh & Nicholas Hollet.
08 Sep 1858	William Brewer md Mary Ann Sapp.
06 Jan 1859	Francis M. Durbin md Genevieve Henley; Wit: Henry Durbin & Elizabeth Henley.
07 Mar 1859	James Trullinger md Mary Frasier; Wit: Margaret & Raphael Durbin.
14 Jun 1859	Francis McNamara md Sarah E. Porter; Wit: Eliz Dial & Joseph Colopy.
08 Aug 1859	Peter Neff md Frances Magers; Wit: John Kelly & Maria Anna Bailes.
02 Jan 1860	Hilary Blubaugh md Sarah Ellen Bailes; Wit: Jos. Colopy & Mary Ann Bailes.
02 Jan 1860	William D. [Darius] Snow md Elizabeth A. [Ann] Blubaugh; Wit: Jacob Rodger & wife.
19 Jan 1860	Phillip Kline md Emiline Sapp; Wit: Jos. Caughlin & Emma Brent.
29 Jan 1860	Michael Trullinger md Sarah M. Bricker; Wit: W. Critchfield & Martha Trullinger.
13 Feb 1860	Nicholas Hollet md Catherine Eifert; Wit: Michael Hollet & Catherine Smith.
14 Feb 1860	Ambrose Logsdon md Maria (Eckenrode) Rimlinger ; Wit: W. Logsdon & Julia Eckenrode.
01 Jul 1860	Henry Raisen md Adaline Bower; Wit: J. N. & M. Allerding.
07 Oct 1860	Peter Walsh md Catherine Connor; wit: Pat Barry & Margaret Keefer.

150

MARRIAGES

07 Oct 1860	Patrick Connors md Melissa [Ellen] Rankin; Wit: Thomas Barry & Margaret Campion.
08 Jan 1861	Ben Eckenrode md Margaret Shaffer; Wit: Joanna Eckenrode & M. Roof.
17 Jan 1861	Edward Colopy md Harriett Farquhar at Mt. Vernon Wit: Edmund & Frances Brent.
20 Jan 1861	Francis M. Gardner md Mary J. Allerding; Wit: John Gardner & Maria Allerding.
16 Apr 1861	Raphael Durbin md Barbara Buck; Wit: Peter Durbin & Maria Buck.
28 May 1861	Elias [P.] Porter md Margaret Durbin, a Baptist; Wit: Henry Durbin & Maria Anna Bailes.
21 Nov 1861	Joseph Francis Millis md Elizabeth White; Wit: Mich Millis & Normanda Sapp.
__ __ 1862	John McNamara md Caroline Beam; Wit: Ben Blubaugh & M. McNamara.
06 Jun 1862	John H. Anthony md Christina Gardner; Wit: John & Catherine Henley.
12 Jun 1862	Gregory Henley md (second) Jane Buckingham; Wit: Absolom Durbin & Penelope Bricker.
15 Jun 1862	Henry Hosfeld md Savina Shaub; Wit: Joseph Millis & Domina Fitzmyre.
29 Jun 1862	Edward W. Brent md Ellen Gertrude McFarland; Wit: Jacob Rowley & Cecilia Brent.
12 Aug 1862	Adam McGough md Maria Taylor; Wit: Henry Durbin & E. Hammond.
24 Aug 1862	Anthony Whisler md Catherine Smith; Jacob Smyth & Barbara Homan.
12 Feb 1863	Henry Whitman md Catherine Gardner; Wit: John Gardner & Marie Gardner.
03 May 1863	Henry Peterson md Anna Whisler; Wit: J. Peterson & Sara _____.
04 Jun 1863	George Beam md Elizabeth Boeshart; WiT: G. C. Henley & Cath Shaub.

14 Jun 1863	Edward Carpenter md Frances Sapp at Mt. Vernon; Wit: Fr. Magers & Catherine Porter.
19 Sep 1863	Laurence Payne md Sarah A. Coleman; Wit: George Payne & wife [Anna Croy].
29 Mar 1864	Michael Homan md Elizabeth Losh; Wit: Martin Homann & Magdalena Losh.
10 Apr 1864	Anthony Smithhisler md Martha E. [Eleanor] Blubaugh; Wit: Francis Hess & Magdalena Shaub.
26 Apr 1864	John McNamara md Emiline Agnes Hammond; Wit: Peter Durbin & Joanna Bricker.
12 Aug 1864	Laurence Hosey md Clara Ellen Beardshear Wit: Emma Brent.
02 May 1865	Ferdinand Eifert md Antoinette Fritz; Wit: Martin Fisher & Maria Sheneberger.
14 Sep 1865	William Anthony md Maria M. Gardner; Wit: A. Whisler & Margaret Breckler.
22 Aug 1865	John Gardner md Mary Breckler; Wit: Jonathan Whisler & Margaret Breckler.
23 Nov 1865	Charles Bengot md Magdalena Shaub; Wit: Philip Smithhisler & Mag. Bigler.
31 Dec 1865	Levi Swarts md Margaret McKenzie; Wit: John Swarts & Catherine Durbin.
01 Jan 1866	Absalom Durbin md Elizabeth Henley; Wit: Peter Durbin & Penelope Bricker.
03 Jan 1866	John W. Beam md Maria Sheneberger; Wit: Nicholas Sheneberger & Philomena Beam.
30 Jan 1866	John Allerding md Apolonia Whisler; Wit: F. & Cath Allerding.
08 Apr 1866	William Sapp md C. R. Ebersole: Wit: Frank Sapp & Matilda A. Noel.
24 Apr 1866	Conrad Hammer md Magdalena Losh; Wit: John Weber & Anna Losh.
27 Aug 1866	Francis Durbin md Susannah Elizabeth Sapp; Wit: Francis Sapp & Joanna Bricker.

MARRIAGES

29 Aug 1866	Anthony Garland md Jane Witt; Wit: H. E. Brent & Maria Walsh.
30 Sep 1866	Martin Homan md Cath Miller; Wit: J. Brent & Julius Tarderville.
11 Nov 1866	Henry Shults md Nora E. Blubaugh; Wit: George Sapp & Angeline Shults.
29 Nov 1866	Leo Blubaugh md Ellen Dial; Wit: Peter Blubaugh & Matilda Dial.
17 Jan 1867	Peter Blubaugh md Margaret Breckler; Wit: Fr. Logsdon & Cath Blubaugh.
12 Feb 1867	Francis Logsdon & Catherine Blubaugh; Wit: Anthony Shaffer & Lucinda Logsdon.
05 Apr 1867	William Henley/Healy md Briget Sheke/Sheehy; Wit: John Dermody & Maria Delany.
15 Sep 1867	Jacob Colopy md Maria E. Myers; Wit: Anthony White & wife.
01 Oct 1867	Philip J. Smithhisler md Maria H. White; Wit: Francis Sapp & Alice Critchfield.
13 Oct 1867	William Sapp md Hattie Bailey; Wit: George Sapp & Jesse Gardner.
29 Oct 1867	Charles Durbin md Eleanor [Frances] Hess; Wit: Levi Colopy & "Bell" [Isabel] Hess.
12 Dec 1867	Richard T. Shreve md Mary Jane Garland; Wit: John T. Roger, Emma Brent.
11 Feb 1868	John Weaver md Maria Anna Losh; Wit: Adam Weaver (bro) & E. Losh.
18 Oct 1868	Charles Logston md Amelia Hays; Wit: J. Dial & Emily Durbin.
24 Nov 1868	Henry Durbin md Catherine Carpenter; Wit: Lyman Durbin & Mellissa Durbin.
20 Jan 1869	Joseph Durbin md Maria Brown; Wit: Bapt Durbin & M. Logsdon.
31 Jan 1869	Baptist Durbin md Angeline Shults; Wit: E. Durbin & Tylor Shults.

13 May 1869	Peter Miller md Isabella Morrison; Wit: Ch. Miller & Eliza Morrison.
01 Nov 1869	John Sylvester Durbin md Maria Paul; Wit: Francis Sapp & Barbara Paul.
17 Nov 1869	Henry Shaub md Maria Boeshart; Wit: Lewis & Cath Boeshart.
05 Jan 1870	John Sapp md Matilda Lybarger; Wit: Francis Durbin & wife.
18 Jan 1870	Jacob Wepler md Christina Fesler; Wit: Joseph Fesler & Rachel Wepler.
24 Apr 1870	Gregory Henley md Rachel Blubaugh; Wit: Peter Blubaugh & wife.
21 Jun 1870	William F. Todd md Maria Shields; Wit: Emma Brent & J. Bricker.
12 Sep 1870	Joseph Boeshart md Maria Rosa Homan; Wit: Lewis & Cath Boeshart.
09 Oct 1870	James Smith md Maria E. Blubaugh; Wit: Christopher Swingle & F. Blubaugh.
23 Nov 1870	A. J. Zimmerman md Frances Welsh; Wit: John & Rosa Zimmerman.
16 Jan 1871	John Davidson md Harriet [Ellen] Sapp.
02 Feb 1871	Marion B. Thoma md Bridget McNamara; Wit: Ben Blubaugh & wife.
14 Feb 1871	John B. Mattingly md Mary D. Engle; Wit: Michael Berky & D. J. Engle.
15 Feb 1871	Landen Welker md Viola Lybarger; Wit: Henry Durbin & wife & Dilly.
16 Feb 1871	Lewis Boeshart md Margaret Homan Wit: Adam & Catherine Boeshart
11 Apr 1871	Christopher Swingle & Florence J. Blubaugh; Wit: Roman Sapp & Fr. Blubaugh.
25 Apr 1871	John Krownapple md Margaret Losh; Wit: Anthony Crownapple & Maria Losh.

154

MARRIAGES

03 Jul 1871	Edward Yeager md Ellen Ferrel; Wit: Jos. Yeager & Maria Metzger.
14 Aug 1871	Jacob Fesler md Catherine Paul; Wit: John Durbin & wife.
15 Aug 1871	Leo J. Gardner md Catherine Blubaugh; Wit: John Breckler & Flora Sapp.
11 Sep 1871	John P. Breckler md Flora Sapp; Wit: Sherman White & S. Baker.
12 Sep 1871	Augustus Gaume md Mary M. [Matilda] Colopy; Wit: Emma Squires & Levi Colopy.
14 Nov 1871	Xavier Beck md Mary Fesler; Wit: Martin Weber & Philomena Bliel.
08 Feb 1872	Charles Henley md Frances Helen Giffin; Wit: Lewis Henley & Penelope Bricker.
11 Feb 1872	John Baptist Bricker md Rosanna Hyatt; Wit: Will Welsh & Jane Bricker.
12 Feb 1872	Francis A. Gardner md Sarah Zimmerman; Wit: Dan Zimmerman & Ellen Miller.
07 Apr 1872	Joseph Zimmerman md Helen Miller; Wit: Levi Colopy & Melissa Durbin.
24 Apr 1872	Francis Blubaugh md Elizabeth A. Sapp; Wit: Bapt Durbin Sr. & wife.
01 Sep 1872	Phillip Kline md Julia A. King; Wit: Peter King & Martha Buck.
10 Oct 1872	Vincent Mattingly md Maria C. Durbin; Wit: Mich Mattingly & Maria Sapp.
14 Apr 1873	Leroy Cochran md Isabella Connor; Wit: E. F. Payne & M. Slowley.
14 Apr 1873	Jacob Conlon md Bridget McCormick; Wit: Pat McGovern & Margaret McCormick.
17 Jun 1873	William Kyser md Margaret Filerand; Wit: ___ Blubaugh & Maria Kyser.
09 Sep 1873	James Homan md Margaret Kaylor; Wit: J. Kaylor & Elizabeth Homan.

155

28 Oct 1873	Francis McKenzie md Emma Blubaugh; Wit: Levi Colopy & Maria Smithhisler.
22 Apr 1874	George Durbin md Catherine Buck; Wit: Pius Durbin & Kate King.
03 Aug 1875	Joseph F. Blubaugh md Lillis Jane Smith; Wit: Lysander Simpkins & Clara Sapp.
04 Nov 1875	Isaac Stevens md Laura Elliott; Wit: Thomas Critchfield & Isadora Critchfield.
22 Nov 1875	Wesley Shaw md Clara Sapp; Wit: John Spencer & Penelope Bricker.
10 Feb 1876	Gasper Paul md Martha Piar; Wit: Martin Riplo & Philomena Bliel.
15 Feb 1876	Martin P. Hammond md Mary Keziah Sapp; Wit: John Thomas Durbin & Hattie Porter.
22 Feb 1876	John M. Smith md Eunice Agnes Carey; Wit: John Alexander & Jane Blubaugh.
25 Apr 1876	Benedict Durbin md Josephine Smithhisler; Wit: Lyman Durbin & Mary Engle.
02 May 1876	Eugene Gaume md Sara Eugenia Durbin; Wit: William Durbin & Cath Smithhisler.
11 Jul 1876	Peter King md Anna Miller; Wit: Gasper Miller & Maria King.
04 Sep 1876	Daniel Bricker md Josephine Smithhisler; Wit: John Smithhisler & Molly Murphy.
17 Oct 1876	John William Alexander md Phedora J. [Jane] Blubaugh; Jacob Blubaugh & Maria Engle.
14 Nov 1876	George Phillips md Catherine Weber; Wit: Rick Arnold.
16 Nov 1876	Anthony Crownapple md Adela Losh; Wit: Maria Losh & John Fritz.
03 Jan 1877	William [E.] Durbin md Catherine Smithhisler; Wit: Michael Smithhisler.
12 Feb 1877	John Smithhisler md Mary Murphy; Wit: Michael Smithhisler & _____ Payne.

MARRIAGES

04 Jun 1877	John Taylor Shults md Alice Jane Rice Wit: Frederick Rice & Sarah Wanders.
26 Jun 1877	Charles H. Miller md Della J. Engle; Wit: Robert Engle & _____ Durbin.
22 Jan 1878	Hubert Boner md Margaret Blubaugh; Wit: John & Maria Breckler.
14 Feb 1878	Martin Reigle md Angeline Durbin; Wit: Basil Blubaugh & Cath Riegle.
14 Feb 1878	Andrew A. Durbin md Martha Ellen Losh; Wit: _____ Weaver & M. Engle.
06 Aug 1878	James R. Blubaugh md Victoria F. Smith; Wit: Augustus Blubaugh.
07 Oct 1879	Louis G. Welker md Lucy Colopy; Wit: Jacob Colopy & Anna Connelly.
07 Oct 1879	John McMahon md Victoria Snow; Wit: _____ Snow & _____ McMahon.
25 Nov 1879	[Benjamin] Oliver Arnold md Emma J. Gaines; Wit: Augustus Blubaugh.
03 Feb 1880	Michael J. Smithhisler md Victoria B. Arnold; Wit: Henry Smithhisler & Helena Arnold.
12 Apr 1880	Zachary Blubaugh md Margaret Helen Engle; Wit: Augustus Blubaugh & Maria Blubaugh.
13 Apr 1880	Levi Whitman md Maria M Gardner; Wit: John Dible & Elizabeth Whitman.
19 Aug 1880	Loran Dial md Mariann Ross; Wit: William Welker & Clarence McKenzie.
05 Oct 1880	Louis D. Welker md Maria Elizabeth Richards; Wit: Basil Blubaugh & N. King.
27 Oct 1880	Levi F. Colopy md Melissa A. Durbin; Wit: Hugh Connelly & Helen A. Arnold.
25 Nov 1880	Samuel F. Davis (non cath) md Elizabeth Blubaugh; Wit: Jacob Blubaugh & Jane Davis. (Samuel promised not to interfer with wife's religous duties or religous training of the children.)

27 Nov 1880	[William] Thomas Critchfield md Emma [Florence] Sapp; Wit: Richard Arnold & Maria Blubaugh.
27 Sep 1881	William N/M Engle md Amelia Colopy; Wit: Elinor Colopy & Eugene Durbin.
29 Sep 1881	A. G. Welker md Anna E. Conley; Wit: Roman Sapp & Albin Colopy.
08 Nov 1881	John B. Durbin md Mary A. Blubaugh; Wit: Raymond Arnold & Mame Engle.
02 May 1882	George Norman South md Susan Rachel McKenzie ; Wit: Jacob McKenzie & Mary McKenzie.
09 Aug 1882	William Edward Hopwood md Ellen Stevens; Wit: Jacob Bectel & Alice Critchfield.
07 Nov 1882	Patrick Purcell md Helena Sapp; Wit: Thomas Hays & Eugenia Sapp.
28 Nov 1882	Daniel Flecknoe md Mary Simpkins; Wit: Charles Stowe & Frances Simpkins.
23 May 1883	James Edward Colopy md Margaret J. McMahon; Wit: Clement Durbin & Isabella Colopy.
05 Sep 1883	Henry Smithhisler md Catherine Hanagan; Wit: Francis Smithhisler & Isabella Hanagan.
06 Nov 1883	Benjamin Durbin md Mrs. Sarah Elizabeth [Porter] McNamara; Wit: Lloyd Logsdon & Frances (Fanny) Diamond.
20 Nov 1883	W. A. Mattingly md Louisa Larabee; Wit: ____ Mattingly & Josephine Durbin.
27 Nov 1883	Calvin Magers md Ellen Arnold; Wit: Basil Blubaugh & Anna Rice.
23 Sep 1884	Lloyd Logsdon md Frances Diamond; Clement & Selora Durbin.
01 Dec 1884	Julian Sapp md Catherine Wiggins; Wit: Daniel Diamond & Selora Durbin.
15 Jan 1885	Peter Smith md Louisa Gardner; Wit: Augustus Whitman & ____ Smith.

MARRIAGES

17 Feb 1885	Joseph [Hill] Colopy md Mrs. Eliza (Baker) Porter widow (non cath); Wit: Jonathan Colopy & wife.
05 Jul 1885	Stephen Durbin md Helen Gamble; Wit: Ella Vance & Anna Piar.
06 Oct 1885	Philip Homan md Sara Catherine Sheneberger; Wit: Ed Carpenter & _____.
19 Jan 1886	Philip Millis md Josephine Weaver; Wit: Frances Smithhisler & Alicia King.
08 Mar 1886	Patrick Finneran md Isabella Henegan; Wit: Francis Hanagan & Catherine Berry.
01 Aug 1886	Francis Arnold md [Frances Slusser] Wit: Martin Hammond & Joseph Losh.
10 Aug 1886	Bernard J. Mattingly md Genevieve Sapp; Wit: ____ Mattingly & Lucy Sapp.
28 Sep 1886	Benjamin F. Durbin md Theodora [Jane] McNamara; Wit: George Smithhisler & Francis Durbin.
12 Oct 1886	William H. McNamara md Lora H. Banbury.
16 Oct 1886	Daniel Diamond md Rachel Blubaugh; Wit: Henry Blubaugh & ____ Logsdon.
14 Nov 1886	John McGough md Elizabeth Burris.
21 Feb 1887	Henry B. Eckenrode md Eugenia B. Durbin; Wit: Purcel Durbin & Josephine Durbin.
26 Apr 1887	Albert Logsdon md Selora Durbin; Wit: John Engle & Eugene Durbin.
10 May 1887	Giles A. Butts md Eva M. McCarter; Wit: M. Butts & _____ Butts.
24 May 1887	Lewis A. Mickley md Charlotte A. Logsdon; Wit: J. E. Greer & Alice King.
28 ___ 1887	George W. Parker md Artensia E. Engle; Wit: Charles Engle & Maria Engle.
02 Aug 1887	Henry D. Blubaugh md Anna V. Durbin; Wit: Edward & Catherine Durbin.
01 Nov 1887	William Welker md Barbara Knout.

10 Jan 1888	Jacob Lower md Mary Shults; Wit: Sherman Blubaugh & Ida Blubaugh.
11 Apr 1888	Clement E. Durbin md Mary Catherine Durbin; Wit: Thomas Durbin & Eugenia Durbin.
17 Apr 1888	William Engle md Catherine Pipes; Wit: John McGough & Ellen Vance.
01 May 1888	Leo J. [Judson] Arnold md Lydia Anna McCleary.
__ Sep 1888	Lawrence V. Blanchard md Florence A. Engle (non cath). Wit: Robert Hutson & Ella Vance.
14 Dec 1888	Clement A. Blubaugh (s/o Hilary & Sarah [Ellen] Blubaugh) md Mary [Ella] Welker (d/o George & Maria Welker); Wit: Edward Charles Durbin & Gertrude Maria Durbin.
10 Sep 1889	Charles C. Logsdon (s/o David Logsdon [& Rebecca Uhl]) md Alice Critchfield (d/o Hiram Critchfield [& Harriet Porter]; Wit: Jacob Gillaine & Joanna Jones.
28 Nov 1889	Thomas Blubaugh (s/o Zachary Blubaugh [& Lydia Colglesser]) md [Margaret] Sophia Shuman (d/o John Shuman); Wit: Francis Durbin & Agatha Swingle.
27 May 1890	William [Elias] Smithhisler (s/o Michael Smithhisler & Mary Millis) md Theodora ["Dora"] Burris (d/o Lyah Burris); Wit: Sherman Blubaugh & Lovina Smithhisler.
21 Oct 1890	Thomas B. Durbin (s/o John L. Durbin & Margaret Colopy) md Mary Jane Durbin (d/o Benjamin Durbin & Margaret McNamara); Wit: Francis Durbin & Alberta Durbin.
22 Oct 1890	Francis Durbin (s/o Charles Durbin) md Eva Asher (non cath, d/o Thomas Asher); Wit: George Logsdon & Martha Homan.
07 Jan 1891	Alva Frizzell (non cath) (s/o George Frizzell) md Gertrude Durbin (d/o Francis Durbin); Wit: Francis Hanagan & Alberta Henley.

MARRIAGES

13 Jan 1891	Sherman William Blubaugh (s/o John J. Blubaugh & Mary P. Dial) md Lorena G. Smithhisler (d/o George Smithhisler); Wit: George Smithhisler & w/o Julius Durbin & Victoria Blubaugh.
15 Apr 1891	Ulyssus G. Church (non cath, s/o Joseph Church) md Martha Homan (d/o Michael Homan); Wit: Charles Weaver & Margaret Homan.
02 Jun 1891	Jacob Carlin (s/o Michael Carlin) md Elizabeth Kauf (non cath), d/o John Kauf; Wit: Jacob O'Hern & wife.
05 Jun 1892	James [Logsdon] (s/o George Logsdon) md Margaret [Homan] (d/o Michael Homan); Wit: George Logsdon & Maria Weaver.
09 Apr 1893	Harley C. Drake (non cath) md Agnes Blubaugh (d/o Henry Blubaugh; Wit: George Logsdon & Rebecca Logsdon.
30 Aug 1893	Julius A. [Smith] (s/o James Smith & Maria E. Blubaugh) md Rose Elizabeth [Colopy] (d/o Joseph Colopy & Mary Jane Durbin); Wit: Elmer Parker & Josephine Durbin.
19 Sep 1893	Edward [Burns] (s/o Jacob Burns) md Emma [Sapp] (d/o Francis Sapp & Mary Ann Carney); Wit: Charles Burns & Maria Sapp.
09 Jan 1894	Ligouri [Blubaugh] (s/o Leo Blubaugh & Ellen Dial] md Mary Theresa [Coleman] (d/o John Coleman & Ann Liffer); Wit: Edward Durbin & Maria Durbin.
23 Jan 1894	Francis [Roland Gaume] (s/o Augustus Gaume & Matilda Colopy) md Frances [Isabel Durbin] d/o John Durbin & Lucy Sapp); Wit: Lewis Gaume & Josephine Durbin.
02 Apr 1894	Rollin [Henegan] (s/o Patrick Henegan) md Delila (non cath) [Smith] (d/o John Smith); Wit: Henry & Catherine Smithhisler.
16 Apr 1894	Edward [C. Durbin] (s/o Raphael Durbin) md Mary E. [Blubaugh] (d/o Leo Blubaugh & Ellen Dial); Wit: Francis & Gertrude Durbin).
05 Jun 1894	Joseph [Fritz] (s/o Jacob Fritz) md Helena [Blubaugh] (d/o John Blubaugh); Wit: Francis Stoltz & Ida Blubaugh.

06 Jun 1894   Theodore [Durbin] (s/o John Durbin & Lucy Sapp) md Anna Lou [Purcell] (d/o Charles Purcell); Wit: Edward Gardner & Josephine Durbin.

12 Jun 1894   Raymond [Arnold] (s/o Richard Arnold) md Mary [Engle] (d/o Joseph Engle & Susanna Durbin); Wit: Elmer Parker & Elizabeth Durbin.

23 Aug 1894   Joseph [C. Harlett] (s/o Joseph Harlett) md Ida Frances [Blubaugh] (d/o John J. Blubaugh & Mary P. Dial); Wit: Francis Harlett & Victoria Blubaugh.

16 Oct 1894   Stephen [Lamy Blubaugh] (s/o Peter Blubaugh & Margaret Breckler) md Isabella [Sapp] (d/o Francis Sapp); Wit: Jerome Gardner & Maria Sapp.

06 Nov 1894   George [Logsdon] (s/o George Logsdon) md Maria Almeda [McFadden] (d/o Harrison McFadden); Wit: Benjamin Logsdon & Lucy Hammond.

26 Nov 1894   Adam C. Beltz (non cath) md Frances E. Durbin; Wit: Julius Bailes & Philena Durbin.

27 Nov 1895   Paul Welker (non cath) md Mary Amelia Beck Wit: William Grassbaugh & Alberta Durbin.

07 Jan 1896   John Kelly md Emma Beam; Wit: Julius Bailes & Helena Beam

24 Jan 1896   Thomas Swartz md Maria Workman (non cath); Wit: Elmer Parker & Frances Parker.

12 Feb 1896   Alva B. Kemp md Helena B. Peters; Wit: William Peters & Joanna Gardner.

12 May 1896   John F. Gardner md Emma Josephine Durbin; Wit: Edward Gardner & Maria Weaver.

13 May 1896   Julius Bailes md Philena J. Durbin; Wit: Fidelis Sapp & Agnes Durbin.

24 Jun 1896   Francis Durbin md Agnes Swingle; Wit: Peter Durbin & Bertha Swingle.

27 Oct 1896   John Kuhn md Flora Collins; Wit: Jacob & Margaret Miller.

MARRIAGES

24 Nov 1896	William Grassbaugh md Bertha Durbin; Wit: Joseph Grassbaugh & Elizabeth Durbin.
16 Feb 1897	Gregory Henley md Honora Peters; Wit: John Henley & Ida Whistler.
15 Jun 1897	Edward [L.] Gardner md Mary [F.] Weaver; Wit: Augustus Gardner & Rosa Weaver.
29 Sep 1897	William Peters md Jane Gardner; Wit: Germanus Gardner & Maria Trotter.
29 Sep 1897	Germanus Gardner md Maria Trotter; Wit: William Peters & Joanna Peters.
05 Oct 1897	William Henry Blubaugh md Clara Peters; Wit: William Peters & Joanna Peters.
25 Jan 1898	Philip Dawson (non cath, s/o Jacob & Henrietta Dawson) md Jennie Butts (d/o Henry Butts & Anna Smith). Wit: Charles Workman & Elizabeth Butts.
23 Aug 1898	Henry [Bernard] Young (non cath) & Anna Frances Fesler; Wit: Laudin Grassbaugh & _____ Fesler.
24 Nov 1898	James W. Gaines md Mary E. Shults; Wit: Samuel Shults & Anetta Banberry.
25 Dec 1898	William Mickly (non cath) and Aurelia Logsdon; Wit: Ben & Maria Logsdon.
12 Jan 1899	David Swarts md Anna Mavis (non cath); Wit: Mavis's brother & sister.
01 Feb 1899	Francis McElroy md Maria McGough; Wit: John Durbin & Elizabeth Strapp.
09 Feb 1899	[Robert] Elmer Parker md Elizabeth Gaines; Wit: Walter McKenzie & Frances Parker.
19 Sep 1899	George Stevens (non cath) md Isabella Innis' Wit: Emma Starner & Elizabeth Strapp.
20 Oct 1899	Francis Shults md Elmira Jackson (non cath); Wit: Eliz Strapp & Agnes Durbin.
25 Oct 1899	Joseph Grassbaugh md Elizabeth B. Durbin; Wit: Ludger Durbin & Frances Grassbaugh.

25 Oct 1899	Mark Durbin md Jessie F. Cunningham; Wit: George Fesler & Laudonica Cunningham.
16 Apr 1900	Henry Coleman (non cath) md Margaret Shults.
16 Aug 1900	Stephen Logsdon md Henrietta Schaub; Wit: Lewis Mickly & wife Maria.
02 Sep 1900	Clayton Peterson md Rebecca Bailes; Wit: Lloyd Logsdon & wife Frances.
03 Oct 1900	William M. Kelly (s/o) John Kelly) md Frances E. Beam (d/o John Beam; Wit: Albert Beam & Lucy Shults.
10 Oct 1900	Quincy M. Simpson (non cath) md Frances Gertrude Smith (d/o James E. Smith & Maria Blubaugh); Wit: John & Rosa Smith.
24 Oct 1900	[Paul] Benjamin Logsdon (s/o George Logsdon) md Helena Elizabeth Fesler (d/o Jacob Fesler); Wit: George Fesler & Maria Gardner.
29 Nov 1900	John Laflin (non cath) md Margaret Rosanna [Lower] Schaub; Wit: John M. Lower & wife.
28 Aug 1901	Herman Albers (of Mercer Co.) md Martha Gardner; Wit: Francis & Maria Gardner.
03 Sep 1901	John B. Parker (s/o Robert Parker) md Lucy Sapp (d/o George Sapp & Delia Ann White); Wit: George ____ & Bertha Sapp.
14 Oct 1901	Edwin [Guy] Blubaugh (s/o Joseph Blubaugh) md Laura Belle Workman (d/o Stephen Workman); Wit: Benjamin Logsdon & Veronica Blubaugh.
15 Apr 1902	John S. Durbin (s/o Raphael Durbin & Barbara Buck) md Rose E. Sapp (d/o Clement Sapp & Lillian King); Wit: Eugene McKinney & Clara Sapp.
29 Sep 1902	Joseph Shuman (non cath) md Anna Blubaugh (d/o John); Wit: Charles Schuman & Rosa Blubaugh.
29 Sep 1902	John W. Fesler md Mary Agnes Durbin (d/o George Durbin & Normanda Workman); Wit: ____ & Elizabeth Fesler.

MARRIAGES

07 Oct 1902	Benjamin [Walter] Logsdon (s/o Francis Logsdon & Catherine Blubaugh) md Eva S. Vincent (non cath); Wit: Veronica Blubaugh.
17 Feb 1903	Francis Bailes (s/o William Bailes) md Lucy Ellen Shults (d/o Henry Shults & Nora E. Blubaugh); Wit: Leo & Angeline Shults.
22 Oct 1903	James [Raymond] Shults (s/o Henry Shults & Nora E. Blubaugh) md Bertha Baker (new convert); Wit: Charles Shults & Eliz Fesler.
04 Nov 1903	Eugene McKinney (s/o Charles McKinney) md Lucy Hammond (d/o Martin Hammond & Mary Keziah Sapp); Wit: Charles McKinney & Rosa Hammond.
24 May 1904	George Sapp md Georgia Bickel (non cath); Wit: Joseph Blubaugh & wife Lilly Blubaugh.
16 Nov 1904	Peter [Michael] Durbin (s/o John C. Durbin & Margaret Colopy) md Mary E. Swingle (d/o Christopher Swingle & Florence J. Blubaugh); Wit: Sylvester Durbin & Jane Swingle.
16 May 1905	John Kunesh md Frances Margaret Losh (d/o John Losh & Sarah Breckler); Wit: Edward Kunesh & Agnes Breckler.
07 Jun 1905	George J. Fesler md Mary [Charlotte] Gardner (d/o John Gardner & Maria Breckler); Wit: William Fesler & Helena Gardner.
23 Nov 1905	Charles Durbin (s/o Elijah & Margaret Durbin) md Mary [Louisa] Smithhisler (d/o Michael & Maria Smithhisler); Wit: Sherman Blubaugh & wife Rena.

End of marriage records copied.

FIRST COMMUNIONS AND CONFIRMATIONS

On the 20th of September 1853 Archbishop Purcell confirmed the following 19 boys and 28 girls who also received their first communion.

John Canavan
John Julius Brent
Nicholas Hollet
Jos Eifert Michael Hollet
Stephen Jerome Blubaugh
Elias Porter
Francis Sapp
Patrick Gillane
M. Adam Mague [McGough?]
Lawrence Allerding
Bazil Durbin
Michael Trullinger
William Sapp
Edward Brent
Joseph Sapp
Joseph Buckingham
Lawrence Richmond
Henry Raisin

Margaret Isabella Durbin
Matilda Gardner
Christianna Gardner
Eliza Hosfeld

Elizabeth Henley
Mary Magdalena Beam
Sarah Hosfeld
Sarah Elizabeth Mague
Mary Frances Critchfield
Catherine Sapp
Ann Theresa Blubaugh
Elizabeth [Eliza] Jane Davidson
Genevieve Henley
Margaret Durbin
Isadora Smyth
Mary Arnold
Cecilia Brent
Sarah Elizabeth Porter
Mary Isabell Davidson
Martha Eifert
Mary Eifert
Normanda Mary Sapp
Martha Frances Sapp
Rebecca McKenzie
Mary Jane Buckingham
Eliza Jane Pratt
Delila Ann Sapp
Ann Arnold.

On the 20 Sep 1857 Archbishop Purcell confirmed in St Lukes 57 children [names not given.]

On the 26 Nov 1861 Archbishop Purcell gave confirmation to 66 children [names not given.]

ST. LUKE'S RECORDS

Confirmation list 2 Sep 1877 by Rt. Rev. Bishop Rosecrans

Boys
Frank Smithhisler
Steven Durbin
Edward "Eddie" Carpenter
John Engle
George Carter
Robert Welker
Leo Bennett Blubaugh
George B. Blubaugh
Benjamin F. Durbin
Sherman William Blubaugh
Henry D. Blubaugh
Clement A. Blubaugh
Ed Durbin
Francis Joseph Durbin
Charles William Parker
Robert S. Parker
Jerome Elroy Gardner
Clement Engle
Elmore Colopy
Giles A. Butts
Frank Arnold
Frank Smithhisler (2)

Girls
Mary O. Shults
Mollie Smithhisler
Frances King
Anna King
Mary Logsdon
Selora A. Durbin
Frances Durbin
Mary Durbin
Eugenie Durbin
Ellen Engle
Louisa Larley
Milla Colopy
Iva Jane Colopy
Ella Sapp
Jennie Sapp
Mary Brewer

Confirmation list 24 May 1880 by Rt. Rev. Bishop Watterson

Hugh Boner
Laurence Blanchard
John Blubaugh
Joseph Durbin
Julius Bailes
Ben Parker
Joseph Francis Swarts
William Smithhisler
W. H. Blubaugh
Joseph Butts
Elias Smithhisler

Lamy Blubaugh
John Logsdon
Justin Blubaugh
John Durbin
Richard Carter
J. B .Parker
Dennis Durbin
Thomas McMahon
Liguori Blubaugh
Lamy Arnold

Thomas Critchfield
Sherman Welker
Charles Blubaugh
R. Durbin
Ch. George Logsdon
James Edw Colopy
Julian Arnold
Pat McMahon
Pius Engle
Raymond Smithhisler

168

FIRST COMMUNIONS AND CONFIRMATIONS

Confirmation list 24 May 1880 by Rt. Rev. Bishop Watterson (cont)

Mary Blubaugh
Anna King
Honora Durbin
Elizabeth B. Durbin
Frances Gardner
Mary Smithhisler
Mary McMahon

Sarah Carter
Sadie Welker
Gertrude Durbin
Sarah Jane Logsdon
Emely Olive Sapp
Fannie Durbin
Frances Durbin
Frances Blubaugh

Dora McNamara
Jennie Durbin
Mary C. Durbin
Florence McKenzie
Ella Swarts
Ella Durbin
Mary Butts

Confirmation list 13 May 1883 by Rt. Rev. Bishop Watterson

Ed Durbin
Julius Smith
Ch Shults
George Welker
Fidelis Sapp
James Durbin
Sam Shultz
Louis Engle
John Welker
Ben Logsdon
James Logsdon
Julius Durbin
Charles Weaver
Fulton Critchfield
William Bailes [adult]
_____ Stevens [adult]

Bertha Sapp
Rosa Smithhisler
Sarah Porter
Inia Smithhisler
Milla Beck
Gertrude Durbin
Barb Jane Durbin
Jennie Blubaugh
Philena Durbin
Vic Blubaugh
Jennie Gardner
Lorena Smithhisler
Louise McNamara
Bertha Durbin
Agatha Swingle
Anne Logsdon
A___ Swarts*
_____ Swarts*
Maria Colopy [Adult]

*Margaret Frances Swarts & Mary Alice Swarts were baptized 30 Jun 1872.

ST. LUKE'S RECORDS

First Communion _ _ 1886

Rollin Henegan
Peter Durbin
F. Sapp
F. Butts
Austin Gardner
John Durbin
Elmer Parker
Tom Durbin
Adam Weaver
Fred Durbin
Mark Durbin
Charles Gardner
William Durbin
Tom Durbin (2)

Emely Blubaugh
Rebecca Logsdon
Mary Weaver
Bessie Colopy
Mary Blubaugh
Fannie Parker
Emily Bailes
Jennie Butts
Bessie Butts
Mary Sapp
Mary Gardner
Aggie Durbin
Frances Gardner
Aggie Blubaugh
Bertha Swingle
Katie Shultz
Nana Smithhisler
Lucy Durbin
Josie Durbin

Confirmation list 20 Nov 1887 by Rt. Rev. Bishop J. A. Watterson

Rollin Henegan
Peter Durbin
Fk. Sapp
Fk. Butts
Austin Gardner
John Durbin
Elmer Parker
Tom Durbin
Mark Durbin
Charles Gardner
William Durbin
Tom Durbin
Fredrick Durbin

Emely Blubaugh
Rebecca Logsdon
Mary Weaver
Bessie Colopy
Mary Blubaugh
Fannie Parker
Emily Bailes
Jennie Butts
Bessie Butts
Mary Sapp
Emma Sapp
Mary Gardner
Aggie Durbin
Frances Gardner
Aggie Blubaugh
Bertha Swingle

Katie Shults
Nana Smithhisler
Lucy Durbin
Josie Durbin
John McGough (adult)
Dallas Smith (adult)
George Sapp (adult)
John McKenzie (adult)
Albert Logsdon (adult)
Mary Gert Blubaugh (adult)
Victoria Blubaugh (adult)
Mary Anne Smith (adult)
Elizabeth McGough (adult)
Hellen Durbin (adult)
Catherine Sapp (adult)
Mary Butts (adult)

FIRST COMMUNIONS AND CONFIRMATIONS

First Communion 11 May 1890

Francis Bailes
Walter McKenzie
Rudger Durbin
Charles Durbin
Thomas Bricker
Bernard Blubaugh
Frank Durbin
Julius Durbin
Curtiss Sapp
Guy Blubaugh
Harry Shaw
Albert Beam

Anna McGough
Mary Rice
Mary Shults
Bertha McKenzie
Metta Blubaugh
Anastasia Gardner
Isabella Sapp
Lucy Hammond
Dolly Gardner
Lucy Miller
Jennie Swingle
Mary Logsdon
Mary Swingle
Rena Weaver
Maggie Shults
Angeline Shults
Mary Engle
Mary Carter (adult)
Theodora Burris (adult).

First Communion 19 Jul 1891

Benjamin Logsdon
Henry Homan
Louis Fesler
Albert Fesler
Charles R. Sapp
Francis Gilbert [adult]
Raymond Durbin
Leo Durbin
George Fesler
Stephen Logsdon
Hyman Sapp
Edward Swingle
Francis Gilbert (adult)

Nora Durbin
Lucy Shults
Rilla Blubaugh
Martella Durbin
Rose Hammond
Veronica Blubaugh
Ettie Sapp
Rose Weaver
Rose Sapp
Isabelle Parker

171

ST. LUKE'S RECORDS

Confirmation list 26 Jul 1891 by Rt. Rev J. A. Watterson

Francis Bailes
Walter McKenzie
Ledger Durbin
Charles Durbin
Thomas Bricker
Bernard Blubaugh
Francis Durbin
Julius Durbin

Curtiss Sapp
Guy Blubaugh
Harry Shaw
Albert Beam
Benjamin Logsdon
Henry Homan
Louis Fesler
Albert Fesler
(John Breckler - sponsor)

Charles R. Sapp
Francis Gilbert [adult]
Raymond Durbin
Leo Durbin
George Fesler
Stephen Logsdon
Hyman L. Sapp
Edward Swingle

Anna McGough
Mary Rice
Mary Shults
Metta Blubaugh
Anastasia Gardner
Isabella Sapp
Lucy Hammond
Dolly Gardner
Lucy Miller
Jennie Swingle

Mary Logsdon
Mary Swingle
Rena Weaver
Maggie Shults
Angeline Shults
Bertha Engle
Mary Carter [adult]
Theodora Burris [adult]
Nora Durbin
(Mrs. George Sapp - sponsor)

Lucy Shults
Rilla Blubaugh
Martella Durbin
Rose Hammond
Veronica Blubaugh
Ettie Sapp
Rose Weaver
Rose Sapp
Isabelle Parker

First Communion 24 Jun 1894

Harry Smithhisler
Sylvester Durbin
John Swarts
William Sapp
James Miller
Mark Miller
Jacob Shults
Leo Shults

George Swingle
Clarence Sapp
William Collins
John Smith
Clare Welker
John Logsdon
James Dick
John Gardner

Leo Blubaugh
George Beck
Marcus Arnold
George Hammond
Charles Swarts
Marion Singer

Elsie McKenzie
Anna Durbin
Ellen Arnold
Alice Welker
Josephine Allerding
Gertrude Smith
Anna Blubaugh
Rose Blubaugh

Jane Swarts
Lulu Purcell
Almeda McFadden
Frances Losh
Stella Blubaugh
Amelia Sapp
Leah Arnold
Mary Durbin

Maud Durbin
Mary Bailes
Rebecca Bailes
Catherine Blubaugh
Margaret Blubaugh
Mary South

FIRST COMMUNIONS AND CONFIRMATIONS

Confirmation list 15 Dec 1894 byRt. Rev. J. A. Watterson

George Harry Smithhisler
William Sylvester Durbin
John Ambrose Swarts
William Sapp
James Miller
Mark Miller
Jacob Raymond Shults
William Leo Shults
George Swingle
Clarence David Sapp
William Collins
John Lamy Smith

Alice (Elsie) McKenzie
Anna Louisa Durbin
Musie Ellen Arnold
Alice Welker
Josephine Mary Allerding
Gertrude Frances Smith
Anna Mary Blubaugh
Rose Ellen Blubaugh
Lulu Purcell
Almeda McFadden
Frances Mary Losh

Clare Elliott Welker
John Lamy Logsdon
Earl James Dick
John Stephen Gardner
Leo Raymond Blubaugh
George Louis Beck
Marcus John Arnold
George Hammond
Marion Singer
Vincent Piar

(Levi Colopy - sponsor)

Stella Frances Blubaugh
Amelia Sapp
Mary Anna Durbin
Maud Elizabeth Durbin
Mary Elizabeth Bailes
Rebecca Alice Bailes
Catherine Mary Blubaugh
Margaret Blubaugh
Mary South
Theodora Smithhisler
(Melissa Colopy - sponsor)

First Communion 15 May 1898

Walter Durbin
William Blubaugh
Charles Blubaugh
Francis Breckler
Purcell Smithhisler
William Bricker
Cosmas Blubaugh
Charles Colopy
Odo Sapp

Theodore Logsdon
Christopher Swingle
Charles Hammond
Charles Durbin
Harry Magers
Homer Bailes
Albert Shults
James Gaines

First Communion 15 May 1898 (cont)

Rita Sapp
Clora Sapp
Lena Gardner
Lena Sapp
Mary Sapp
Rose Smith
Stella Miller
Mary Arnold
Nora Fesler
Isabelle Smithhisler
Mary Durbin

Margaret Bricker
Ida Blubaugh
Butille Alexander
Lucy Swingle
Margaret Losh
Rose Durbin
Ida O'Hearn
Mary Durbin
Clara Homan
Isadora King
Mary Audrey Payne

Confirmation list 13 Jul 1898 by Rt. Rev. J. A. Watterson

Walter Durbin
Basil William Blubaugh
Charles Aloysius Blubaugh
Francis Breckler
Joseph Purcell Smithhisler
William Bricker
Cosmas Blubaugh
Charles Aloysius Colopy
Odo Sapp
Theodore Logsdon
Christopher Swingle
Charles Hammond

Charles Durbin
Harry Magers
Peter Homer Bailes
Albert Peter Shults
James William Gaines
Charles Fesler
Joseph Albinus Singer
David Sylvester Heiple
William Fesler
Albert Kemp
John Kelly
(Levi Colopy - sponsor)

Rita Sapp
Clora Sapp
Lena Gardner
Lena Sapp
Mary Teresa Sapp
Rosa Smith
Mary Stella Miller
Mary Arnold
Nora Fesler
Isabelle Smithhisler
Margaret Bricker
Ida Mary Blubaugh
Bertille Alexander
Lucy Swingle
Margaret Losh

Rosa Durbin
Ada Clara O'Hearn
Mary Durbin
Clara Homan
Isadora King
Mary Audrey Payne
Mary Elizabeth Fesler
Mary Teresa Blubaugh
Almeda Martha Winterringer
Matilda Fesler
Florence Blanchard
Eva Maria Welker
Jane Frances Phillips
Mary Durbin
(Melissa Colopy - sponsor)

FIRST COMMUNIONS AND CONFIRMATIONS

First Communion 28 Apr 1901	Confirmation list 5 May 1901 by Rt. Rev. Henry Moeller
Lamy Arnold	John Lamy Arnold
Earl Blanchard	Earl Leo Blanchard
Bernard Blubaugh	James Bernard Blubaugh
Joseph Blubaugh	Joseph John Blubaugh
Julius Blubaugh	Julius Blubaugh
William Blubaugh	William Joseph Blubaugh
Raymond Carpenter	Raymond Lewis Carpenter
Joseph L. Colopy	Joseph Levi Colopy
Stanton Colopy	Germanus Stanton Colopy
Charles Drouhard	Charles William Drouchard
Charles Durbin	Charles Levi Durbin
Clement Durbin	Clement Paul Durbin
Hubert Gardner	Hubert Albert Gardner
Charles Homan	Charles Andrew Homan
Louis Lower	Louis Albert Lower
Cyril Millis	Cyril Henry Millis
Edward Piar	Edward Joseph Piar
Thomas Sapp	Thomas Edward Sapp
Frederick Shults	Frederick Ansel Shults
Charles Smith	Charles Francis Smith
	Clayton Joseph Peterson
	Joseph McElroy
	Desilva Sylvester Peterson
Selora Arnold	Selora Jane Arnold
Bertilla Bailes	Bertilla Agnes Bailes
Lucy Alice Blubaugh	Lucy Florence Blubaugh
Rosa Blubaugh	Rose Mary Blubaugh
Stella Blubaugh	Stella Gertrude Blubaugh
Veronica Blubaugh	Veronica Cecilia Blubaugh
Anna Bricker	Anna Gertrude Bricker
Jane Ona Bricker	Jane Frances Bricker
Rosa Butts	Rosalie Frances Butts
Frances Drouhard	Frances Rosalia Drouhard
Alice Durbin	Aloysia Maria Durbin
Blanche Durbin	Blanche Lovina Durbin
Ethel Durbin	Ethel Lucinda Durbin
Monica Logsdon	Mary Monica Logsdon

**First Communion
28 Apr 1901 (cont)**

Clara Losh
Rosa Lower
Adella Mickley
Mary Mickley
Elizabeth Sapp
Frances Donna Shults
Blanche Smithhisler
Katherine Swingle
Jessie Frances Durbin

**Confirmation list 5 May 1901 by
Rt. Rev. Henry Moeller (cont)**

Clara Louisa Losh
Anna Rose Lower
Adella Cecilia Mickley
Mary Elizabeth Mickley
Elizabeth Agnes Sapp
Frances Donna Shults
Blanche Mary Smithhisler
Florence Catherine Swingle
Jessy Frances Durbin
Magdaline Frances Hogland
Honora Anna Durbin
Mary Florence McElroy
Harriet Mary Logsdon
Mary Elizabeth Burgess
Elizabeth Fesler
Emma Catherine Starner

**First Communion & Confirmation 8 May 1904
by Rt. Rev. James Hartley, Bishop of Columbus**

Geo Wm Blubaugh
Louis Grover Durbin
Jonathan Dwight Magers
Fidelis Fenton Durbin
Stephen Joseph Breckler
Bernard Leonard Hammond
Wm Mark King
John Ambrose Durbin
Lawrence King
Wm Bernard Piar
John Aloysius Blubaugh
Judson Cletus Durbin

Sylvester Raymond Blubaugh
Jeremiah Edmund Colopy
William Dennis Shults
Anthony Raymond Blubaugh
Raymond Walter Schaub
Robert Eugene Hammond
John Thomas Losh
Harry Lee Schaub
William Alexander Losh
Raymond Walter Lower
Albert Priessnitz (a)

Domitilla Cath Smithhisler
Mary Darlla Colopy
Ethel Edith Arnold
Maud Mary Alexander (b)
Bertha Veronica Sapp
Pauline Cecilia Durbin
Eulalia Agnes Blubaugh (b)

Bernadette Agnes Durbin
Ethel Mary Logsdon
Bertha Almeda Blubaugh ©
Rose Veronica Gilbert
Catherine Gertrude Butts
Agatha Mary Butts
Grace Gertrude Drouhard (b)

176

FIRST COMMUNIONS AND CONFIRMATIONS

First Communion & Confirmation 8 May 1904
by Rt. Rev. James Hartley, Bishop of Columbus (cont)

Mary Ester Smithhisler
Agnes Anastasia Blubaugh (b)
Cecilia Dorothy Piar
Lucy Mary Homan
Margery Ruth Lower
Bertha Catherine Lower
Mary Parker (e)
Juanita Sapp (e)

Mary Frances Blubaugh (b)
Lucy Alice Lower
Louise Agnes Bash (d)
Philomena Lower
Alice Mary King
Jessie Mary Priessnitz (a)
Laura Blubaugh (e)
Louisa Schaub (e)

(a) 1st comm. 14 Oct 1904
(b) at Mt.Vernon
(c) at Fredericktown
(d) at Glenmont
(e) converts also confirmed

Communicants enrolled in the Scapular of Our Lady of Mt. Carmel 4 Apr 1908

Mrs. Emilia Bailes
Mrs. John Lower
Mrs. Frank Logsdon
Mrs. Mones Butts
Mrs. John R. Banbury

Mrs. James J. Logsdon
Mrs. James Blubaugh
Miss Bertha Blubaugh
Mr. Walter Hawk

First Communion 7 Jul 1909

Aloysius Durbin
Justin Durbin
Bernard Durbin
Roy Henry Lower
Charles Lower
Edward Mickley
Frank Mickley
Sanford Hammond
Clarence Hammond
Donald Colopy

Ralph Colopy
Raymond Butts
Charles Breckler
Corwin Blanchard
Lewis Smith
Augustine Smithhisler
Ferdinand Logsdon
Stephen Losh
Edward Gilbert
Oscar Piar

ST. LUKE'S RECORDS

First Communion 7 Jul 1909 (cont)

Alice Blubaugh
Agnes Blubaugh
Mary Blubaugh
Monica Blubaugh
Isabel Blubaugh
Edna Blubaugh
Mary Butts
Lena Durbin

Esther Durbin
Lena Lower
Hattie Lower
Valeria Priessnitz
Edith Priessnitz
Antonette Smithhisler
Rhea Smith
Rose Hoagland

First Communion 3 Oct 1909

1. Jonathan Arnold
2. Herman Blubaugh
3. Francis Blubaugh
4. Andrew Blubaugh
5. Purcell Butts
6. Frederick Durbin

7. Chaucy Durbin
8. Cornelius Henley
9. Clarence Kemp
10. Benjamin Losh
11. Harley Sapp
12. Edward Py

1. Mary Blubaugh
2. Mary Blubaugh
3. Ocia Blubaugh
4. Virgie Blubaugh
5. Charlotte Blubaugh
6. Agnes Bailes
7. Elizabeth Butts
8. Florence Blanchard
9. Beatrice Durbin
10. Constance Durbin
11. Rose Durbin
12. Virgilia Gardner

13. Hilda Gardner
14. Pauline Hammond
15. Cora Lower
16. Ethel Lower
17. Mary King
18. Madeline King
19. Edna Kelley
20. Ethel Piar
21. Martha Smithhisler
22. Mary Waddell
23. Dorothy Schaub

FIRST COMMUNIONS AND CONFIRMATIONS

Confirmed 14 Nov 1909 by
Rt. Rev. James J. Hartley

Confirmation Sponsors

1. Aloysius Alphonsus Durbin
2. Justin Thomas Durbin
3. Bernard Augustine Durbin
4. Henry Roy Paul Lower
5. Charles Henry Lower
6. Edward Martin Mickley
7. Frank Paul Mickley
8. Sanford Henry Hammond
9. Clarence Edward Hammond
10. Donald Eugene Colopy
11. Ralph John Colopy
12. Raymond ( ) Butts [sick]
13. Charles Cleophas Breckler
14. Corwin Aloysius Blanchard
15. Lewis James Smith
16. Augustine James Smithhisler
17. Ferdinand Jerome Logsdon
18. Stephen Otto Losh
19. Edward William Gilbert
20. Oscar Albert Piar
21. Jonathan Paul Arnold
22. Herman Sylvester Blubaugh
23. Francis ? Blubaugh
24. Andrew Thomas Blubaugh...(abs)
25. Purcell Paul Butts.....(sick)
26. Frederick Leo Durbin
27. Chaucy Joseph Durbin
28. Cornelius Joseph Henley
29. Clarence Henry Kemp
30. Benjamin Francis Losh
31. Harley Ambrose Sapp......(abs)
32. Edward Joseph Py

1. C. A .Blubaugh
2. Joseph Grassbaugh
3. Raymond Arnold
4. Albert Py
5. Frank Bailes
6. Frank Logsdon
7. B. O. Arnold
8. William Durbin
9. John Welsh
10. Giles Butts
11. C. Durbin
12 [none]
13. John F. Colopy
14. Pius Engle
15. Joseph C. Colopy Jr.
16. Charles Durbin
17. Paul B. Logsdon
18. Clement Durbin
19. Samuel Shults
20. Thomas Blubaugh
21. Liguori Durbin
22. Augustine Blubaugh
23. Henry Fesler
24. Ayman Sapp
25. Louis Welker
26. John F Gardner
27. Francis Esley
28. Chris Swingle Jr.
29. Gregory Henley
30. S. L. Blubaugh
31. Charles Shults
32. Henry Lower.

Confirmed 14 Nov 1909 by Rt. Rev. James J. Hartley (cont)	Confirmation Sponsors
1. Alice Clare Blubaugh	1. Elenora Durbin
2. Agnes Mary Blubaugh	2. Angela Shultz
3. Mary Clara Blubaugh	3. Clara Trogus
4. Monika Teresa Blubaugh	4. Cath Swingle
5. Isabel Helen Blubaugh	5. Mrs. Charles P. Durbin
6. Edna Gladys Blubaugh	6. Mrs. Chris Swingle
7. Mary Anna Butts	7. Mrs. Thomas King
8. Lena Cecelia Durbin	8. Mary Durbin
9. Esther Clara Durbin	9. Mrs. Clara Blubaugh
10. Lena Rose Lower	10. Mary Lower
11. Hattie Frances Lower	11. Mrs. Julius Bailes
12. Valeria Monika Priesnitz	12. Pauline Durbin
13. Edith Bridget Priesnitz	13. Alice Durbin
14. Antionette Clara Veronica Smithhisler	14. Clara Grassbaugh
15. Rhea Clara Smith	15. Rose Smith
16. Rose Clara Hoagland	16. Mrs. A. B. Kemp
17. Mary Florence Blubaugh	17. Mrs. Joseph Blubaugh
18. Mary Catherine Blubaugh	18. Mrs. John Kelley
19. Ocia Catherine Blubaugh	19. Mrs. Frank Durbin
20. Virgie Teresa Blubaugh	20. Mary Evers
21. Charlotte Rebecca Blubaugh	21. Mrs. Mary Sapp
22. Agnes Margaret Bailes	22. Mrs. Mark Durbin
23. Elizabeth Martha Butts	23. Mrs. Louis Welker
24. Florence Cecilia Blanchard	24. Mrs. Charles Logsdon
25. Beatrice Catherine Durbin	25. Esther Smithhisler
26. Constance Teresa Durbin	26. Mrs. Raymond Arnold
27. Rose Dorothy Durbin	27. Blanche Durbin
28. Virgilia Mary Gardner	28. Frances Gardner
29. Hilda Marie Gardner	29. Mrs. B. F. Durbin
30. Pauline Cecilia Hammond	30. Mrs. Francis Esley
31. Cora Clara Lower	31. [none given]
32. Ethel Teresa Lower	32. Mrs. Rose Durbin
33. Mary Agnes King	33. Mrs. Mones Butts
34. Madeline Mary King	34. Agnes Fesler
35. Edna Mary Kelley	35. Jennie Durbin
36. Ethel Gertrude Piar	36. Margaret Blubaugh
37. Martha Elizabeth Smithhisler	37. Maud Durbin
38. Mary Hilda Virginia Waddell	38. Mrs. Edward Durbin

DEATHS, FUNERALS AND BURIALS

Early death records for St. Luke Roman Catholic Church are nearly non-existent, encompassing burials 1840 & 1841, deaths April 1844 through May 1847, burials June 1847 through July 1848. Later deaths/burials start in July 1876 and are fairly complete through September 1947. Additional information may be found in Richard DeLauder's *Cemetery Records of Knox County Ohio* (Volume 1-1991, Volume 2-1992).

Burials.

25 May 1840	Aaron McKenzie.
25 May 1840	Gabriel McKenzie s/o Gabriel.
07 Aug 1840	Theodore Chonidall age 42.
15 Aug 1840	_____ Jones age 74.
21 Aug 1841	_____ Douche.

Record of Deaths (or burials).

07 Apr 1844	Maria Priscilla Magers
11 Apr 1844	Patrick Welsh.
__ __ 1844	Rachel Logue w/o Daniel.

08 May 1845	David Durbin Sr.
22 May 1845	N. Dresbaugh Jr.
22 May 1845	Jacob Welsh Sr.
02 Jul 1845	Michael McNamara Sr.
03 Jul 1845	Thomas Welsh Jr.
13 Jul 1845	Francis Durbin Jr.
21 Sep 1845	[John] Ryan infant.
21 Sep 1845	Miss Farrell.
__ Dec 1845	Miss Engle.
__ Dec 1845	Miss Jones.

05 Feb 1846	Elizabeth Murphy.
07 Mar 1846	infant of Elias McKenzie.
12 Mar 1846	Timothy Colopy Sr. at Mt.Vernon.

15 Mar 1846	Rachel Blubaugh.
30 Apr 1846	Henry M. Porter.
03 May 1846	Rachel Croy.
11 May 1846	Edward Payne infant.
07 Jun 1846	Anthony Sterner s/o ____.
15 Jul 1846	___ Fitzpatrick.
21 Jul 1846	N. Durbin infant d/o Bapist [Durbin] & Catherine King.
31 Aug 1846	N. Sapp infant d/o Samuel Sapp & Rachel Major [Magers].
08 Nov 1846	Sarah [C. Colopy] Black [age 16 yrs 1m 19d; bur 10 Nov].
02 Mar 1847	Daniel Boyle.
__ May 1847	infant of Nicholas Smith.
29 Jun 1847	Patience Blubaugh 42 yr.
01 Jul 1847	Elias Engle.
04 Jul 1847	infant Wagner [Waggoner].
11 Jul 1847	Anthony Fisher.
11 Jul 1847	infant Brent.
02 Aug 1847	infant Edmund Hernetty.
27 Aug 1847	infant Alexandria Blubaugh d/o Benjamin Blubaugh & [Elizabeth] Durbin.
02 Sep 1847	Anna Maria Graeme [Gaume ?]
05 Sep 1847	Maria Frances Hotsfer.
09 Sep 1847	infant Lauler.
28 Sep 1847	Maria Anna Haverick.
30 Sep 1847	Rachel Carter.
12 Nov 1848	_____ Durbin.
15 Nov 1847	infant Peter Miller 4 mo 6 d.
__ Dec 1847	Lydia ____.
14 Dec 1847	Peter Fishash 2 d.
28 Feb 1848	infant s/o Elias McKenzie.
__ Mar 1848	infant d/o Lewis Sapp
24 Aug 1850	Peter Fisher b 30 Jun, s/o Martin Fisher & Mary King.

DEATHS

Deaths (Burials):

08 Jul 1876	Anna [Louise] Durbin [d/o John Durbin & Lucinda Sapp.]
25 Dec 1876	William Engle.
01 Feb 1877	Gasper Sheneberger, [bur St Michaels cemetery].
22 Mar 1877	Catherine Durbin [w/o George].
20 Jul 1877	Leo Fidelis Durbin 6 yr, [s/o Francis Durbin & Genevieve Henley.]
07 Feb 1878	Edward Durbin, [s/o John S. Durbin & Mary Paul].
07 Feb 1878	Charles Durbin, [s/o John S .Durbin & Mary Paul].
02 Mar 1878	Maria Louisa Durbin, [d/o Benedict Durbin & Josephine Smithhisler].
21 Aug 1878	Francis McNamara.
29 Nov 1878	Angela Durbin.
04 Jan 1879	Walter Durbin.
23 Jan 1879	Isadora [Smith] Critchfield, [w/o William Thomas Critchfield].
23 Mar 1879	Elsa A. Parker 2 yr.
27 Mar 1879	Clarence Blubaugh
25 Apr 1879	Joseph Blubaugh.
22 Jul 1879	Baptist Durbin [s/o John].
26 Nov 1879	William Weaver, [s/o Adam Weaver & Elizabeth Mary Ernest].
23 Jul 1880	Mary Isabel Blubaugh 19 yr, [d/o John J. Blubaugh & Mary P. Dial].
22 Aug 1880	Henry Durbin 45 yr, [s/o Basil Durbin & Aparilla Buckingham]
15 Dec 1880	Benjamin Blubaugh.
26 Sep 1881	Lamy J. Smithhisler 9 mo, [s/o Michael J. Smithhisler & Victoria B. Arnold].

02 Oct 1881	Barbara Durbin [w/o Raphael Durbin & d/o Eberhard & Adeline Buck]
	Maria Durbin [d/o Raphael Durbin & Barbara Buck].
	Martha Buck [d/o Eberhard & Adeline Buck].
	(Above all drowned)
10 Nov 1881	Christopher Bricker 72 yr.
24 Nov 1881	[Thomas] Lamy Arnold 14 yr, [s/o Jonathan Arnold & Mary Blubaugh].
02 Dec 1881	Charles W. Beam [s/o J. Beam & M. Sheneberger].
13 Dec 1881	Catherine Blubaugh [65yrs 10m 13d, w/o Stephen Blubaugh].
07 Jan 1882	Eugenia Colopy 3 yr.
23 Jan 1882	[Loretta] Sapp 4 yr, [d/o C. & F. Sapp].
20 Feb 1882	William Basil Smith 8 yr, [s/o J. & M.].
24 Mar 1882	Helena Magers.
01 May 1882	Nancy Bricker 72 yr, [w/o Christopher].
01 May 1882	infant Colopy.
03 Sep 1882	Mary Domitila Bricker,[d/o Daniel Bricker & Josephine Smithhisler].
05 Sep 1882	William Dial 72 yr.
13 Oct 1882	_____ Bricker
17 Oct 1882	Walter Smithhisler [age 4y 4m 2d,.s/o George A. & Sarah Smithhisler].
27 Dec 1882	Jacob Shults 75 yr.
02 Jan 1883	Catherine [Arnold] McKee, [w/o George T. McKee].
23 Jan 1883	John Baptist Logsdon 15 yr, [s/o C. & S. G.]
28 Feb 1883	Margaret Durbin 40 yr, [w/o Benjamin Durbin].
07 Feb 1884	James McKenzie.
29 Mar 1884	Elizabeth Colglesser 83 yr, [former wife J. Blubaugh].
04 Jul 1884	infant [Myrtle] Parker 1 yr, [d/o Thomas Soloman Parker & Mary Victoria Burris].
22 Aug 1884	Peter Durbin.
20 Sep 1884	Angeline Brewer 20 yr.
29 Sep 1884	infant Colopy 1 d.
17 Nov 1884	George Durbin 65 yr.

DEATHS

02 Feb 1885	Frances Elizabeth Durbin 5 yr.
01 Mar 1885	Elizabeth Weaver 69 yr, [w/o Adam Weaver].
18 Mar 1885	Richard Arnold.
28 Mar 1885	infant Timothy Sapp 1 yr.
28 Mar 1885	Elizabeth Blubaugh 75 yr.
14 Apr 1885	John Homan 3 d.
18 Jul 1885	Rachel Henley 65 yr.
22 Jul 1885	John Durbin 54 yr, [s/o Baptist Durbin & Catherine King].
26 Sep 1885	Thomas [Bernard] Logsdon 13 yr, [s/o George Logsdon & Catherine Durbin].
18 Oct 1885	Sarah Louisa Arnold 3 yr.
01 Jan 1886	Jacob Smith 74 yr.
03 Jan 1886	Stephen Durbin 23 yr.
06 Jan 1886	Jonathan Sapp 72 yr.
09 Feb 1886	Joseph Henry Durbin b 27 Nov 1885, [s/o John B. Durbin & Mary A. Blubaugh].
28 Feb 1886	Elizabeth Engle 62 yr, [w/o Martin Engle. Cemetery Book states 54yr 7mo 17da].
11 Mar 1886	Mary A. [Breckler] Shults 78 yr, [w/o Jacob Shults].
02 Apr 1886	Robert Smith 20 yr.
25 Apr 1886	Joseph Edward Gardner 3 mo, [s/o Thomas Gardner & Emma Peters].
26 Apr 1886	Rebecca Dial 77 yr, [w/o William Dial].
07 Jul 1886	Clara Blubaugh 2 yr, [d/o James Blubaugh & Victoria F. Smith].
15 Jul 1886	Henry Walter Blubaugh 4 yr, [s/o James Blubaugh & Victoria F. Smith].
23 Jul 1886	Martha E. Blubaugh 1 yr, [d/o James Blubaugh & Victoria F. Smith].
06 Aug 1886	Jacob Welker 66 yr.
27 Nov 1886	Rebecca Logsdon, [w/o David Logsdon].
18 Jan 1887	Francis McNamara 87 yr.
17 Feb 1887	Charlotte [Heckler] Blubaugh 60 yr, w/o Stephen.
15 May 1887	Cyrus Stevens.

17 May 1887	Ward Smith.
28 Jun 1887	Gregory Henley 26 yr,
23 Jul 1887	Thomas B McKenzie 45 yr.
18 Aug 1887	Levi [Clyde] Colopy 1 yr, [s/o Levi Colopy & M. A. Durbin.
09 Jan 1888	Maria Sapp 72 yr.
31 Mar 1888	Joseph Losh 74 yr
17 Apr 1888	Elizabeth Homan 70 yr, [w/o Paul Homan].
12 May 1888	Martin Engle 66 yr.
30 Jun 1888	Elizabeth Rice 5 yr.
16 Sep 1888	Sarah Weaver 29 yr.
23 Sep 1888	Edna Smithhisler 1 yr, [d/o Henry & Catherine].

Burials:

13 Dec 1888	Samuel Durbin 81 yr.
03 Feb 1889	Charles B. Blubaugh 2 yr, [s/o James Blubaugh & Victoria F. Smith].
08 Jun 1889	Eberhard [Buck] 82 yr.
05 Jul 1889	Apollonia Sheneberger 61 yr.
09 Jul 1889	Mrs. Keziah White 81 yr, [w/o Anthony White].
23 Jul 1889	James McKenzie abt 40 yr, [s/o John]..
02 Sep 1889	Paul Homan 89 yr.
10 Oct 1889	Emmanuel Gilbert infant.
24 Nov 1889	David White 79 yr.
13 Jan 1890	Jacob Colopy 88 yr.
14 Feb 1890	[William] Everett Rice 14 yr, [s/o Israel & Elizabeth].
24 Mar 1890	Rachel [Arnold Porter] Durbin 77 yr.
02 Apr 1890	John Swingle 80 yr.
26 Aug 1890	Harriet Critchfield 74 yr, [w/o Hiriam].
31 Oct 1890	Isaac Dial 94 yr.
20 Nov 1890	Allison Bailes 89 yr, [w/o John].
11 Dec 1890	Sarah Ellen Blubaugh 52 yr, [w/o Hilary D.].
18 Dec 1890	James Barry Colopy 1 yr.

DEATHS

02 Mar 1891	Ella B. Durbin 1 yr, [d/o John Durbin & Mary Blubaugh].
23 Mar 1891	Mary [Colopy] Sapp 86 yr, [w/o Levi].
20 Apr 1891	James White 64 yr.
19 May 1891	Agnes R. Blubaugh 18 yr, [d/o John J. Blubaugh & Mary P. Dial].
02 Jun 1891	Christopher Swarts 55 yr.
11 Dec 1891	Frances Losh 77 yr, [w/o Joseph].
28 Dec 1891	William E. Welker 70 yr.
01 Jan 1892	Mary A. [Buckingham] Durbin 79 yr, [w/o Bazil].
10 Jan 1892	Jerome Blubaugh 40 yr.
28 Feb 1892	Jacob Skilling 93 yr.
09 Jun 1892	Margaret Sapp 8 yr.
06 Aug 1892	Anastasia Gardner 15 yr, [d/o Francis M. Gardner & Mary J. Allerding].
25 Oct 1892	Helen Durbin 2 yr.
30 Oct 1892	Maria Smith 91 yr.
24 Feb 1893	John McKenzie 59 yr.
22 May 1893	Isabella Durbin 80 yr.
30 Sep 1893	Edward Critchfield 23 yr.
07 Nov 1893	Michael Porter 84 yr.
12 Feb 1894	Henry Peters 63 yr.
03 Apr 1894	Samuel Shrimplin 80 yr.
06 Sep 1894	Anna [Losh] Weaver 50 yr, [w/o John].
15 Dec 1894	Thomas McMahon 67 yr.
20 Feb 1895	Jonathan Arnold 76 yr.
12 Mar 1895	John Porter 83 yr.
22 Apr 1895	Adam Weaver 91 yr.
16 May 1895	William Collins 34 yr.
01 Jun 1895	Margaret Durbin 59 yr.
19 Jun 1895	Althea Blubaugh 41 yr.
13 Sep 1896	Maria Colopy 1 yr.
14 Sep 1896	John J. Smithhisler 1 yr, [s/o Henry & Catherine]
30 Dec 1896	Amanda South 63 yr.

19 Feb 1897	Francis M. Durbin 66 yr.
05 Jun 1897	Gertrude [Rosetta] Durbin 1 yr, [d/o John B. Durbin & Mary Blubaugh.]
19 Jun 1897	Francis Durbin 28 yr.
29 Jun 1897	Marie Magers 1 yr, [d/o Calvin Magers & Ellen Arnold].
03 Sep 1897	Daniel Carter 54 yr.
13 Dec 1897	Julius Peterson 2 yr.
21 Mar 1898	Frances E. Beltz 36 yr, [w/o Adam C.].
24 Mar 1898	Anna V. Blubaugh 35 yr.
02 Apr 1898	Joseph Smithhisler 1 yr, [s/o Henry & Catherine]
24 Sep 1898	James Michael Durbin 1 yr, [s/o Frederick Durbin & Martha Eckenrode].
07 Dec 1898	Mary A. Smithhisler 70 yr, [w/o Michael].
07 Feb 1899	Benjamin Eckenrode 74 yr.
04 May 1899	Anne Elizabeth Butts 26 yr, [d/o Henry & Amme M.].
29 May 1899	Mary Parker 12 yr, [d/o Thomas Sololomon Parker & Mary Victoris Burris].
29 May 1899	William A. Durbin 1 yr, [s/o John B. Durbin & Mary Blubaugh].
06 Jul 1899	Alfred Durbin 20 yr, [s/o George & Catherine].
29 Oct 1899	Charles Peterson 5 yr, [s/o D & R & g's of Rachel Peterson].
07 Nov 1899	Sarah [Ann Sapp] Bradfield 70 yr, [w/o James W.].
29 Nov 1899	John S. Durbin 70 yr
07 Feb 1900	James Millis 78 yr.
12 Apr 1900	Joseph Engle 70 yr.
21 May 1900	Harriet Blubaugh 73 yr, [w/o John].
21 Nov 1900	Catherine Smithhisler 38 yr, [w/o Henry P.]
27 Dec 1900	[Charlotte] "Charity" [Critchfield] McKenzie 58 yr.
01 Feb 1901	James J. Skilling 72 yr.
10 Jun 1901	Helen Blubaugh 40 yr.
24 Aug 1901	Mary Beam 59 yr.
30 Aug 1901	Mary (Barry Henegan) Colopy 62 yr.
06 Sep 1901	Isabella Sapp 57 yr.

DEATHS

28 Dec 1901	Rachel Piar 73 yr.
04 Jan 1902	Robert H. Sapp 40 yr.
15 Jan 1902	Simeon Durbin 64 yr.
27 Feb 1902	Maria Blubaugh
02 Mar 1902	Margaret Millis 77 yr.
15 Mar 1902	Martin Porter 43 yr.
03 May 1902	Frances D. Durbin 58 yr.
14 Nov 1902	Catherine Marshall 74 yr.
16 Nov 1903	Rebecca Parker 64 yr.
15 Dec 1903	James E. Colopy 49 yr.
28 May 1904	Joseph Jefferson Peterson 38 yr.
18 Jun 1904	Raymond W Schaub 18 yr.
21 Jul 1904	Elizabeth McKenzie 93 yr.
07 Dec 1904	Margaritta Eckenrode 70 yr.
21 Mar 1905	Mary Losh 54 yr.
22 Mar 1905	William Kemp 1 yr.
08 Jul 1905	Vincent Piar 79 yr.
14 Jul 1905	Alexander Durbin 57 yr.
15 Jul 1905	Eliza Arnold 83 yr [w/o Richard].
23 Sep 1905	Walter Henry Mickley 1 yr 20 da.
04 Oct 1905	John J. Durbin 32 yr.
15 Jan 1906	Rachel Welker 83 yr.
14 Feb 1906	Mary Ann Durbin.
07 Aug 1906	Rebecca Smith 79 yr.
01 Sep 1906	Delia Ann Sapp 74 yr.
22 Oct 1906	Benjamin Durbin 78 yr 5 mo 11 d.
07 Mar 1907	Lucinda Durbin 76 yr.
30 Apr 1907	Johanna [Phillips] McMann.
12 Aug 1907	Melissa A. Colopy (Mrs. Levi).
27 Oct 1907	Purcell Henry Smithhisler 23 yr 1 mo 2 da (killed by electricity on Lake Shore Traction RR near Freemont OH on 25 Oct 1907).

21 Dec 1907	Richard Carter 69 yr.
25 Feb 1908	Henry C. Shults.
19 Mar 1908	Agnes Maria Arnold 2y.
08 Apr 1908	Mary Ann Harden 69 yr.
20 Jun 1908	Mary Nora Durbin 29 yr.
21 Oct 1908	Laurence King 20 yr, [s/o Julius & Olive].
29 Mar 1909	Levi Colopy.
06 Apr 1909	Raphael Durbin.
14 Apr 1909	Elizabeth Grassbaugh.
23 Apr 1909	Sarah McCoy.
02 Jun 1909	William Henry Blubaugh.
17 Aug 1909	Susanna Engle
06 Sep 1909	Walter McKenzie infant.
24 Nov 1909	Herman Albers.
10 Dec 1909	Gregory Hammond infant.
10 May 1910	Normanda Durbin 70 yr.
11 May 1910	Sarah C. Logsdon 70 yr.
03 Oct 1910	Margaret Durbin 73 yr.
22 Jul 1910	Caroline Skilling.
25 Jul 1910	Laurence King.
09 Sep 1910	John Smith 24 hrs, [s/o Julius A. & Rose E.].
28 Dec 1910	Maria Florence McElroy.
18 Jan 1911	Julius Logsdon 1 da, [s/o James & Margaret].
20 Feb 1911	Jonathan Colopy.
03 Mar 1911	Leo Judson Arnold.
03 Apr 1911	John J. Losh.
20 Apr 1911	Lucinda Dick.
27 Apr 1911	Francis Simpson.
01 May 1911	Robert Carl Parker.
26 May 1911	Walter S. Arnold.
18 Aug 1911	John Laflin.
22 Aug 1911	Olive Grace Logsdon.
20 Nov 1911	Francis M. Gardner.

DEATHS

06 Jan 1912	Mary Carter (Mrs. Richard).
08 Feb 1912	George Sapp.
25 Mar 1912	Lydia Carter (Mrs. Raphael).
03 Apr 1912	Raphael Carter.
09 Jul 1912	Maria Helen Piar.
17 Aug 1912	Mary [Ella] Blubaugh 43 yr [w/o Clement].
28 Sep 1912	Raymond Cletus Butts 19 yr [s/o Giles].
30 Oct 1912	Hannah King 84 yr (w/o Laurence).
19 Jun 1913	Maria Arnold 90 yr.
03 Nov 1913	Caecilia Piar 20 yr.
04 Nov 1913	Anna Clara Sapp 1½ yr.
12 Dec 1913	Mary Jane Stevens 88 yr.
17 Jan 1914	Andrew T. Blubaugh 20 yr.
18 Aug 1914	John Weaver 70 yr.
07 Oct 1914	Ralph Marcellus Welsh 52 da.
02 Dec 1914	Elizabeth Kelly 75 yr.
24 Dec 1914	Charles Clement Logsdon 75 yr.
09 Apr 1915	John Gardner Sr. 73 yr.
12 Apr 1915	John J. Blubaugh 88 yr.
19 Apr 1915	John Michael Smithhisler 90 yr.
10 May 1915	Mary Elizabeth [Buck] Logsdon 71 yr.
31 May 1915	Stephen Blubaugh 85 yr.
01 Sep 1915	Leona Fesler 18 da.
10 Nov 1915	Robert William Sapp 2 da.
03 Dec 1915	Landon Edward Welker 76yr.
13 Dec 1915	Matilda Welker 80 yr.
20 Dec 1915	John W. Beam 72 yr.
28 Feb 1916	Benjamin Oliver Arnold 61 yr.
04 Mar 1916	Ethel (Logsdon) Durbin 24 yr, from Akron OH.
04 May 1916	Catherine (Smithhisler) Durbin 60 yr.
14 Sep 1916	Ann [Whisler] Peters 82 yr.
22 Sep 1916	Florence Swingle 63 yr.
27 Oct 1916	Joseph Hill Colopy 81 yr.

31 Jan 1917	Charles Pius Durbin 70 yr.
24 Apr 1917	Anna Maria Butts 82 yr.
03 May 1917	Alice Gertrude Logsdon 72 yr.
08 Jun 1917	Clinton Paul Wohler 9 yr.
23 Aug 1917	Thomas Wilfred Parker 8 yr.
29 Aug 1917	Elias Porter 79 yr.
19 Oct 1917	Thomas L. Wiggins 36 yr.
15 Jan 1918	Rose Mary Colopy 4 mo.
22 Jan 1918	Julius Eugene Durbin 8 da.
09 Feb 1918	Francis Sapp 79 yr.
23 Mar 1918	George Durbin 80 yr.
05 Apr 1918	Mary J. Gardner 82 yr.
13 May 1918	Mary O. Lower 51 yr.
22 Jul 1918	Sarah Margaret Warner 87 yr.
25 Sep 1918	Margaret Porter 76 yr.
30 Sep 1918	Paulina Gronka 16 yr.
05 Oct 1918	Helen I. Smith 16 yr.
14 Oct 1918	Francis Wall d 6 Oct 1918 at Camp Jackson, SC.
24 Oct 1918	George W. Sapp 73 yr.
21 Dec 1918	Julian Bennett Sapp 61 yr.
19 Feb 1919	Charles H. Miller 69 yr.
25 Apr 1919	Clarence Augustus Smith 2 mo.
28 Apr 1919	William M. Kelley 55 yr.
09 Jun 1919	Lewis D. Welker 63 yr.
23 Aug 1919	Josephine Frances Robinson 39 yr, died 20 Aug at Greer, OH.
28 Nov 1919	Jacob Smith 74½ yr.
22 Dec 1919	Jacob Frederick Heffelfinger 1 da.
05 Feb 1920	Leo Raymond Blubaugh 37 yr, fall from roof.
06 Feb 1920	Clara L. Losh 30 yr at Akron, OH.
23 Feb 1820	Francis Mickley 27 yr.
01 Apr 1920	Mary Ann Swingle 56 yr, w/o George Swingle of Brink Haven, OH; died 30 Mar at St John Hospital, Cleveland, OH.
26 Apr 1920	Henry Butts 85 yr (old soldier).

DEATHS

08 Jul 1920	Francis Logsdon 79 yr (old soldier).
03 Feb 1921	John C. Durbin 81 yr.
16 Mar 1921	Mary Ann Sapp 75 yr 6 mo.
31 Mar 1921	George Logdson 84 yr (old soldier).
02 Apr 1921	Lewis Weber 2 hrs.
07 Jun 1921	Mary P. Lower 60 yr.
17 Jun 1921	Mary Ellen Durbin 50 yr at Mt. Carmel hospital.
07 Sep 1921	Raymond Otto Weber 5 mo.
20 Dec 1921	Barbara Helen Kemp 49 yr at Mt. Carmel.
10 Feb 1922	Dr. Andrew Durbin Welker 74 yr at Gambier OH.
06 Mar 1922	Elizabeth Helen Blubaugh 19 yr.
13 Mar 1922	George Leo Blubaugh 21 yr.
25 Mar 1922	Mary Catherine Shults 2 hrs (premature birth).
13 Apr 1922	Charles Albert Shults 53 yr.
01 Jun 1922	John Peter Breckler 74 yr.
29 Aug 1922	Charles Thomas Colopy 8 yr, kicked by horse in chest 26 Aug.
15 Nov 1922	Raymond Arnold 61 yr.
18 Nov 1922	infant [Joseph O.] Arnold stillborn at Mt. Vernon.
02 Jan 1923	Benjamin W. Logsdon 42 yr.
09 Feb 1923	Frances Lucille Banbury 18 yr.
07 Apr 1923	John Taylor Shults 74 yr.
07 Jul 1923	Mary Charlotte Blubaugh 84 yr.

Funerals:

30 Oct 1923	William Bailes 86 yr, d 27 Oct.
__ Nov 1923	Emma J. Kelley 57 yr, d 20 Nov 1923 at Mt. Vernon.
28 Jan 1924	Clinton Joseph Grassbaugh 22 yr, d 24 Jan; killed at Wooster, OH.
01 Apr 1924	Mary Louise Piar d/o Omar Piar; died soon after birth.
23 Apr 1924	Thomas Blubaugh d 20 Apr.
09 Sep 1924	Rev. Francis Schaub 54 yr, died 5 Sep.
18 Dec 1924	Joseph F. Blubaugh 73 yr.
31 Dec 1924	Maria E. Smith 73 yr.

23 Feb 1925	Anthony B. Blubaugh 24 yr.
07 May 1925	Della Butts 57yr.
11 May 1925	Elizabeth Welker 68 yr.
20 Jun 1925	Clara Blubaugh 58 yr.
14 Aug 1925	Louisa Ferenbaugh Winterhalter 5 mo.
19 Sep 1925	Sarah E. Losh 64 yr.
30 Nov 1825	Lewis Mickley 63 yr.
22 Dec 1925	Margaret Almeda Winterringer 76 yr, w/o John.
30 Dec 1925	Delilah Susanna Durbin 71 yr.
03 Feb 1926	Ina Catherine Grassbaugh 6 yr.
17 May 1926	Sarah Elizabeth Durbin 85 yr, d in Cleveland, OH 14 May.
23 Sep 1926	Lawrence V. Blanchard 59 yr.
07 Dec 1926	Catherine Welker 84 yr 8 mo.
10 Mar 1927	James W. Gaines 46 yr at Columbus, OH.
27 May 1927	Clement Sapp 47 yr at Mt. Carmel.
30 Jul 1927	Anita May Lower 47 or 97 yr, at Mt. Vernon.
19 Nov 1927	James R. Blubaugh 70 yr.
07 Jan 1928	Lucy W. Gardner 49 yr.
19 Jan 1928	Nora Ellen Shults 79 yr.
18 Feb 1928	Bertha [Olive] Grassbaugh 56 yr.
31 Mar 1928	Frederick Rice 74 yr at Creston, Iowa.
21 Apr 1928	Robert Henry Conroy 7 mo 14 d at Ft. Wayne, IN.
20 Jun 1928	Lillis Blubaugh 80 yr at Mt. Vernon, OH.
16 Aug 1928	Joan Maria Blubaugh 22 yr, at Kenmore, OH.
25 Sep 1928	Jacob Fesler 84 yr.
28 Sep 1928	Thomas J. McMahon; murdered at his home 6pm Sat 22 Sep 1928, found by sheriff Wed 26 Sep at 9 am; buried Fri 28 Sep at 10 AM.
20 Nov 1928	Raymond Durbin 49 yr.
28 Nov 1928	Elizabeth Blubaugh 31 yr; killed in auto accident on way to church.
11 Dec 1828	Edward Welsh 65½ yr.

194

DEATHS

02 Jan 1929	Joseph Boeshart infant ½ hr [s/o Edward].
08 Jan 1929	Mary K. Hammond 72 yr.
06 Jun 1929	Brigitta Welsh 76 yr.
10 Oct 1929	Ethel Lower Conroy 32 yr.
01 Feb 1930	John F. Colopy 65 yr.
08 Feb 1930	John Thomas Durbin 81 yr.
11 Mar 1930	Thomas Solomon Parker 71 yr; buried Workman Cemetery, Danville, OH.
18 Apr 1930	Peter Paul 88 yr, (Good Friday).
03 Jun 1930	William A. Schaub 52 yr.
07 Jun 1930	Anna Piar 65 yr.
16 Sep 1930	Sarah A. Blubaugh 73 yr.
23 Dec 1930	Flora A. Breckler 76 yr.
10 Mar 1931	Barbara Rose Mary Colopy 3½ mo.
31 Mar 1931	Lewis Francis Mickley 1 yr.
25 Apr 1931	Catherine Fesler 83 yr.
08 Jun 1931	Anna Lou Durbin 59 yr, died 5 Jun in Akron ,OH.
10 Oct 1931	Victoria Blubaugh 75 yr ?
04 Feb 1932	Mary Paul Durbin 92 yr.
14 Mar 1932	Matilda Ann Bailes 84/86 yr.
02 Jul 1932	Edwin Guy Blubaugh 54 yr at Mt. Vernon.
02 Dec 1932	E Jennie Jones 86 yr at Mt. Vernon.
06 Dec 1932	Charles Engle 76 yr; of Millwood, died in Columbus, OH.
__ __ 1932	John B. Durbin 74 yr.
17 Mar 1933	Robert Smithhisler 62 yr.
20 May 1933	William Franklin Mickley 80 yr; killed by Erie RR near Wadsworth, OH.
12 Jun 1933	Samuel Shults 63 yr.
24 Jun 1933	Paul L. Arnold 22 yr.
29 Jun 1933	Robert Elmer Parker 60 yr.
11 Aug 1933	Della Mickley Magers 45 yr at Mt. Vernon.
13 Sep 1933	James J. Logsdon 63 yr.
24 Oct 1933	Jennie Durbin 62 yr, found dead in bed.
06 Nov 1933	Christopher John Swingle 84 yr.

26 Jan 1934	Bessie Parker 74 yr at, [buried at Mt. Calvery, Mt. Vernon].
01 Feb 1934	John W. Fesler 54 yr, d 29 Jan.
05 Mar 1934	Henry Blubaugh 69 yr at Mt.Vernon.
05 Apr 1934	Giles A. Butts 69 yr.
30 Apr 1934	Aurelia Isabella Sapp 29 yr, d 27 Apr at Akron, OH.
26 May 1934	Theodore Durbin 73 yr, at Akron, OH.
07 Jun 1934	Agnes Bertille Piar 44 yr.
16 Aug 1934	Catherine Jane Sapp 76 yr.
26 Oct 1934	Curtis L. Sapp 58 yr.
18 Mar 1935	Sherman William Blubaugh 69 yr.
18 May 1935	Charles C. Breckler 41 yr.
07 Sep 1935	Mary L. (Smithhisler) Durbin 83 yr.
30 Oct 1935	James D. Parker 72 yr at Mt. Vernon.
09 Nov 1935	William E. Durbin 80 yr.
30 Dec 1935	John Calvin Magers 78 yr.
04 Jan 1936	Alma Virginia Durbin 22 yr.
19 Feb 1936	Martha Ellen Durbin 80 yr.
09 Mar 1936	Ethel Frances Blubaugh 11 yr; killed by auto after alighting from school bus.
01 Apr 1936	Martin P. Hammond 85 yr.
21 Apr 1936	Paul Benjamin Logsdon 66 yr.
22 Apr 1936	Deliah A. Banbury 94 yr.
12 May 1936	Arthur Francis Sapp 16 yr.
18 Jul 1936	Blubaugh infant premature birth at Mt. Vernon.
22 Aug 1936	Mable (Easterday) Blubaugh 43 yr, killed in auto accident at Monroe Mills, OH.
25 Sep 1936	Helena E. Logsdon 61 yr in Columbus, OH.
03 Dec 1936	Mary Gardner 90 yr.
18 Feb 1937	Carlos Z. Sapp 20 yr.
09 Mar 1937	Francis L. Smithhisler 74 yr.
04 May 1937	Rosa Durbin 57 yr.
09 Jun 1937	Cecilia Margaret Losh 7 yr.
29 Sep 1937	Margaret R. Sapp 83 yr.
09 Nov 1937	John Lamy Logsdon 56 yr.

DEATHS

13 Nov 1937	Catherine N. Logsdon 90 yr at Columbus, OH.
19 Jan 1938	George Martin Swingle Sr. 86 yr.
12 Mar 1938	Thomas King 75 yr.
17 Mar 1938	Alice J. Shults 81 yr.
22 Mar 1938	Lorena G. Blubaugh 66 yr, died 18 Mar.
11 Apr 1938	Joseph Grassbaugh 65½ yr.
28 Jun 1938	Matilda Patton.
09 Aug 1938	Thecla Elenore Durbin 57 yr.
28 Oct 1938	Joseph Harlett 71 yr, died 25 Oct.
31 Oct 1938	Lucy Florence Blubaugh 48 yr, died 27 Oct.
12 Nov 1938	John Thomas Blubaugh 1½ hrs, stillborn s/o Elmer & Laverne
05 Dec 1938	Julia (Hunter) Lower 63 yr.
12 Dec 1938	John W. Lower 80 yr.
31 Jan 1939	John F. Gardner 73 yr.
13 Apr 1939	Lucy Mary Finan 1½ yr; burned in home fire.
23 Apr 1939	Helen E Colopy 38 yr; burned to death in fire near Mt. Vernon, OH.
21 May 1939	Lyman P. Holdbrook 91 yr at Canton, OH.
01 Jun 1939	Robert Eugene Blubaugh 5½ yr, auto accident in front of home.
04 Oct 1939	Helena Victoria Weber 42 yr, died 1 Oct.
22 Nov 1939	Genevieve Durbin 100 yr, died 20 Nov. at Barberton, OH.
08 Jan 1940	James Augustin Blubaugh 84 yr, died 8 Jan.
02 Mar 1940	Joseph M. Grunden 71 yr, died 29 Feb.
20 Mar 1940	Henry Smithhisler 80 yr, died 17 Mar at Lorain, OH.
03 Apr 1940	Joseph C. Blubaugh 22 yr, died 31 Mar.
15 May 1940	Mary Magdalena King 42 yr, died 31 Mar.
14 Aug 1940	Hanna J. Holdbrook 92 yr, died 11 Aug at Canton, OH.
20 Aug 1940	Walter Celestine Durbin 1 d.
06 Sep 1940	Clement A. Blubaugh 73 yr, died 4 Sep.
16 Sep 1940	Maria Florence Gnunden 60 yr, died 14 Sep.
15 Nov 1940	George W. Blubaugh 48 yr, died 16 Nov.
16 Jan 1941	Lewis D. Engle 69 yr, died 14 Jan.

28 Jan 1941	Charlotte Mickley 73 yr, died 28 Jan.
11 Feb 1941	Ellen Magers 84 yr, died 8 Feb.
08 Mar 1941	Marion Edward Singer 66 yr, died 6 Mar, found on route 36 at Millwood, OH.
20 Mar 1941	Jack Kelly 89 yr, d 17 Mar., car fell on him.
29 May 1941	Francis Leo Boeshart 17 yr, died 26 May.
04 Jun 1941	Hillery David Piar 81 yr, d 1 Jun.
03 Jul 1941	Lamy Wallace Rice 11 wks, died 2 Jul.
16 Jul 1941	Bernadette Anna Weber 8 yrs, died 14 Jul.
19 Sep 1941	Naomi Margaret Sapp 28 yr, died 19 Sep at Mansfield, OH.
16 Oct 1941	Agnes Fesler 68 yr, died 13 Oct.
10 Jan 1942	William E. Smithhisler 75 yr, died 6 Jan.
09 Feb 1942	Alice Elizabeth Losh 39 yr, died 5 Feb.
18 Mar 1942	Dennis Lee Banbury 8 d, died 16 Mar.
20 Mar 1942	Samuel F. Blubaugh Jr., died 18 Mar.
28 Mar 1942	Edward C. Durbin 75 yr, died 25 Mar.
23 May 1942	Fidelis E. Sapp 71 yr, died 20 May.
02 Jun 1942	Mones I. Butts 75 yr, died 30 May.
12 Sep 1942	Marcus J. Arnold 62 yr, died 9 Sep.
15 Sep 1942	Jacob Lower 82 yr, died 12 Sep at Mt. Vernon.
24 Oct 1942	Florence Blanchard 75 yr, died 21 Oct.
14 Dec 1942	Josephine Lower 44 yr, died 11 Dec.
13 Jan 1943	Joseph A. Durbin 74 yr, died 9 Jan.
29 Mar 1943	Lucy A. Blubaugh 56 yr, died 25 Mar.
14 Jun 1943	2nd Lt. Paul Joseph Durbin 24 yr, died 10 Jun in airplane crash at Woody Field, GA.
17 Jul 1943	Mary Catherine Lower 76 yr, w/o Joseph Lower died 15 Jul at Mt. Vernon.
13 Dec 1943	William J. Mickley 76 yr, died 9 Dec. at Wadworth, OH.
22 Dec 1943	John W. Welsh 84 yr, died 19 Dec.
31 Jan 1944	Hilary D. Blubaugh 45 yr, died 28 Jan.
17 Mar 1944	Mary Louisa Durbin 15 d, died 16 Mar.
19 Jun 1944	Regina Mary Grassbaugh 34 yr, died 15 Jun at Sarasota Springs. NY.

DEATHS

07 Sep 1944	Mary Margaret Breckler 53 yr, died 4 Sep at Zanesville, OH.
29 Nov 1944	Walter Jacob Blubaugh 5 d, died 22 Nov. at Mt. Vernon.
21 Dec 1944	Peter Michael Durbin 71 yr, died 18 Dec.
12 Feb 1945	Michael John Smithhisler 89 yr, died 9 Feb. at Columbus, OH.
03 Mar 1945	Eva Catherine Butts 77 yr, died 28 Feb.
21 Mar 1945	Charles Mason 64 yr, died 18 Mar.
13 Jun 1945	Cletus Edward Kirwen died 11 Jun at Helena OH.
31 Aug 1945	Mary E. Farrell 82 yr, died 29 Aug.
23 Oct 1945	Mary Agnes Durbin 87½ yr, died 19 Oct.
27 Oct 1945	Roger Paul Banbury 11 da, died 25 Oct.
03 Nov 1945	Angeline Crow 70 yr, died 31 Oct.
07 Jan 1946	Della Jane Miller 91 yr, died 3 Jan.
01 Mar 1946	Mary C. Arnold 61 yr, died 23 Feb.
18 Mar 1946	Emma J. Arnold 93 yr 8 mo, died 14 Mar.
07 Jun 1946	John M. Schaub 65 yr, died 4 Jun at Cleveland.
14 Aug 1946	Basil Blubaugh 89 yr, died 11 Aug.
04 Aug 1946	Regina Maria Hawk 11 yr.
04 Dec 1946	Margaret J. Colopy 84 yr, died 01 Dec at Fulton, OH.
23 Jan 1947	Catherine Swingle 59 yr, died 20 Jan.
03 Feb 1947	Thomas B. Durbin 81 yr, died 31 Jan.
07 Feb 1947	Florence Milla Sapp 76 yr, died 4 Feb. at Columbus, OH.
17 Mar 1947	Henry A. Lower 80 yr, died 14 Mar.
01 Apr 1947	Vida Mae Durbin 11 mo, died 31 Mar.
21 Jul 1947	Julius B. King 92 yr, died 18 Jul.
22 Jul 1947	Gerald Benedict Durbin 39 yr, killed in auto crash 18 Jul.
16 Aug 1947	William Grassbaugh 76 yr, died 12 Jul.
09 Oct 1947	**All records from this date forward to be placed in new books. Deaths, First Communion, Confirmation, etc. to be entered in separate books. Joseph R. Casey Visitator**

NAME INDEX

This name index lists the spellings that exist in the hand-written records, therefore check all conceivable variations. Some uncommon surname variants found within these records, as recognized by the authors, are presented in the Preface, pages vii and viii. Given names with illegible surnames, and those without a surname, are presented on page 256. Parentheses appearing in this index enclose identified maiden names.

ARNOLD cont.
Elias 3, 4, 5, 8, 29, 32,
44, 45, 48, 49, 52, 55,
57, 59, 65, 147, 148
Elias Jr. 27, 31, 60
Elias Sr. 65
Eliza 189
Eliza (Harden) 53
Elizabeth Ellen 69
Ella 103
Ellen 35, 124, 135, 158,
172, 188
Ellen "Elsa" Anna 41
Ellen "Elsie" 21, 32
Elsie 145
Emma J. 199
Ethel Edith 176
Ethel Maria 140
Frances 140
Francis 119, 140, 159
Frank 168
Harvey 107
Helen "Ellen" 115
Helen A. 157
Helena 111, 157
Isaac 54
Jacob Austin 58
Jane 32
Jane Selora 123
Joanna 32
John 8, 11, 13, 18, 20,
29, 38, 60, 63, 101
John Albert 53
John Alton 56, 145
John Lamy 175
Jon 4
Jonathan 53, 60, 63, 64,
69, 72, 75, 76, 77, 78,
79, 80, 84, 89, 96, 101,
108, 109, 111, 113,
128, 147, 178, 184,
187
Jonathan Gaines 134,
139
Jonathan Paul 179
Joseph O. 193

Julia Anna 11
Julian 117, 168
Julius 84, 140
Lamy 168, 175
Leah 172
Leah Maria 111
Leo 59
Leo Judson 67, 106,
120, 160, 190
Levina (Logsdon) 53
Lewis 99
Louisa 35
Lovina 45
M. Catherine 106
Marcus 172
Marcus J. 109, 198
Marcus John 173
Margaret 11, 33
Maria 101, 104, 114,
115, 128, 133, 135,
137, 140, 146, 191
Mary 30, 167, 174
Mary C. 199
Mary Helen 113
Mary Matilda 20
Mathilda 42
Matilda 35, 41, 48, 52,
56, 59, 63, 67, 70, 73,
78, 147
Musie Ellen 173
Paul L. 195
Rachel 11, 17, 20, 26,
35, 37, 41, 53, 65, 67
Raymond 112, 133,
137, 140, 158, 162,
179, 193
Raymond, Mrs. 180
Rebecca 9, 15, 19, 24,
34, 43, 63
Rich 107, 111
Richard 34, 45, 51, 53,
54, 58, 60, 67, 84, 99,
102, 146, 158, 162,
185, 189
Rick 156
Roman 65

Rowena Frances 140
Sara 13, 42, 52
Sarah 60, 63, 148
Sarah Catherine 49
Sarah Louisa 185
Selora 175
Selora Jane 175
Thomas L. 85
Thomas Lamy 116, 119,
184
Victoria 72, 100
Victoria B. 109, 111,
157, 183
Walter S. 190
William 5, 55

ARON
Jacob 111

ASCOT
Theresa 31

ASHBURN
Ellis 42, 49, 55, 58, 69,
146
George 58
Levi 49
Maria Elizabeth 55
Martha 42
Rosa 69

ASHER
Eva 160
Eve 126
Thomas 160

BACUS
Ann 141

BAER
Mary 23

BAILES
Agnes 178
Agnes Bertilla 123
Agnes Margaret 180
Allison 186
Bertilla 175
Bertilla Agnes 175
Charles Francis 103
Emilia 177

203

204

205

207

209

BROWN
 Maria 153
 Marianne 33
BROWNE
 George 123
 George Dickeson 123
BRUNEMANN
 J., O. S. F. ix
BUASON
 Julia 141
BUCHINGHAM
 Daniel 24
BUCK
 Abalona 27
 Adaline 57, 184
 Adeline (Draper) 45
 Amelia 123, 133
 Barbara 45, 78, 82, 85,
  88, 91, 94, 107, 151,
  164, 184
 Barbara Anna 98, 103
 Cath 91
 Catherine 54, 99, 156
 Eberhard 184, 186
 Eberhart 27, 45, 52, 54,
  57, 68
 F. M. 102
 Joseph 46
 Maria 45, 151
 Martha 85, 102, 155,
  184
BUCKHART
 Francis 42, 43
BUCKINGHAM
 _____ 24, 32
 Abigail 7
 Absolam 29
 Absolem 8
 Absolom 4, 11, 17, 18,
  22, 24, 36, 42, 64, 146
 Ambrose 55
 Anna 24, 59
 Anna "Nancy" 35

Aparilla 7, 10, 11, 17,
 26, 183
C. 59
Catherine 29, 44, 67
Charles Bowling 11
Dan 35, 38, 41, 44
Daniel 32, 36, 38, 48,
 51, 52, 53, 59, 64, 146
Esther Jane 18
Jane 34, 48, 50, 51, 55,
 59, 147, 151
Joan 38
Joanna 41, 50, 51, 52,
 64, 148
John Absalom 64
Joseph 35, 167
L. Guy 121
Margaret 26
Margaret Elizabeth 38
Maria 29, 42, 51
Maria Aparilla 41
Mary Jane 167
Nancy 17, 48
Nancy Jane 24
Penelope 16, 19, 30, 34
Rebecca 35, 38
Rosanne 24
Sara 17, 19, 146
Sarah 38, 46, 53, 67
Sarah Catherine 48
BULLOCK
 James Vincent, O. P. ix
BUMPUS
 Frederick 150
BURGESS
 Mary Elizabeth 176
BURNS
 Charles 161
 Edward 161
 Jacob 161
 Peter 122
BURR
 Elizabeth 39, 41, 50

BURRIS
 Elizabeth 120, 159
 Josiah 123
 Lyah 160
 Mary 116
 Mary Victoria 111, 141,
  184, 188
 Theodora 123, 171, 172
 Theodora "Dora" 160
BUTLER
 Delilah 131
 Mariann 31
BUTT
 Henry A. 93
BUTTS
 _____ 118, 159
 Agatha Maria 122
 Agatha Mary 176
 Amme M. 188
 Anna E. 95
 Anna M. (Smith) 95
 Anna Maria 192
 Anne Elizabeth 188
 Bessie 170
 Catherine Gertrude 176
 Cyril Francis 93
 Della 194
 Elizabeth 127, 163, 178
 Elizabeth Martha 180
 Eva Catherine 199
 F. 170
 Fk. 170
 Giles 179, 191
 Giles A. 120, 123, 129,
  132, 138, 159, 168,
  196
 Giles Allen 82
 Henry 82, 98, 163, 188,
  192
 Henry A. 85, 88, 95
 Hubert Purcell 132
 Jennie 163, 170
 Joseph 168
 M. 118, 159
 Maria 126

COLOPY cont.
Joseph C. Sr. 179
Joseph E. 78
Joseph H. 85, 122
Joseph Hill 159, 191
Joseph L. 175
Joseph Levi 122, 175
Julius Leander 95
Levi 78, 81, 82, 83, 87,
 89, 91, 95, 96, 99, 100,
 105, 108, 110, 122,
 124, 126, 131, 136,
 137, 142, 153, 155,
 156, 173, 174, 186,
 189, 190
Levi "Clyde" 186
Levi Claude 117
Levi F. 114, 117, 157
Levi Francis 20
Lucy 71, 109, 110, 157
Lucy Leona 120
Margaret 83, 85, 88,
 92, 95, 101, 106, 109,
 160, 165
Margaret J. 199
Maria 5, 11, 18, 22, 30,
 32, 41, 169, 187
Maria Anna 116, 120
Maria Matilda 36
Mark 104
Mary 27, 56
Mary "Barry" (Henegan)
 188
Mary Adele 81
Mary Darlla 176
Mary Margaret 135
Mary Matilda 103, 155
Matila 84
Matilda 30, 44, 45, 76,
 78, 81, 87, 107, 161
Melissa 110, 122, 124,
 126, 137, 173, 174
Melissa A. 189
Milla 168
Mrs. 22
Nancy 22

Ralph 177
Ralph John 179
Robert Emmett 126
Rose Elizabeth 95, 132,
 136, 142, 161
Rose Mary 192
Sara 7, 12, 22
Sara Catharine 6
Sarah 5, 15, 46, 47
Sarah Catherine 52,
 146
Sarah Jane 5
Stanton 175
Stephen Callistus 141
T. 97
Thomas J. 114
Tim 12
Timothy 15, 21, 43
Timothy Sr. 181
William 5
CONDON
Frances 141
Patrick 141
Sarah 141
CONKLIN
Mary 115
CONLEY
Anna E. 158
CONLON
Jacob 155
CONNELLY
Anna 157
Elizabeth Edna 119
Florence Joan 126
Hubert 119, 122, 126
Hubert Lamar 122
Hugh 157
Math 103
Matilda 96
CONNELY
Anna 30
Patrick 30

CONNOR
Catherine 150
Isabella 155
CONNORS
Patrick 151
CONROY
Daniel P. 138
Ethel Lower 195
Howard 138
Robert Henry 194
COOK
Joseph Reuben 60, 148
COOPER
Julia 25
COX
Eliza 88
Elizabeth 113
Maria Elizabeth 97
Michael 97
Sara Jane 97
CRABAUGH
Henry 43
William 43
CRAMER
Edward 49
CRAWFORD
Elizabeth 47, 146
CRITCHFIELD
Alice 153, 158, 160
Barbara "Charlotte" 99
Charlotte 76, 80, 103
Charlotte "Charity" 110
Edward 91, 187
F. C. 77
Frederick 133
Fulton 169
Harriet 36, 38, 148, 186
Hiram 23, 27, 40, 49,
 53, 160
Hiriam 186
Isadora 100, 156
Isadora (Smith) 183
Jacob 133

214

215

DURBIN cont.
Charles Levi 175
Charles Michael 104
Charles P., Mrs. 180
Charles Pius 192
Charles Raymond Basil
  106
Chaucy 178
Chaucy Joseph 179
Clement 114, 119, 122,
  123, 136, 139, 158,
  175, 179
Clement E. 126, 130,
  134, 140, 160
Clement Elmer 80
Clement Paul 121, 175
Constance 178
Constance Maria 140
Constance Teresa 180
Cornelius Purcell 77
Dan 3, 14, 19, 21
Dan Basil 14
Daniel 7, 8, 10, 11, 12,
  14, 16
David 28, 32
David Sr. 181
Delila Helen 11
Delilah Susanna 194
Dennis 20, 85, 168
Dilly 154
Dorothy 88
E. 153
Ed 168, 169
Edw. 121
Edward 125, 129, 135,
  142, 159, 161, 183
Edward C. 132, 135,
  142, 161, 198
Edward Charles 160
Edward Moitrier 104
Edward, Mrs. 180
Eizabeth 132
Eleanor 7
Elenora 180
Elias 14, 19, 21, 23

Elijah 4, 12, 15, 18,
  145, 165
Eliz 124
Eliz J. 88
Eliza 55
Elizabeth 6, 8, 11, 12,
  14, 20, 21, 26, 29, 42,
  46, 51, 54, 73, 78, 106,
  130, 141, 162, 163,
  182
Elizabeth (Lybarger) 8
Elizabeth (Reams) 7
Elizabeth B. 163, 169
Elizabeth Bertha 92
Ella 169
Ella B. 187
Ellen 60
Ellen "Helen" 21, 50,
  145
Elphina 7
Emily 11, 153
Emma Cecila 60
Emma Josephine 95,
  137, 162
Esther 178
Esther Clara 180
Ethel 175
Ethel (Logsdon) 191
Ethel Lucinda 175
Ethel Lucy 123
Eugene 158, 159
Eugenia 113, 160
Eugenia B. 159
Eugenie 168
F. 106
Fannie 169
Fenton F. 127
Fenton Fidelis 124
Fidelis Fenton 176
Flora 14
Fr. 88, 89, 90, 95
Frances 90, 103, 119,
  121, 126, 133, 140,
  168, 169
Frances D. 189
Frances E. 162

Frances Elizabeth 185
Frances Ellen 83
Frances Isabel 133, 161
Frances Isabella 79
Francis 70, 72, 74, 76,
  83, 85, 86, 87, 94, 97,
  98, 99, 106, 107, 110,
  113, 117, 120, 123,
  126, 152, 154, 159,
  160, 161, 162, 172,
  183, 188
Francis A. 105
Francis Anthony 101
Francis Joseph 85, 168
Francis M. 9, 74, 77,
  80, 83, 90, 101, 105,
  150, 188
Francis N. 121
Francis Raphael 103
Francis Raymond 87
Francis Sr. 181
Frank 119, 171
Frank, Mrs. 180
Fred 170
Frederick 132, 139,
  141, 178, 188
Frederick Leo 179
Fredrick 170
Genevieve 75, 94, 98,
  197
George 4, 18, 46, 77,
  79, 83, 85, 88, 90, 94,
  95, 99, 106, 107, 111,
  117, 156, 164, 183,
  184, 188, 192
Gerald Benedict 199
Gertrude 87, 121, 135,
  141, 142, 160, 161,
  169
Gertrude Margaret 94
Gertrude Maria 160
Gertrude Rosetta 136,
  188
Gregory Pius 104, 110
H. 80, 83
Hanna 25

217

DURBIN cont.
Margaret 6, 12, 18, 34, 42, 62, 65, 69, 77, 79, 80, 82, 83, 91, 94, 95, 98, 101, 107, 114, 115, 136, 150, 151, 165, 167, 184, 187, 190
Margaret (McNamara) 86
Margaret Isabel 132
Margaret Isabella 78, 167
Margaret Monica 104
Margarita 105, 106
Margarite 14
Maria 7, 8, 11, 13, 14, 15, 17, 18, 28, 35, 38, 42, 47, 53, 60, 64, 65, 83, 92, 103, 108, 111, 35, 161, 184
Maria (Gorsage) 14
Maria (Winebrenner) 9
Maria Anna 58, 65, 68, 69, 72, 73, 75, 76, 82, 83, 103, 104, 106, 111, 148, 149
Maria C. 155
Maria Caroline 71
Maria Catherine 17, 34
Maria Elizabeth 78
Maria J. 83, 86, 89
Maria L. 84
Maria Louisa 103, 183
Maria Lucy 101
Maria Pauline 111
Maria Samantha Mary (Reynolds) 70
Maria Teresa Frances 80
Marianna 41, 81
Mark 99, 164, 170
Mark, Mrs. 180
Martella 171, 172
Martha 34
Martha Ellen 196

Martin 3, 4, 6, 9, 12, 13, 14, 21, 39, 40, 52
Mary 77, 168, 172, 174, 180
Mary A. (Buckingham) 187
Mary Agnes 95, 164, 199
Mary Angela 108
Mary Ann 112, 189
Mary Anna 173
Mary Aparilla 89
Mary C. 169
Mary Catherine 63, 88, 123, 126, 130, 134, 140, 160
Mary Clara 115
Mary Ellen 193
Mary Honora 108
Mary Isabella 93
Mary Jane 78, 86, 95, 133, 140, 160, 161
Mary Louisa 198
Mary Margaret 106
Mary Nora 190
Mary Paul 195
Mary Vesta 113
Maud 172, 180
Maud Elizabeth 173
Maude Elizabeth 114
Melissa 155
Melissa A. 114, 117, 157
Melissa Anna 41
Mellissa 153
Miranda 50
N. 44, 182
Nancy 14, 16, 23
Nancy "Anna" 78
Nora 171, 172
Normanda 106, 190
Oliva Josephine 88
Olive Bertha 92
Olive J. 125, 129, 139
Olive Josephine 118
Parmelia Anna 11

Patrick Thomas 120
Paul Joseph, 2nd Lt. 198
Pauline 180
Pauline Caecilia 114
Pauline Cecelia 126
Pauline Cecilia 176
Peter 65, 67, 69, 71, 74, 77, 78, 79, 80, 81, 83, 84, 85, 86, 88, 89, 93, 95, 99, 100, 104, 105, 106, 151, 152, 162, 170, 184
Peter Michael 95, 165, 199
Philena 125, 162, 169
Philena J. 136, 162
Philina Joan 90
Pius 89, 91, 92, 97, 101, 107, 111, 156
Pius Gregory 49
Purcel 159
R. 168
Rachel 16, 35, 47, 68, 72, 89, 98, 100, 146
Rachel (Arnold) Porter 186
Rachel Loretta 61
Ralph 93, 141
Raphael 65, 67, 75, 76, 78, 79, 80, 82, 85, 88, 91, 94, 98, 101, 103, 106, 107, 150, 151, 164, 184, 190
Raymond 171, 172, 194
Raymond Rollin 113
Rebecca 19, 34, 42, 49, 55, 58, 69, 146
Rebecca Joannna 70
Richard 23
Rosa 26, 28, 31, 32, 35, 46, 49, 64, 85, 174, 196
Rosa Anna 43
Rosalie Elizabeth 118
Rosann 11, 132

219

DURBIN cont.
Rosanna 8, 9, 12, 13,
  49, 55, 56
Rosanna (Lybarger) 16
Rosanne (Lybarger)
  Walker 6
Rose 174, 178
Rose Dorothy 180
Rose, Mrs. 180
Rudger 171
Sam 4, 10, 85, 86, 88
Sam, of Ben 4
Samuel 6, 8, 11, 14, 16,
  21, 23, 28, 34, 36, 39,
  41, 44, 47, 53, 56, 68,
  82, 90, 98, 100, 106,
  114, 115, 186
Samuel W. 20, 26
Sara 6, 13, 18, 21
Sara Agnes 17
Sara Elizabeth 120
Sara Eugenia 103, 156
Sarah 12, 14, 38, 52,
  71, 86, 89, 90
Sarah (Sapp) 9
Sarah Ann 29
Sarah Catherine 22, 74,
  84, 94
Sarah Elizabeth 68, 194
Sarah Ellen 83
Sarah Jane 69
Selora 114, 120, 122,
  125, 129, 133, 136,
  142, 158, 159
Selora A. 168
Selora Alphonsa 82
Simeon 69, 82, 96, 106,
  110, 189
Solomon 12, 68, 70, 71,
  74, 80, 88, 94, 103,
  105, 149
Stephen 21, 79, 159,
  185
Steven 168
Susan 23

Susanna 54, 59, 65, 67,
  69, 72, 77, 84, 89, 92,
  96, 99, 105, 148, 162
Sylvester 142, 165, 172
Sylvester Aloysius 109
Teresa 148
Thecla Elenore 197
Theodore 76, 121, 133,
  138, 140, 162, 196
Theresa 15
Theresa Honora 15
Thomas 111, 112, 114,
  124, 125, 126, 160
Thomas B. 127, 133,
  134, 135, 140, 160,
  199
Thomas Bernard 83
Thomas Bulger 97
Tom 170
Vida Mae 199
Walter 173, 174, 183
Walter Celestine 197
Will 92
William 12, 71, 103,
  108, 113, 128, 136,
  141, 149, 156, 170,
  179
William A. 188
William Alphonso
  Liguori 140
William Bernard 71,
  104, 110, 115, 118,
  123, 128, 156, 196
William Eberhard 98
William Eugene 66
William Sylvester 173
DURN
  Annie 38
DUVALL
  Sarah M. 130
DYER
  Maria A. 138
EAGAN
  Margaret 30

EARNEST
  _____ 43
  George 142
  Jacob 24, 29
  Joseph 24
EARNST
  Jacob 23
  Magdalena 23
EASTERDAY
  Mabel 126
EBERLING
  Catherine 43
  Elizabeth 41
  Joseph 43
  Magdalena 43
EBERLY
  Catarina 147
EBERSOLE
  C. R. 152
ECKENROD
  John 84
ECKENRODE
  Agnes 84, 95
  Agnes E. 140
  Agnes Evelyn 88
  Ben 75, 82, 88, 89, 91,
    151
  Benjamin 83, 84, 96,
    188
  David 4
  David William 89
  Edward Mark 95
  Emma 140
  Eva 36
  Harriet 70, 75, 149
  Henrietta 36
  Henry 4, 18, 24, 56
  Henry B. 159
  Joanna 151
  John 88, 91, 95
  John Julius 91
  Julia 150
  Margaritta 189
  Maria 46, 52

220

EWING
Eliza 11
Elizabeth 15
FAHY
Anthony Dominic, O. P
ix
FAIRASEN
Barbara 25
FARELL
Henry 37
William 37
FARQUHAR
Harriet 78, 80, 84, 87,
91, 95, 104
Harriett 151
FARRELL
John 39, 41
Laura 39
Mary E. 199
Miss 181
FATLER
Alice 127
Ida 127
FENWICK
Edward, Father 1
FERENBAUGH
_____ 51
Eliza 16
Fidele 34
Fidelis 16
James Leo 34
Joseph Anthony 16
Josephine 45
Peter 45, 147
FERREL
Ellen 155
FERRY
Martin 31
FESLAR
Jacob 93
FESLER
_____ 163

Agnes 180, 198
Albert 171, 172
Anna 29
Anna Frances 96, 163
Catherine 195
Charles 174
Christina 43, 154
Eliz 165
Elizabeth 96, 164, 176
George 164, 171, 172
George J. 165
Helena Elizabeth 164
Helena Elizabeth "Lena"
100
Henry 179
Henry Albert 93
Jacob 96, 100, 103,
108, 155, 164, 194
John Joseph 93
John W. 164, 196
Jos. 96
Joseph 23, 27, 29, 43,
96, 97, 101, 154
Joseph Jr. 27, 93, 102
Laurence 23, 27
Leona 191
Louis 171, 172
Mary 23, 101, 155
Mary Ann 102
Mary Elizabeth 174
Matilda 174
Matilda Amelia 108
Nora 174
Rose Katherine 103
Salome Stark 23
William 165, 174
FILERAND
Margaret 155
FINAN
Lucy Mary 197
FINNERAN
Isabel Pauline 124
Patrick 124, 159
FIRMACK
Cunta 141

FISCHER
Martin 54
Peter 54
FISHASH
Peter 182
FISHER
Anthony 45, 182
Bernard 52
Catherine 48
Celestius Peter 65
Elizabeth 58
John 49
M. A. 116
Maria 46, 52, 62, 64
Maria Anna 79
Martin 45, 49, 52, 56,
58, 60, 65, 152, 182
Martin Jr. 45
Mary 56
Michael 60
Peter 182
FITZ
Mag. 148
FITZGERALD
Robert 146
FITZMYRE
Domina 151
Fitzmyre F. 147
Fr. 84
Francis 81, 148
Margaret 81
FITZPATRICK
___ 182
Margaret 25
Maria 5, 25
FLARETY
Jacob 74
FLATZ
Benjamin 36
Joseph 36
FLECKNOE
Daniel 158

222

GARDNER cont.
John F. 137, 162, 179,
    197
John Francis 82
John Julius 76
John Sr. 191
John Stephen 173
Joseph Edward 116,
    185
Joseph Henry 72
Josephine 138
Julia Jane 90
Lena 174
Leo 80, 90, 92
Leo J. 94, 95, 97, 100,
    155
Louisa 114, 158
Lucy W. 194
M. Anna 50
Maria 34, 57, 60, 80,
    137, 140, 141, 164
Maria Anna 45
Maria Barbara 29
Maria Elizabeth 62
Maria M. 152, 157
Maria Velma Virgillia
    139
Maria Virgilia 134
Marie 151
Martha 164
Martha Teresa 91
Martin 76
Mary 124, 170, 196
Mary Barbara 84
Mary Catherine 84
Mary Charlotte 105,
    165
Mary Elizabeth 97
Mary J. 192
Mary Louisa 114
Mary Magdalena 45
Mary Margaret 70
Matilda 66, 70, 75,
    149, 167
S. Christina 87
Sara (Zimmerman) 92

Stephen Marcus "John"
    109
Thomas 114, 116, 119,
    185
Virgilia 178
Virgilia Mary 180
William Dennis 100
GARETY
Elizabeth 31
Thomas 31, 145
GARLAND
Anna 80
Anthony 153
Charles Richard 80
Elizabeth 80
Jacob 80
Julia Anna 72, 75, 149
Julie Anna 70
Mary Jane 153
GARNER
Margaret 33
GARRET
David 146
GAUM
Ethel Lutila 133
Frances 136
Francis 136
Francis Roland 133
GAUME
Ameda Gertrude 103
Anna Maria 182
Augustus 103, 107,
    155, 161
Eugene 103, 110, 156
Francis Roland 107,
    161
Jacob Monty 103
Lewis 161
GAYE
Elizabeth 25
GESSLING
Francis 118
Marg 71

GIFFEN
Frances H. Ellen 109
Frances Helen 103
GIFFIN
Ellen 94
Frances Helen 94, 113,
    155
GILBERT
Edward 177
Edward William 179
Emmanual 122
Emmanuel 186
Francis 122, 125, 126,
    130, 171, 172
George 125
Hannah 61
Rosa Veronica 126, 176
William Edward 130
GILLAINE
Jacob 160
Joseph 26
Patrick 167
GILLANE
Paul 26
GILLMORE
Walter H. 125
GIMBLE
Andrew 62
Anthony 68
GLASSBERGER
Henry William 12
Glassberger
Thomas 12
GLAZER
Adaline 57, 65
GLESSON
Margaret 22
GNUNDEN
Maria Florence 197
GOODBALLER
Felicia 75

226

HENLEY cont.
  Gregory 83, 139, 151,
    154, 163, 179, 186
  Jennifer 62
  John 103, 151, 163
  Lewis 90, 155
  Mary 62
  Mary Ellen 65
  Rachel 185
  William 113, 153
HENRY
  Joseph 31
  William 141
HERNETTY
  Edmund 182
HESS
  Anna Harriet 66
  Eddie 119
  Eleanor Frances 87, 153
  Elizabeth 52
  Francis 33, 78, 152
  Henrietta 136, 137
  Honora Frances 36
  Ida Catherine 82
  Isabel "Bell" 153
  Isabella 92, 94, 98, 107,
    110, 112, 114, 119,
    121
  John 87
  Margaret 87
  Maria 27, 28
  Maria Isabella 52
  Marianna 51
  Marie 33
  Sam 86, 87
  Samuel 36, 52, 66, 69,
    76, 82
  Sara Agnes 69, 122,
    127, 131, 138
  Sarah Agnes 112, 115,
    118
  Veronica 86
  William Daniel 76

HESSLER
  Benjamin 37
  Naomi 37
HIBBETS
  Henrietta 92
HIBBETTS
  Elizabeth 98
  Henrietta 98
  Jacob 98
HIGHMAN
  Sylvester 132
HINAMAN
  Wm 4
HINEMAN
  Peter 4
HINES
  Jacob Michael 67
  Thomas 67
HIXON
  Elizabeth 119, 122, 126
HOAGLAND
  Rose 178
  Rose Clara 180
HOGAN
  Anna 43
  Helen 41
  Margaret 43
  Michael 41
HOGLAND
  Magdaline Frances 176
HOGLIN
  Rebecca 113, 117
HOLDBROOK
  Hanna J. 197
  Lyman P. 197
HOLDEN
  Catherine A. 147
HOLLER
  Catherine 28
  Jacob 15, 27, 54, 145
  Magdalena 15
  Mich 72

HOLLET
  Cath 75
  James Michael 77
  Jos Eifert Michael 167
  Margaret 40
  Michael 150
  Nicholas 40, 56, 75, 77,
    149, 150, 167
  Ursula 56
HOLLIGAN
  Timothy 63
HOMAN
  Barbara 61, 151
  Bertha Agnes 135
  Cecilia Frances 89
  Charles 175
  Charles Andrew 175
  Clara 174
  Clara Gertrude 118
  Edwin Stephen 102
  Elizabeth 32, 73, 87,
    101, 114, 115, 118,
    119, 155, 186
  Elizabeth (Neuth) 26
  Eva Catherine 36
  Frances 120, 125
  Henry 171, 172
  Jacob 118
  James 97, 155
  John 65, 185
  Louisa 97
  Lucy Mary 128, 177
  Magdalena 26
  Margaret 134, 154, 161
  Maria Rosa 154
  Martha 127, 129, 160,
    161
  Martin 25, 71, 80, 86,
    87, 89, 93, 153
  Mary Matilda 86
  Michael 26, 32, 36, 96,
    102, 114, 127, 152,
    161
  Michael Philip 71
  Paul 25, 32, 65, 71, 93,
    100, 186

LUCAS
  Levi Aloysius 100
  Samuel 100
LYBARGER
  Elizabeth 11, 16, 20
  George 6
  Jacob 97
  Laura Isadora 97
  Maria Roush 42
  Mary 46
  Mary Magdalena 36
  Matilda 95, 105, 108,
    112, 154
  Matilda S. 92
  Rosanna 9
  Rosanne 24
  Viola 154
MACKEY
  Rachel 142
MADAY
  Lewis 133
MAGER
  Simeon 72
MAGERS
  _____ 55
  Ambrose 47, 52, 54, 55,
    58, 60, 62, 64
  Amelia 21
  Anna 47
  Ben J. 91
  Benedict 34, 35, 36, 40,
    46, 47, 55, 56, 57, 59,
    60, 61, 62, 67, 69, 70,
    71, 72, 73, 74, 146
  Benjamin 39, 43, 146
  Calvin 115, 124, 135,
    158, 188
  Catherine 5, 12
  Cecila 65
  Della Mickley 195
  Drusilla 13
  Dwight Jonathan 124
  Eliza 7, 17, 28
  Eliza Ellen 76

Elizabeth 8, 23, 33, 37,
  46
Ellen 198
Ellen Rebecca 60
Fr. 152
Frances 150
Francis 55, 65
Francis Xavier 61
Gabriel 29
Harry 173, 174
Harry Francis 115
Helena 184
Henrietta 46, 146
Henry Milton 43
Hester Ann 48, 51, 57,
  62, 147
Jane 43
John 8, 37, 61, 64, 65
John Calvin 196
John Peter 20
Jonathan Dwight 176
Laurence 39, 47, 48,
  52, 55, 65, 67, 147
Lawrence 38
Lewis 21
Lucinda 40
Lucy Emila 52
Lydia 16, 75, 77, 101,
  123
Manuel 67
Margaret 5, 10, 12, 16,
  37, 41
Margaret Helen 72
Margaret (Sapp) 8
Maria 55, 56, 67, 69,
  77
Maria Alice 76
Maria Elias 57
Maria Elizabeth 65
Maria Isabella 52
Maria Priscilla 181
Marie 135, 188
Martha 5
Mary 13

Nathan 5, 7, 8, 9, 11,
  13, 17, 18, 23, 24, 26,
  28, 52, 63, 76
Nathan S. 4
Nathan W. 3, 19
Nathaniel 5, 8
Peter 5, 7, 149
Rachel 7, 182
Raphael 40, 147
Rebecca 22, 26, 29, 41
Richard F. 10
Simon 76
Susanna 9, 15, 20, 44
W. 59, 69
William 5, 10, 12, 13,
  15, 16, 20, 23, 29, 34,
  37, 38, 46, 55
William N. 3, 55
William R. 8
Winifred 5, 7, 8, 9, 13,
  17, 18, 55, 61, 63, 64,
  65
Winifred (Logsdon) 18
Winnie 8
Wm 20
Wm N. 4
MAGUE
  M. Adam 167
  Sarah Elizabeth 167
MAJOR
  Nathan 11
  Rachel 182
MAJORS
  Drusilla 13
  Margaret 12
  Nathan 9, 13, 17
  Susanna 9
  William 13, 16
  Winifred 9, 13
  Winifred (Logsdon) 17
MANI
  Elizabeth 116
  Gainor 116
MANSFIELD
  Catherine 49

234

235

McKENZIE cont.
Joseph Hyacinthas 10
Laurence 59
Lewis 16
Margaret 5, 7, 8, 9, 13, 41, 85, 88, 92, 98, 104, 145, 152
Maria 14, 15, 17, 23, 32, 58
Maria (Dial) 10
Maria Cecilia 97
Maria Elizabeth 50
Maria Elizabeth 52
Mary 10, 158
Mary (Dial) 145
Mary Anna Cath 84
Mary Elizabeth 53
Mary Helen 47
Moses 4, 5, 7, 9, 10, 15, 16, 21, 38
Nathan 10, 17, 18
Nathan Benedict 59
Nathaniel 10
Paula 37
Peter 20
Polly 14
Rachel 52, 59
Rachel Susanna 32, 80
Raphael Hilary 21
Rebecca 15, 17, 63, 69, 72, 79, 82, 86, 90, 108, 112, 167
Rebecca A. 75, 101
Rebecca Maria 16
Samuel 3, 5, 6, 8, 10, 11, 13, 19, 37, 82
Samuel P. 84
Sara 9, 15
Sara Helen 10
Sarah 6, 7, 10, 15
Sarah Margaret 51
Siril 9
Stephen 28
Stephen Aloysius 61
Stephen Elias 20
Susan Rachel 158

Susanna 7, 10, 52, 59, 65, 67, 147
Sylvester 10
Thomas 35, 98
Thomas B. 186
Walter 163, 171, 172, 190
William 6
William Francis 37
William Marcellus 99
McKEOGH
Ellen (Durbin) 13
Patrick 13
McKINNEY
Charles 165
Eugene 164, 165
McMAHON
____ 157
John 108, 157
Lloyd 142
Mabel 129
Margaret J. 116, 120, 124, 126, 135, 139, 158
Maria Gertrude 108
Mary 169
Pat 168
Paul 142
Thomas 168, 187
Thomas J. 194
McMANN
Johanna (Phillips) 189
McMOHAN
Margaret J. 131
McMULLEN
Catherine 45
Margaret 48
Michael 45, 48
Thomas 25, 45
Thomas Henry 25
McNAMARA
____ 44
Anna 37, 55, 56
Barbara 37

Bridget 15, 46, 154
Brigett 54
Catherine 15, 40, 47, 51, 55, 146
Christina 81, 101
Clement 83
Dora 169
Eliz 107, 112
Francis 37, 46, 54, 56, 64, 70, 75, 77, 81, 85, 94, 101, 149, 150, 183, 185
Francis Bernard 101
Francis K. 46
George G. 56
John 83, 151, 152
Joseph Florin 44
Louise 169
M. 151
Margaret 37, 46, 70, 71, 75, 80, 81, 82, 85, 86, 92, 149, 160
Margaret A. 87
Margaret Anna 79
Margaret Edith 101
Maria 37, 81
Mary 46
Matthew 54
Michael 15
Michael, Sr. 181
S. E. 83
Sarah Elizabeth (Porter) 158
Theodora J. 128
Theodora Jane 85, 121, 124, 138, 159
Victoria Letitia 94
W. E. 84
William 15, 37
William H. 159
William Henry 75
McNAMEE
Abraham 130
Anna 28
McVAY
Jacob 147

240

241

SAPP cont.
Margaret R. 196
Maria 6, 13, 14, 15, 36, 53, 67, 71, 97, 115, 116, 121, 131, 149, 155, 161, 162, 186
Maria (Colopy) 8, 13
Maria (Durbin) 12
Maria Anna 66
Maria Elizabeth 38, 45, 48, 118
Maria Josephine 71
Martha 14, 15, 18, 22, 26, 32, 33, 43, 47, 51, 53, 58, 145
Martha Frances 53, 67, 71, 167
Martha J. 55
Martha Jane 6
Martin 18
Martina Isabella 78
Mary 20, 56, 97, 170, 174
Mary (Colopy) 187
Mary Ann 13, 18, 81, 150, 193
Mary Anna 149
Mary Ellen 58
Mary Frances 97
Mary K. 121
Mary Keziah 103, 107, 111, 115, 124, 130, 135, 138, 156, 165
Mary L. 92
Mary Teresa 174
Mary, Mrs. 180
Matilda Lybarger 89
N. 182
Naomi Margaret 198
Nelson 58, 59
Normanda 32, 64, 69, 71, 151
Normanda Mary 167
Odo 114, 173, 174
Rachel 6, 7, 10, 13, 16, 18, 26, 38, 55, 62

Rachel Normanda 59
Raymond 136
Raymond J. 136
Raymond Monterville 98
Rebecca 145
Rita 174
Robert 35, 38, 39, 40, 43, 50
Robert H. 189
Robert Jacob 9
Robert William 191
Roman 67, 92, 154, 158
Rosa 107, 141
Rose 171, 172
Rose E. 164
Rose Estelle 112
Rosella 83
Samuel 7, 9, 15, 20, 22, 182
Sara 6, 21, 97
Sara Ann 35, 41, 70, 146
Sara Anna 53, 63, 67
Sara Elizabeth 53
Sarah 12, 14, 34, 83
Sarah Ann 47, 58, 79
Sarah Anna 35, 85
Sarah Elizabeth 60
Sarah Rebecca 67
Silvern 30
Simeon 7, 18, 66, 68, 71, 77, 79, 83, 94, 149
Simon 8, 30, 68, 75, 148
Simon H. 3, 23, 33, 40
Simon Hartley 6, 10, 13, 18, 26, 38, 62, 68
Solomon 18
Susan 82, 110
Susan (Millis) 79
Susan Anna 77
Susan Willis 77
Susanna 7, 11, 15, 17, 42, 85, 97, 107, 113, 117, 149

Susanna (Magers) 7
Susanna Elizabeth 12
Susannah Elizabeth 152
Thomas 7, 175
Thomas Bernard 105
Thomas Edward 124, 175
Timothy 13, 60, 104, 107, 117, 185
William 127, 152, 153, 167, 172, 173
William Francis 14
Winifred 36
SCHAFFER
Albina Helen 59
George 59
SCHAUB
Adam 23
Dorothy 178
Francis, Rev. 193
Harry Lee 176
Henrietta 164
John M. 199
Louisa 177
Magdalena 23
Margaret Rosanna (Lower) 164
Raymond W. 189
Raymond Walter 176
William A. 195
SCHISLER
Amelia 91
SCHLASELT
Henrietta 141
SCHMIDTT
Catherine 146
SCHONENBERGER
Michael 23
Regina 23
SCHOP
Ablonia 147
SCHULTZ
Jacob 68

246

WILLENPUC
John 22
WILLIAMS
Sarah 66
WILLIS
Susan 75, 83, 148
Susan A. 71
Susanna 68
WILSON
Catherine 12, 26
WILTON
Catherine 31
WINEBRENNER
Eva 17
Maria 17
WINKLE
Catherine 61
Thomas 61
WINTERHALTER
Louisa Ferenbaugh 194
WINTERRINGER
Almeda Martha 174
John 194
Margaret Almeda 194
WITMAN
John 148
WITT
Jane 153
WIZERNANDT
Phebe 44
WOHLER
Clinton Paul 192
WOLLENSNEIDER
Elizabeth 31
Jacob 29
WORK
Bridget 21
WORKMAN
Charles 163
Laura Belle 164
Maria 162

Normanda 83, 88, 90,
95, 99, 164
Raphael 79
Stephen 164
YEAGER
Bernard 48
Edward 155
Jos. 155
Joseph 48
YOUNG
Henry Bernard 163
Nicholas Dominic, O. P.
ix
Nicholas, Rev. 1
Otto C. 117
YUNKAWIG
Barbara 43
YUNKER
Helen 39
Theresa 43
ZACHARY
William 53
ZATPILLER
Catherine 70
ZIEGLER
Clara 130
ZIMBLE
Andreas 70
ZIMMERMAN
A. J. 154
Amelia Agnes 97
Benjamin 15
Dan 155
Frederick 35, 43, 44,
46, 47
Frederick Jr. 15, 22
Helena 97
John 4, 154
John Frederick 46, 47
Joseph 93, 96, 97, 155
Maria 22
Rosa 154
Sarah 15, 95, 155

ZINK
Barbara 100
ZUMMA
John 4

UNKNOWN
SURNAMES
Amanda 114
Barbara 12
Charlotte 138
Elias 74
Eliza 15
Elizabeth 139
Elizabeth Anna 50
Eudie 119
Frances 23
George 164
Helen 123
Henry 54
Israel 51
Jacob 54
Jacob Leander 68
Joanna 81
John 74
Lewis Franklin 81
Lucinda 40
Lydia 182
Magdalena 16
Margaret 102
Maria 48
Maria 54
Maria Elizabeth 109
Rebecca 123
Sara 151
Theodore Francis 61
Ursala 50

256

www.ingramcontent.com/pod-product-compliance
Lightning Source LLC
Chambersburg PA
CBHW071850270326
41929CB00013B/2169